Kings and Priests

Kings and Priests

Scripture's Theological Account of Its Readers

UCHE ANIZOR

With a Foreword by Daniel J. Treier

☙PICKWICK *Publications* · Eugene, Oregon

KINGS AND PRIESTS
Scripture's Theological Account of Its Readers

Copyright © 2014 Uche Anizor. All rights reserved. Except for brief quotations in critical publications or reviews, no part of this book may be reproduced in any manner without prior written permission from the publisher. Write: Permissions, Wipf and Stock Publishers, 199 W. 8th Ave., Suite 3, Eugene, OR 97401.

Pickwick Publications
An Imprint of Wipf and Stock Publishers
199 W. 8th Av.e, Suite 3
Eugene, OR 97401

www.wipfandstock.com

ISBN 13: 978-1-62564-482-4

Cataloging-in-Publication data:

Anizor, Uche.

    Kings and priests : scripture's theological account of its readers / Uche Anizor ; with a foreword by Daniel J. Treier.

    xviii + 256 p. ; 23 cm. Includes bibliographical references and index.

    ISBN 13: 978-1-62564-482-4

    1. Bible—Hermeneutics. 2. Bible—Reading. 3. Bible—Criticism, interpretation, etc. 4. Bible—Theology. I. Title.

BS476 A57 2014

Manufactured in the U.S.A.

Unless otherwise indicated, all Scripture references are taken from the New Revised Standard Version Bible, copyright © 1989, Division of Christian Education of the National Council of the Churches of Christ in the United States of America. Used by permission. All rights reserved.

To Melissa, my patient wife

Ὑμεῖς δὲ γένος ἐκλεκτόν, βασίλειον ἱεράτευμα, ἔθνος ἅγιον, λαὸς εἰς περιποίησιν, ὅπως τὰς ἀρετὰς ἐξαγγείλητε τοῦ ἐκ σκότους ὑμᾶς καλέσαντος εἰς τὸ θαυμαστὸν αὐτοῦ φῶς.

—1 Pet 2:9

Contents

Foreword by Daniel J. Treier   ix
Acknowledgments   xiii
List of Abbreviations   xv

1. On Locating the Readers of Scripture   1

PART ONE: Royal Priesthood and "Reading" in Biblical-Theological Perspective

2. Royal Priesthood Meets the Word of God: A Biblical-Theological Sketch   27

3. Virtuous Royal Reading: The King as the Ideal "Exemplarist" Reader of Scripture   51

4. Reading *Pro Ecclesia*: The Priest as the Ideal "Didactic" Reader of Scripture   82

PART TWO: Royal Priesthood and "Reading" in Christ's Church

5. Royal Priestly Reading in Christological Perspective: Jesus Christ as the Ideal Reader   103

6. Martin Luther, the Priesthood of All Believers, and the Word of God: Toward a Theology of Readers   137

PART THREE: Royal Priesthood and "Reading" in Covenant Life

7   Divine Dramatics: Royal Priesthood as a Theological Account of the Readers of Scripture   165

8   Response and Responsibility: Royal Priesthood as an Ethical Account of the Readers of Scripture   197

Bibliography   237
Index   251

Foreword

How can we put *Kings and Priests: Scripture's Theological Account of its Readers* into a larger perspective regarding theological interpretation of Scripture (hereafter TIS)—maybe even a larger perspective than its author intends at this point? In my view, Dr. Anizor's project makes both formal and material contributions to the current discussion.

First, at a formal level, *Kings and Priests* embodies possible harmony rather than tension between biblical theology and TIS. Dr. Anizor supplements contemporary accounts of TIS, and indeed offers an example, by way of tracing a key theme in biblical theology. In this regard, contrasts between his approach and those of several others are fairly evident.

For understandable reasons, some TIS proponents have written extensively at a hermeneutical level, either developing their own proposals or analyzing those of others, without themselves doing monograph-length biblical theology: Todd Billings, Kevin Vanhoozer, I myself, and arguably even Francis Watson could serve as examples whose hermeneutical focus in their TIS advocacy confines their engagement with biblical theology to chapter or article length.

Other TIS proponents, meanwhile, cultivate more critical distance from biblical theology. Joel Green is a renowned biblical scholar, and remains insistent about the importance of history, but he also critiques certain kinds of historical work and the ways in which they tend to influence biblical theology. Stephen Fowl distances himself even farther from biblical theology, viewing it as academically normed in a way that, instead, requires the church to pursue its own, fundamentally different, interpretative interests. On this view—a view that has no little anecdotal evidence to support it—mainstream biblical theology struggles with or even simply opposes attempts to read the Bible as Christian Scripture, in particular as the witness to a unified story revealing the Triune God.

For *Kings and Priests* to advocate and enrich TIS by way of sustained work in biblical theology, then, constitutes an important formal contribution. Dr. Anizor is alert to theological interests such as divine action and human response, covenant, and Christ's threefold office, while undertaking careful, historically engaged, exegesis of texts such as Exod 19:6 and Old Testament kingship material. Sympathetic to traditional formularies such as the threefold office, he remains unafraid to rework their details and emphases in light of what he thinks the biblical texts teach. Yet this scrupulous work in biblical theology is undertaken with robustly Trinitarian faith, confident in Scripture's unified witness to that drama of redemption.

Second, at a material level, then, *Kings and Priests* reframes TIS in terms of how readers imagine their identity in Christ. If Scripture identifies its ideal readers as a royal priesthood fulfilling Israel's hope in her Messiah, then certain practices follow by implication. Scripture reading will be integrally connected to being chosen for pursuing and promoting holiness. Scripture reading will evoke various ministries of communication. Scripture reading will attend regularly to prayerful participation in Jesus's priesthood. Scripture reading will require cultivating virtue even while relying on the mediation of Jesus; the most pertinent virtues will center on fearing and delighting in our holy God. Scripture reading will focus upon participating in God's covenant, the most definitive relationship and framework for life.

Therefore, Scripture reading will never stray too far from its oral foundations. Orality is metaphorically foundational to Scripture's self-presentation: God speaks, we hear and are enlivened to obey. But orality is more than metaphor: many if not most biblical texts incorporate oral traditions or components into their very composition. Most encounters of biblical texts with initial audiences would have been oral, and the hermeneutical consequences of this point can be vital, as illustrated in Richard Bauckham's work on the Book of Revelation. Most subsequent reading of Scripture in the tradition has been vocal and aural at the very least, if not consistently communal, given literacy rates and liturgical framing. Paul Griffiths and others have shown how the replacement of reading out loud with individual subvocalization coheres with modern shifts toward "consumerist" rather than truly "religious" reading, with attendant spiritual consequences. Thus Dr. Anizor's work, arriving at implications involving orality, provides another theological rationale for the biblical priority placed upon public reading of Scripture—to which many of our churches surely should pay more attention.

Kings and Priests is an evangelical Protestant book, though neither arrogant nor isolationist. Its interest in and approach to biblical theology reflect those evangelical roots. So too does a final material contribution: Dr. Anizor begins to rehabilitate the Protestant doctrine of the priesthood of all believers. The covenantal, oral, and other contexts of royal priesthood sketched herein will prevent that doctrine from being perverted into the isolated priesthood of each and every individual. Yet the context of union with Christ in his threefold office will prioritize personal participation in the royal priesthood as the backdrop for Scripture reading—a churchly practice, in which each believer has a prayerful share of privilege and responsibility. If Dr. Anizor hints at the embrace or even partial resolution of such tensions as divine sovereignty and human responsibility, then we can recognize still another one at stake here, in contemporary tendencies to lurch between communal and individual emphases. The priesthood of all believers has been a casualty of those recent Protestant mood swings.

Kings and Priests is not overdramatic, spelling out all its implications thoroughly and telling everyone else how they are wrong. For the most part, it is a theologically sensitive exercise in workmanlike biblical theology. Precisely that steady faithfulness gives it the formal and material significance sketched above. We may hope that Dr. Anizor himself, and others, will take up the implications hinted at here and work them out more thoroughly in years to come. Above all, of course, we must hope that churches themselves become more fully acquainted with, and more faithful to, their identity as a royal priesthood.

Daniel J. Treier

Acknowledgments

It is difficult to imagine anyone getting through a project like this without the help of many selfless and helpful others. I am grateful for the many expected and unexpected gifts of grace that accompanied me throughout this sometimes tortuous journey.

First, I'd like to thank my families—Anizor and Angelikas—for their regular encouragement, even though they often did not understand the nature of my doctoral work. Thanks for supporting me and never expressing doubt (especially when finances were lean) about whether this was the right course for us to follow.

A word of thanks to my professors at Southern Seminary for providing models of Christian scholarship that stirred up, rather than diminished, the desire to be a right reader of Scripture. In particular, I'd like to thank Gregg Allison for initially suggesting that I pursue some sort of theology of the reader.

The doctoral program at Wheaton College provided the ideal environment for me to grow into a PhD student. My gratitude extends to the generous donors, especially Mrs. June Cecelia Anderson, for significantly reducing the financial burden of doing doctoral work. I am also grateful to my 2007 cohort for providing companionship in a non-competitive environment, while, by their lives, prodding me to pursue excellence in the many areas of my own life. Similar things may be said of cohorts before and after mine. Jordan Barrett also deserves a special note for befriending me and providing an outlet to talk candidly about theology, theologians, church, and everything else. I needed that kind of friendship more than he can imagine.

My sincere gratitude goes to Talbot School of Theology for not only including me among its stellar faculty, but for also providing me with two semesters of a reduced load so that I might complete this project. I pinch myself regularly, astonished that this is where I get to work. It has been a privilege to serve alongside these men and women.

Thanks to Nicholas Perrin for providing thoughtful feedback on this project, much of which has saved me from great embarrassment. Thanks to Todd Billings for surfacing a number of issues in this project that needed clarification. His charitable and insightful comments were invaluable.

To Daniel Treier, my doctoral mentor, I am so greatly indebted. He took on a very shaky new student and tactfully, patiently, and graciously guided me through life change, coursework, and this project during time at Wheaton. I can hardly express my gratitude for the many times he pulled me from the brink of despair by his very timely sage and encouraging words. It was also a pleasure to have our family lives intertwined—an unexpected, but enriching experience. He models excellence as an evangelical husband, father, and scholar. I continue to learn so much from observing his life and work.

My two children—Zoe and Eli—who were born during the writing of this thesis, I cannot think about this project without thinking about the joy they brought during those years.

Finally, my wife and best friend, Melissa, was the chief source of encouragement on those days when giving up seemed imminent. I am grateful for all the sacrifices she made that I might finish this race. Her example is a constant reminder that I must not only read the Scriptures, but also live them. She is the sunshine of my every day. To her I dedicate this book.

Abbreviations

AB	Anchor Bible
AOTC	Abingdon Old Testament Commentary
AnBib	Analecta biblica
ANET	*Ancient Near Eastern Texts Relating to the Old Testament*. Edited by James B. Pritchard. 3rd ed. Princeton, 1969
ANF	*Ante-Nicene Fathers*. Edited by Alexander Roberts and James Donaldson. Buffalo, 1885–1896. 10 vols. Repr. Peabody, 1994
ApOTC	Apollos Old Testament Commentary
AThR	*Anglican Theological Review*
BBMS	Baker Biblical Monograph Series
BC	*The Book of Concord*. Edited by Robert Kolb and Timothy J. Wengert. Minneapolis, 2000.
BECNT	Baker Exegetical Commentary on the New Testament
BJS	Biblical and Judaic Studies
BS	Barth Studies
BSac	*Bibliotheca Sacra*
BSL	Biblical Studies Library
BST	The Bible Speaks Today
BTB	*Biblical Theology Bulletin*
CBC	Cambridge Bible Commentary
CBET	Contributions to Biblical Exegesis and Theology
CBQ	*Catholic Biblical Quarterly*
CBQMS	Catholic Biblical Quarterly Monograph Series
CCSS	Catholic Commentary on Sacred Scripture

CD	Karl Barth, *Church Dogmatics*. Edited and translated by G. W. Bromiley and T. F. Torrance. 4 vols. London, 2009
CEB	*Commentaire Évangélique de la Bible*
CGTC	Cambridge Greek Testament Commentary
CH	*Church History*
ConBNT	Coniectanea biblica: New Testament Series
EKKNT	Evangelisch-katholischer Kommentar zum Neuen Testament
ETR	*Études Théologiques et Religieuses*
EUS	European University Studies
FC	Fathers of the Church
FKD	Forschungen zur Kirchen- und Dogmengeschichte
FOTL	Forms of the Old Testament Literature
HSM	Harvard Semitic Monographs
HTKAT	Herders theologischer Kommentar zum Alten Testament
HTKNT	Herders theologischer Kommentar zum Neuen Testament
IBC	Interpretation: A Bible Commentary for Teaching and Preaching
ICC	International Critical Commentary
IJST	*International Journal of Systematic Theology*
Int	*Interpretation*
ITC	International Theological Commentary
JBL	*Journal of Biblical Literature*
JETS	*Journal of the Evangelical Theological Society*
JPSTC	Jewish Publication Society Torah Commentary Series
JR	*Journal of Religion*
JSHJ	*Journal for the Study of the Historical Jesus*
JSNT	*Journal for the Study of the New Testament*
JSNTSup	Journal for the Study of the New Testament: Supplement Series
JSOT	*Journal for the Study of the Old Testament*

JSOTSup	Journal for the Study of the Old Testament: Supplement Series
LCL	Loeb Classical Library
LD	Lectio divina
LHBOTS	Library of Hebrew Bible / Old Testament Studies
LW	*Luther's Works.* Edited by Jaroslav Pelikan and Helmut T. Lehmann. 56 vols. St. Louis and Philadelphia: Fortress Press, 1955–1986.
NAC	New American Commentary
NICNT	New International Commentary on the New Testament
NICOT	New International Commentary on the Old Testament
NIGTC	New International Greek Testament Commentary
NIVAC	NIV Application Commentary
NovTSup	Novum Testamentum Supplements
NPNF1	*Nicene and Post-Nicene Fathers*, Series 1. Edited by Philip Schaff. New York, 1886–1889. Reprint, Peabody, MA, 1994
NPNF2	*Nicene and Post-Nicene Fathers*, Series 2. Edited by Philip Schaff and Henry Wace. New York, 1890. Reprint, Peabody, MA, 1994
NSBT	New Studies in Biblical Theology
NTAbh	Neutestamentliche Abhandlungen
OBO	Orbis biblicus et orientalis
OTL	Old Testament Library
PNTC	Pillar New Testament Commentaries
RevExp	*Review and Expositor*
SA	*Smalcald Articles*
SC	*Small Catechism*
SHCT	Studies in the History of Christian Thought
SBAB	Stuttgarter biblische Aufsatzbände
SBJT	*Southern Baptist Journal of Theology*
SBLAB	Society of Biblical Literature Academia Biblica
SBLDS	Society of Biblical Literature Dissertation Series

SHBC	Smyth & Helwys Bible Commentary
SHCANE	Studies in the History and Culture of the Ancient Near East
SHR	Studies in the History of Religions (supplement to *Numen*)
SJT	*Scottish Journal of Theology*
ST	Thomas Aquinas, *Summa Theologiae*. London, 1964–1976
TDOT	*Theological Dictionary of the Old Testament*. Edited by G. J. Botterweck, H. Ringgren, and Heinz-Josef Fabry. Translated by J. T. Willis, G. W. Bromiley, D. E. Green, and D. W. Stott. 15 vols. Grand Rapids: Eerdmans, 1974–2006
TDNT	*Theological Dictionary of the New Testament*. Edited by G. Kittel and G. Friedrich. Translated by G. W. Bromiley. 10 vols. Grand Rapids: Eerdmans, 1964–1976
ThTo	*Theology Today*
TynBul	*Tyndale Bulletin*
VT	*Vetus Testamentum*
WeBC	Westminster Bible Companion
WBC	Word Biblical Commentary
WMANT	Wissenschaftliche Monographien zum Alten und Neuen Testament
WUNT	Wissenschaftliche Untersuchungen zum Neuen Testament
WW	*Word and World*
ZAW	*Zeitschrift für die alttestamentliche Wissenschaft*

1

On Locating the Readers of Scripture

To paraphrase the author of Ecclesiastes: "Of misreading many canonical books there is no end." The recent history of Bible (mis)reading followed on the heels of changing currents in philosophical hermeneutics. Chief among the developments was a rising consciousness of the perceived problems created by the historical and cultural distance between the world of the reader and that of the text.[1] Acknowledging these "problems," Gadamer stated that "the hermeneutic task consists in not covering up this tension [between historical text and present] by attempting a naive assimilation of the two but in consciously bringing it out."[2] Understanding, on his account, is always "the fusion of horizons," whereby the present horizon of the reader is seen *in* the historical text and "grows together" with it as a "continuing tradition."[3] Thus the reader's own historical situatedness cannot be ignored when trying to determine the "meaning" of an historical text. The reader has a voice and it shall, indeed must, be heard.

Such insights from Gadamer and others, however, have been transformed into what one writer has termed "The Reader's Liberation

---

1. See Thiselton, *The Two Horizons*, 51–84 (especially 63–69).

2. Gadamer, *Truth and Method*, 306. Elsewhere he writes: "[T]emporal distance is not something that must be overcome. This was, rather, the naive assumption of historicism . . . In fact the important thing is to recognize temporal distance as a positive and productive condition enabling understanding" (ibid., 297).

3. Ibid., 306. For Gadamer's discussion of effective history, see ibid., 300–302.

Movement,"[4] wherein the author and text have been overthrown and the reader, as a necessary component of understanding and "meaning," is crowned king. A result for biblical interpretation has been that any number of horizons, traditions, or ideologies may be fused with the biblical text to achieve "understanding" without any sense of impropriety.

The issue this situation raises, which the present study addresses, is that of the proper orientation to reading Scripture. Kevin Vanhoozer writes of the current situation: "The interests that control one's reading—be it an interest in the history behind the text, the grammar of the text, or one's existence in front of the text—is [sic] a function of the reader's choice."[5] This concern echoes that of C. S. Lewis, who, in discussing the proper approach to the Psalms, remarked: "Those who talk of reading the Bible 'as literature' sometimes mean, I think, reading it without attending to the main thing it is about; like reading Burke with no interest in politics, or reading the *Aeneid* with no interest in Rome. That seems to me to be nonsense."[6] In bringing any and every interest to bear upon reading Scripture, one is in danger of missing "the main thing."

Stanley Hauerwas' contention that the Bible should be taken from the hands of North American Christians, though controversial *prima facie*, might therefore be somewhat apt. He argues that North American Christians are schooled to believe that they are able to read the Bible without any moral or spiritual transformation. As a result, he observes:

> They read the Bible not as Christians, not as a people set apart, but as democratic citizens who think their common sense is sufficient for understanding the Scripture. They feel no need to stand under the authority of the truthful community to be told how to read. Instead they assume that they have all the "religious experience" necessary to know what the Bible is about. As a result the Bible inherently becomes the ideology for a politics quite different from the politics of the Church.[7]

The American Christian, reared as he is in an atmosphere of democratic individualism, should not be permitted access to the Bible, lest he use it to endorse habits and practices that are foreign to the church of Jesus Christ. Instead of trusting in the intelligence of the so-called "common

---

4. Eagleton, "The Revolt of the Reader," 449–52.
5. Vanhoozer, *Is There a Meaning*, 155.
6. Lewis, *Reflections on the Psalms*, 10.
7. Hauerwas, *Unleashing the Scripture*, 15.

person," the right reading of Scripture requires "having spiritual masters who can help the whole Church stand under the authority of God's Word."[8] The Christian reader of the Bible must read in and with the church, and is ever challenged to examine his "politics" as he approaches the Scriptures. Thus Hauerwas further helps to surface a constellation of issues relating to the reading of Scripture that in part animate this study, such as: (1) the effect of one's theology (or "politics") on interpretation; (2) the use of Scripture to underwrite sinful practices; (3) the posture of the reader toward the text; (4) the relationship between the public and personal reading of Scripture; and, therefore, (5) the role of the church community. These concerns undoubtedly point in the direction of a general question this project seeks to address, namely: What does it mean to be right readers of Scripture?

Although attempts to reform readers date at least as far back as Augustine,[9] an increasing number of writers have recently taken up the task of properly resituating the readers of Scripture. The growing sense is that only particular ways of approaching Scripture accord faithfully with its nature and functions. To be a right reader is to be a *follower* of the Word and this involves particular dispositions, approaches, responses, aims, and practices. To demonstrate that the contribution proposed here builds upon yet supplements previous studies, the following section offers a brief survey of recent approaches.

Contemporary Remedial Approaches

Although there is a polyphony of voices clamoring to be heard, this present work converses primarily with those proposals that attempt to construct thoroughgoing theological and theological-ethical depictions of the reader(s)' hermeneutical situation. Within this group, then, there are at least two tendencies: (1) to privilege divine action or (2) to privilege human response, usually cast as ethical-spiritual-communal formation.[10]

8. Ibid., 16–17.
9. See Augustine, *On Christian Teaching*.
10. One might add a third group, which consists of those who primarily advocate the development of certain "skills" (not methods) to aid in proper interpretation. Included among these is Charles Wood, who argues that responsible Christian readers of Scripture must have the right aim (knowledge of God, in the Calvinian and biblical sense), develop the appropriate skills (an ability to understand the verbal sense of signs, conceptual tools to make use of the signs, and the discernment to apply or not

Though ethics are not absent from the former, and divine agency from the latter, each has a distinct emphasis.[11] We take these up in turn.[12]

---

apply the text to a given situation), and a nuanced understanding of the two main functions of Scripture (as tradition/source and as canon) (Wood, *Formation of Christian Understanding*, 15–29).

11. An example of a recent treatment that is difficult to categorize is Matthew Levering's *Participatory Biblical Exegesis*, which argues that a renewed sense of history as participatory, as the history of the Triune God's renewal of the cosmos, opens up to readers new ways of seeing what is in the text of Scripture as well as a revitalized sense of the mediatorial role of the church in reading the Bible. Cf. Green, *Seized By Truth* and Treier, *Virtue and the Voice of God*, 129–62, which provide helpful summary accounts of some of the dispositions, aims, skills, assumptions, and methods necessary for reading the Bible Christianly.

12. Furthermore, lest I overstate the case, there are indeed a few proposals that seek to present construals of the reader that are both richly theological and ethical. Notable examples might include Vanhoozer and J. Todd Billings. In his earlier study of hermeneutics, Vanhoozer provides a Trinitarian proposal for reforming the reader, arguing first for a reinstatement of authors and texts in light of the God who in Jesus Christ and by his Spirit effectively communicates himself and his desire for covenantal relations with his people (Vanhoozer, *Is There a Meaning*, 206). Readers are recipients of divine communication and, therefore, followers, disciples, and witnesses of the Word (ibid., 374, 378, 441). Accordingly, his recommendations for right reading include (1) seeking interpretative virtues such as honesty about one's pre-understandings and commitments, openness to the ideas of the text, and obedience to the directions of the text (ibid., 376–77); (2) aiming for understanding, first and foremost, not for how the text might be used (ibid., 402); and (3) acknowledging an all-encompassing need for the Holy Spirit in every aspect of interpretation. Though attempting to be thoroughly theological, this early project by Vanhoozer borrows more from general hermeneutical and literary-critical resources, and has a more ethical tone to it (thus, the part of the subtitle: "The Morality of Literary Knowledge") than in *The Drama of Doctrine*. In the latter, he provides a more thoroughgoing theological account, or special hermeneutics for Scripture, that emphasizes the drama of redemption as the decisive context in which all theology and practice occur. Believers are actors in this drama, with God as playwright, the Holy Spirit (and pastors under him) as director, and canonical Scripture as the script. Bible reading in this scenario is not merely about culling truths about God from Scripture but about developing the character and skills requisite for fitting participation in the drama in which God is engaged with his people (Vanhoozer, *Drama of Doctrine*). Billings, in his recent constructive study of theological interpretation, follows a similar course, contending that readers of Scripture are those who participate in the Trinitarian drama of redemption. Reading as one involved in this story demands the development of *phronesis* and the improvisatory skills necessary for proper performance in the drama. Moreover, one must read as part of a community of Jesus' disciples who regularly hear and proclaim the Word of God, thus participating in the triune God's work of reforming the church and renewing creation (Billings, *Word of God for the People of God*, esp. 195–227).

Divine Action and the Readers of Scripture

The notion that the readers and reading cannot be construed without giving priority to the divine action that makes reading a possibility is the operating assumption of authors in this first group of proposals. Since it would be difficult to survey all of the relevant treatments, I will focus on a handful of the most distinctive and/or extensive ones.

In a recent article, Angus Paddison proposes that any account of the readers of Scripture must reckon with God's free revealing activity in Christ. He argues that the Word made flesh provides the soteriological and ontological basis for the possibility of being readers of the Bible:

> The Word of God, seizing hold of us by our humanity, opens up a dialogue between God and humanity. The consequence of this is that readers are capable of believing in and responding to this Word precisely through the prior act of the Word, the act which encloses the reader in communion with God. The Word made flesh reveals who and what the reader of scripture ontologically *is*.[13]

Since God in Christ speaks and saves from within our humanity, the reader and the Word of God exist in a "real and potential correspondence." "The giving of the Word and the reader's reception of the Word," Paddison adds, "constitute a united, saving act where what is given and received is appropriate to each of the agents."[14] Consequently, since Bible readers have already been addressed by the Word (which for Paddison is not identical with Scripture), they must emphasize passive habits of reception rather than active practices of construction. Obedient readers are those who let themselves be addressed by the Word of God when they engage Scripture.[15] Furthermore, the church's reading "around" and "under" the Word is eschatological since it occurs in the presence of the risen and victorious Christ. The Word made flesh, who now reigns, governs and guides the reading of Scripture both as its *telos* and as the sovereign Lord who reveals himself at the behest of his own will. In this light, reading is open-ended and never final; it awaits vigilantly the revelation of God, but never assumes it.[16] In the end, Paddison presents

---

13. Paddison, "Scriptural Reading and Revelation," 439.
14. Ibid.
15. Ibid., 440–41.
16. Ibid., 442–44.

a Christological depiction of readers as those saved, surrounded, and addressed by the Word made flesh. This Word creates the ontological possibility of reading Scripture faithfully, while providing a necessary eschatological orientation to the church's reading practices.

Trevor Hart describes right reading as primarily occurring "in the Spirit," wherein God chooses "to enter into fellowship with us and transforms our character in and through the process of reading."[17] Hart's primary emphasis is not on the competencies of human readers, for they are unable to supply what is necessary. Rather, he lays stress on the capacities of God, who in his freedom chooses to enter into a covenant relationship with us.[18] When the church turns to Scripture, God speaks and draws the community into the world of the text; Scripture's narrative "overlaps" with and becomes part of the community's story. This event of reading and understanding is out of the church's control; it happens because the church is encountering and communing with the God who is the main character of the story.[19] As Hart sums up:

> Reading the Bible as Scripture, then, is never a mere matter of handling texts and the relationships between texts. It is above all a matter of being in the presence and open to the handling of the One who, in some sense, is the final "author" of its message, because he is the one whose story it tells, and it is as we know him, as we dwell in his presence, and as he dwells in us that we see and hear what he is saying and showing to us through it. At this point general hermeneutics falls short, and we must confess the Christian reading of the Bible as Scripture to be *sui generis*.[20]

Reading in the Spirit, therefore, involves being sovereignly brought into fellowship with the One who brought Scripture into being, with the One of whom Scripture primarily speaks.

In a recent monograph, Mark Bowald attempts to mediate critically between approaches in theological hermeneutics which privilege divine agency and those that favor human agency.[21] He maintains that too much of the modern hermeneutical discussion is focused on the

---

17. Hart, "Tradition, Authority, and a Christian Approach," 202.

18. Ibid.

19. Ibid., 203.

20. Ibid., 204.

21. Bowald, *Rendering the Word*; cf. idem, "The Character of Theological Interpretation of Scripture," 162–83.

relationship between readers and texts, ignoring divine agency. He writes, "The problem is that in theological enterprises the very idea of removing oneself from the prior influence of God's agency is, at *best*, awkward. . . . Thus, when doing theology and especially when reading Scripture, it is an ingredient feature of our bearing to assume something like what Kant describes as operational antecedent judgments pertaining to the shape and nature of God's agency."[22] He therefore proposes placing divine action among the constituent factors in interpretation and develops what he calls his "triangular typology" of approaches to theological hermeneutics. Type One prioritizes human action in and with the texts themselves, asking, "What does the human authored text say?" Type Two privileges human agency in the activity of reading, asking, "What do readers do? How should they respond to the texts?" Type Three emphasizes divine agency, asking, "What does God do or say in the composition and reading of Scripture?" Wise and faithful Bible reading involves bringing together the concerns of both Types One and Two, but with an overarching awareness of divine agency throughout the process. Thus Bowald ultimately proposes what he calls "divine rhetorical hermeneutics," which describes the concerns of each type in classical rhetorical categories: Type One as the *logos*, Type Two as the *pathos*, and Type Three as the *ethos* of theological interpretation. In his schema, however, divine agency is not merely an equal party, but rather ubiquitous in the text's composition and every act of reading. God's action is the environment for the production and reception of Scripture. He concludes: "This way of representing the event of theological hermeneutics encourages us to do fuller justice to the fundamental character of divine agency in our thinking about theological hermeneutics. It presents us with the ubiquity of divine agency that permeates all aspects of biblical hermeneutics; the infinite and universal dimension of the trinitarian self-announcement to which Holy Scripture serves."[23] Thus Bowald brings together the concerns of all three types without opting for some cheap form of "balance" or a *via media*.

Finally, in order further to clarify, illustrate, and situate the concerns and orientation of this "pole" of the theological hermeneutical conversation, it will be helpful to examine one of its most forceful and representative proposals—that of John Webster.

22. Bowald, *Rendering the Word*, 25.
23. Ibid., 178.

The British theologian's thesis is relatively straightforward: "The Christian activity of reading the Bible is most properly (that is, Christianly) understood as a spiritual matter, and accordingly as a matter for theological description." Christian description of Scripture reading must first speak of God and then everything else *sub specie divinitatis*.[24] He laments the decline of the use of Christian doctrine to depict the church's Bible reading practices and calls for a renewal of dogmatic descriptions of the hermeneutical situation.[25] Webster argues that contemporary Christian approaches to hermeneutics tend to take one of two courses. On the one hand, there are proposals that seek to show how a particular hermeneutical strategy might provide an account of the Christian reading of Scripture. On the other hand, there are those who propose the appropriateness of a certain hermeneutical theory by linking it to a particular Christian doctrine. However, both of these approaches do not regard Christian doctrine as equal to the task of depicting how the church reads the Scriptures.[26] Following Ricoeur's description of the course of modern hermeneutics, he cites two reasons for the marginalization of doctrine.[27] First is a move Ricoeur refers to as "deregionalization," which denotes the process of subsuming special or regional hermeneutics under one general theory. This shift affects the place of dogmatic construals of hermeneutics by making general hermeneutical theory primary—minimizing the self-descriptions of Christian readers and maximizing the common features between the Christian act of reading and all other acts of reading, and thus envisaging the church's reading of Scripture as merely one instance of a general phenomenon.[28] The second and more serious move is the "radicalization" of hermeneutics, where ontology becomes more prominent than epistemology, such that the focus shifts from knowing to the interpreting self's modes of being in the world. This radicalizing of hermeneutics affects Christian theology and, thus, Christian discussions of hermeneutics by shifting attention away from

---

24. Webster, "Hermeneutics in Modern Theology," 47. Cf. idem, *Holy Scripture*, 68–106. See Scott, "Speaking to Form," 137–59, for a similar proposal.

25. The "hermeneutical situation" is an account of the "complex configuration" of agents involved, their locations, and implied aims; texts; and the acts performed by the agents in relation to the texts (Webster, "Hermeneutics in Modern Theology," 56).

26. Ibid., 49–50.

27. See Ricoeur, "The Task of Hermeneutics," 43–62.

28. Webster, "Hermeneutics in Modern Theology," 53–54.

God, Christ, the Spirit, etc., to the human self and making a non-Christian anthropology of "inwardness" axiomatic. Christian theology thus has little bearing on how one reads a text. What matters is the individual subject's ability to transcend the hindrances of culture and tradition in order to arrive at an understanding of oneself and the text.[29]

In response Webster proposes five principles that underlie a properly Christian construal of the hermeneutical situation: (1) there is no single thing called "understanding" and therefore the need to elaborate a transcendental hermeneutical phenomenology of the interpretive subject should be jettisoned. Hermeneutics needs to be "re-regionalized"; (2) the main task of this re-regionalized hermeneutics is to depict accurately the church's reading of the Bible, not to develop a general theory to ground it; (3) such a depiction requires a Christian hermeneutical ontology that is governed by Christian doctrine; (4) therefore, the Christian construal is not pre-doctrinal, but entirely theological, being determined by and responsible to the Word of God; (5) theological hermeneutics will be confident and faithful when it speaks much about its true axiom: Jesus Christ made present in the Spirit to the church.[30]

Webster moves on to describe the hermeneutical situation positively. He avers that the Christian reading situation is *sui generis* because it involves the Bible as the living voice of God that addresses his people and brings about faith and obedience.[31] Webster lauds some recent proposals in hermeneutics for rightly stressing the ecclesial location of reading acts, but chides them for largely neglecting meaningful talk about divine agency. "Ecclesiality," or even the church, cannot be grasped properly apart from a right description of the action of God. Thus the hermeneutical situation is to be defined in particular and contingent ways—as an episode in the history of God's self-manifestation to and, consequently, redemption of his people. As such the main elements of a theological construal of Christian Bible reading will (1) describe God as "Word," thus emphasizing his will and primacy in communicating himself; (2) speak of the Bible as an instrument of divine action; (3) employ an

---

29. Ibid., 54–56. Inwardness is defined by Webster as "the way in which selfhood is abstracted from backgrounds or frameworks" (ibid., 54–55).

30. Ibid., 57–58.

31. Ibid., 58–59.

anthropology not devoid of spiritual dispositions; and (4) define reading of the Bible as the *church's* reading.[32]

Highlighting that God is Word brings to the fore certain features that are important to the discussion of reading the Bible. First, "Word" underlines that God is self-communicative in what he does and says. Second, this self-communication is free, sovereign, and spiritual, that is, God alone governs the initiation, form, and reception of his Word. Finally, God's self-communication has a purpose, which is to give the knowledge of himself for those to whom he chooses to manifest himself.[33] When God is understood in this way—as the One who is known only on his own terms—Christian doctrine begins to take center stage in depicting the hermeneutic situation.

Turning to the biblical text, Webster's thesis is that "the Bible is an instrument of divine action, a means through which the *viva vox Dei* speaks to the congregation of faithful believers in the course of the history of salvation." Therefore, theological hermeneutics is primarily concerned with hearing God speak.[34]

A Christian description of the readers of Scripture must account for those conditions outside of the reading self that make it possible for there to be a self at all. It must therefore situate readers within the history of redemption and thus a very particular hermeneutical situation. Every act of Bible reading is an event in the history of God's overcoming of sin, and is therefore a moral and spiritual act.[35] Any anthropology of the reader must, therefore, employ concepts like faith, consent, discipleship, and prayer. The reading of Scripture is a responsive activity, called forth, enabled, and sustained by the power of God.[36] While talk of readers' skills and roles has some place, more attention must be given to the language of soul formation—using terms like mortification and vivification. This emphasis on divine action mitigates the potential in much talk of interpretive virtues to "immanentize" or "psychologize" the

---

32. Ibid., 63–64.

33. Ibid., 66–68.

34. Ibid., 72–73. Webster elsewhere argues that the deficiency of many proposals in theological hermeneutics is found in their lack of a theological ontology of Scripture, rooted in the resurrection of Jesus Christ (see Webster, "Resurrection and Scripture," 138–55).

35. Webster, "Hermeneutics in Modern Theology," 77–79.

36. Ibid., 82–83.

eschatological nature of the Christian life and thus minimize the intrusive character of the Spirit's activity for and in us.[37]

Webster concludes his account with a few words about the need to read the Bible in community. One cannot be a wise reader of Scripture apart from the historical practices of the church. Of the latter, Webster stresses the canon, creeds, and traditions as those aspects of Christian practice that govern and guide our reading of Scripture. Moreover, when speaking of the reading community we must speak of the "church" and not some form of "ecclesiality." The latter is vague and general, while the former makes reference to the particular community in which the Word of God is heard and received.[38] It is this community that can properly read the Bible.

Among the many strengths of Webster's account is his forceful and consistent emphasis on divine priority, initiative, and action as that which most fundamentally forms the situation in which readers of the Bible find themselves. To begin with the reading subject(s) is to begin with that which is not the beginning, often leading to truncated and only half-true accounts of readers and their situation. It is God and his free decision to enter into a relationship with his people that most significantly defines the readers of Scripture. Similarly, far from altogether rejecting anthropological considerations, Webster deploys biblical and theological concepts to frame what it is to be human, namely, to be one encountered by the triune God of grace. When speaking of the readers of Scripture, it is with these particular human beings that we are concerned. Moreover, by correlating the deity and self-communication of God with a construal of the nature of the Bible as the living voice of God, Webster's treatment places a strong moral imperative upon readers of the Bible. When Christians take up the Bible, they are immediately confronted by God himself, and this encounter calls for an appropriate response—faith, love, obedience, consent.

Indeed, the primary concern of the theologians in this group is to depict the reader's situation in dogmatic terms—often deploying Trinitarian and Christological categories in order to situate readers vis-à-vis God. Other major emphases include the priority of divine agency and freedom, especially in the establishment of a covenant with his people, the need for the Holy Spirit to transform readers and make reading

37. Ibid., 84.
38. Ibid., 84–86.

effective, Scripture as the instrument in God's work of renewal, and the stress that Bible reading is a unique event. While ethical-spiritual issues in interpretation are a matter of concern, they are treated secondarily in these proposals and are, therefore, often underdeveloped. Furthermore, though some mention is made of the church as the location of proper Bible reading, Webster and others do not develop a more thorough account of the corporate and communal aspects of reading Scripture.[39] For a more extensive treatment of these concerns one must turn elsewhere.

Human Response and the Readers of Scripture

To situate readers rightly involves speech not only about divine agency, but also about the human responses called for by such agency. Readers in the Christian community are summoned by God and in Scripture to embody particular virtues and character that make for faithful and fruitful Bible reading. Therefore, among a second group of theologians, exegetes, and ethicists, theological reflection on the nature of readers of Scripture tends toward the moral, spiritual, and communal formation of readers. What these writers seek to do is offer thick descriptions of the human dimensions of the act of reading Scripture. To illustrate the concerns of this group, I will offer a few of the more noteworthy examples.

Richard Briggs provides an account of the interpretative virtues founded upon rich interaction with Old Testament (OT) literature. His thesis is that the OT in its varied narrative and prophetic episodes presents a portrait of the moral and ethical character that is most to be desired, "and this in turn is the implied character of one who would read these texts, especially one in search of their own purposes and values."[40] In constructing his account of the implied reader of Scripture, Briggs attempts to theologize the interpretive virtues (as they have typically been treated) by presenting OT figures as exemplars of them. Moses (Num 12:3) is the example of humility, Solomon (1 Kgs 3) of wisdom and *phronesis*, Hezekiah (2 Kgs 18–19) of trust, Ruth (Ruth 1–4) and Elisha (2 Kgs 5) of steadfast love and charity, and Isaiah (Isa 6) of receptivity

---

39. On many occasions, the absence of these aspects is likely due to the brevity of the authors' treatments of the subject. In other cases, this does not appear to be the case. This study responds to *published* proposals, not what the authors might say under different circumstances.

40. Briggs, *The Virtuous Reader*, 17.

to divine mystery.⁴¹ Real readers of Scripture are called to aspire, in the context of a Christian community, to embody these virtues, as the possession of them accompanies masterful handling of the Bible.⁴²

Also notable is Eugene Rogers' study of Aquinas and biblical interpretation.⁴³ He argues through Thomas that interpretation as a human act requires a distinction between the *conveniens ratio* (fitting explanation) and the *sensus spiritualis* of a biblical text—the latter being known only to God. When this "usual gap" between God's knowledge and our own is recognized, the reader learns to accept the contingency of all interpretation, and this further produces the necessary virtue of humility.⁴⁴ Moreover, since the literal sense in Thomas can be manifold and underdetermined (since it is God's intended meaning, which may be multiple), other tools must be marshaled to distinguish fitting from unfitting readings. First, readers must bring the proper theological aims to the event of interpretation. For Thomas these aims include unifying the two Testaments, explicating the atonement, and providing a Christian reading of Numbers.⁴⁵ Second, readers must possess the right moral virtues—charity, justice, and prudence—to read texts correctly. The goodness of any interpretation, as with any human act, must be measured by more than the technical and intellectual skill displayed; it must also be judged by its moral character. Readers are to attend to the goodness and fruit of a reading, not merely its truth and skill.⁴⁶ Finally, a reader must bring an active sense of divine agency in revelation through Scripture, a profound faith in God's providence and protection against ultimately distorting interpretations, and thus a spirit of prayer to his many acts of interpretation, in order to render fruitful and fitting readings of the Bible.⁴⁷

Along similar lines, L. Gregory Jones suggests that questions of interpretative method and biblical authority can be addressed more helpfully by attention to the development of habits for effective and faithful

---

41. Ibid., chaps. 2–6.
42. Ibid., 206–10.
43. Rogers, "How the Virtues of an Interpreter," 64–81.
44. Ibid., 70–71. Access to the spiritual sense is then mediated through the church in the form of the community's agreed upon *conveniens ratio* (ibid., 71).
45. Ibid., 75.
46. Ibid., 76–77.
47. Ibid., 80–81.

Bible reading. These habits result from the formation of a "scriptural imagination," wherein the church knows the stories and convictions of the Scriptures so intimately that it then has the freedom creatively to live in and interpret their world as the Bible does.[48] The development of such an imagination, and consequently the habits of wise reading, involves catechesis (i.e., immersion in the stories and judgments of Scripture), critical study (i.e., wrestling with the Bible by use of philological, rhetorical, historical, and literary tools), and social engagement (i.e., experiencing the fruitful tension between one's social reality and the biblical text). In these ways, the Bible is treated as a Word "that journeys with us."[49] In the end, the wise reader of Scripture is one who reads with a Christocentric focus in the company of other disciples of Jesus, recognizing Scripture as given by God with multiple senses, but unified Testaments. She is open to being transformed by Scripture and displays the interpretive virtues of receptivity, humility, truthfulness, courage, charity, and imagination.[50]

As with the first group of proposals, to illustrate better the concerns of this "pole" of the theological hermeneutical conversation, I will examine one of its most cogent and extensive proposals—that of Stephen Fowl—as it takes up and integrates the concerns of the aforementioned accounts.

In the context of addressing the fact that Christians have sometimes used the Bible to underwrite sinful practices, Fowl explains how his theory of underdetermined interpretation does not necessarily aid and abet such practices, but rather fosters faithful readings of Scripture. It is not an overdeveloped theory of textual meaning that precludes improper use of Scripture, but rather the appropriation of a complex web of Christian beliefs and practices.[51] Fowl contends that Christian conviction regarding the pervasiveness and distorting effects of sin summons believers to maintain a certain vigilance over their interpretation. These beliefs about sin make necessary the practices of confession, forgiveness, and reconciliation in the church. Finally, when these practices are

---

48. Jones, "Formed and Transformed," 21.

49. Ibid., 21–27.

50. Ibid., 27–32. For a similar list of traits necessary for proper interpretation, see the nine theses of *The Scripture Project* in Davis and Hays, eds., *The Art of Reading Scripture*, 1–5.

51. Fowl, *Engaging Scripture*, chap. 3.

in good working order, they aid in the formation of virtuous readers who can exercise interpretative charity in disputes and who live truthful, faithful Christian lives.[52]

He develops this argument by making sustained use of the eye metaphor found in Luke 11:34–36. The eye represents one's powers of perception and judgment, according to Fowl: "If these powers are single-mindedly focused on Jesus, then one is full of light." He who is not intently focused on Jesus proves that his eye is defective, resulting in spiritual darkness.[53] The warning of Luke 11:34–36 is that the Christian must consider seriously the state of his eye, lest he become incapable of rendering a proper response to Jesus. What this requires is vigilant, ongoing attention to the faculties by which one perceives and makes judgments about Jesus. This insight relates to reading in that instead of focusing on theories of interpretation, the Christian is called to keep his eye singularly focused on Jesus Christ.[54] Twofold vigilance is then required: one directed at oneself and the church, in the form of honest and critical self-reflection; the other directed similarly, but this time for the purpose of making one better able to focus on God.[55] In fact, what Luke's Gospel makes clear throughout (e.g., 7:36–50; 18:9–14; 18:18–24; 19:1–10) is that those who respond well to Jesus are those who see themselves as sinners whose redemption comes through a singular focus on Jesus. Confessing oneself a sinner

> orients one in such a way that it is possible to begin that process of keeping one's eye single and of redirecting one's eye on those occasions when one begins to confuse darkness with light. This, then, becomes a primary and necessary element which an underdetermined account of biblical interpretation will invoke as a way to counter the habit of reading scripture in ways that underwrite sin.[56]

In the end, if Christians are to read the Bible rightly, they must first recognize themselves as sinners.

Yet seeing ourselves as sinners is not enough to free us from endorsing sinful practices through our reading. Christians must also find

52. Ibid., 74–75.
53. Ibid., 76.
54. Ibid., 77–78.
55. Ibid., 78–79.
56. Ibid., 81.

themselves within a community that practices forgiveness, repentance, and reconciliation, in order that they might be formed into single-minded people. The process is as follows: when a Christian recognizes that she is a sinner within the context of this type of community, she is immediately drawn into God's forgiveness, which leads to repentance and, ultimately, reconciled relationships with God and others.[57] These new patterns and practices help her to become the type of person who can faithfully embody the Scriptures with a single eye. Conversely, when those beliefs and practices are distorted, Christians will be unable to read and live out Scripture without using it for sinful ends.[58]

Not only is it necessary to recognize oneself as a sinner and practice forgiveness, repentance, and reconciliation within a Christian community, one must also grow in virtue in order to become a faithful reader of Scripture. As Christians regularly avail themselves of the above practices, they are transformed by the Spirit into the likeness of Christ, or grow in virtue. The primary virtue Fowl treats is charity, asking how the exercise of charity might aid in resolving interpretative disputes. The charitable interpreter, according to Fowl, will display at least three traits. First, she is willing to listen to differences and reject the temptation to reduce or rationalize the differences away. Second, she will unearth and clarify the true nature of the points of agreement within a dispute. Finally, she will assiduously avoid attributing irrationality to those with which she disagrees.[59] Other virtues include openness—to friendships with outsiders and to the Spirit's often-radical guidance—as well as *phronesis*. Concerning the former, Fowl argues from Acts 10–15 that the decision of the Jerusalem council involved "a complex series of interactions between interpretations of the Spirit's work and Spirit-inspired interpretation and application of scripture."[60] The Jerusalem church would not have arrived at the decision they did had they not been willing to read the signs that the Spirit was also active among Gentiles. Likewise, the contemporary church will only be able to embody Scripture properly

---

57. Ibid., 83–84. Fowl elsewhere adds the communal practices of admonishing and correcting one another, truth telling/seeking, and the exercise of patience as necessary for faithful interpretations of Scripture (see Fowl, *Theological Interpretation of Scripture*, 52, 64–70).

58. Fowl, *Engaging Scripture*, 84.

59. Ibid., 87–91.

60. Ibid., 113.

when it is able to discern the works of the Spirit around them in new situations and in various people, which involves the practice of developing friendships with diverse others, fittingly correlating these with their readings of Scripture.[61]

The strengths of Fowl's account are at least fourfold. First, unlike so many writers in hermeneutics, he attempts to provide a portrait of the reader that is rooted in biblical exegesis, not in philosophical or general hermeneutical reflection. A creative reading of Luke and Acts, for example, provides a biblical basis for a reorientation of readers of Scripture. Second, he rightly sees that some of the most fundamental issues regarding proper reading are moral and spiritual, not simply methodological, and provides an extended account of the spiritual-ethical work involved in helping Christians to approach the Bible rightly. Third, through his albeit controversial reading of Acts 10–15, he provides a concrete way to apply Scripture by the aid of the Spirit, thus making reading an "open" activity. Finally, more than the first group of theologians, Fowl's account of the reader is explicitly and extensively communitarian, and that in at least two ways. On the one hand, he tends to speak of the community as those who read Scripture together (discerning the Spirit, practicing charity, etc.). On the other hand, he speaks of the community as that which forms single-minded and virtuous readers. Therefore, Fowl presents a robust account of the community as at once the subject, school, and context of proper Bible reading.[62]

Theologians in this second group, like Fowl, aim to depict the reader's situation in primarily ethico-spiritual terms—consistently deploying virtue and ecclesial categories.[63] Readers approach Scripture correctly

---

61. For Fowl's extended discussion, see ibid., 86–127. On his treatment of *phronesis*, see ibid., chap. 7.

62. Cf. Fowl and Jones, *Reading in Communion*, which provides a fuller account of the development of Christian communities of character that learn to perform the Scriptures.

63. Other noteworthy ethico-spiritual proposals include the following. Alan Jacobs provides an eloquent Augustinian theology of charitable reading, viewing love of God and love of neighbor as the governing hermeneutical guideline and goal (Jacobs, *A Theology of Reading*). Wesley Kort provides a portrait of right reading that he calls "centripetal reading." The process begins with divesting oneself of any claims that one brings something good or praiseworthy to the act of reading and it then continues with the reception of "saving knowledge" from God, which leads to heart transformation and change in the reader's direction (Kort, *Take, Read*, 28). Also see Paul Griffiths' brief essay on the importance of distinguishing between various types of reading. Here he con-

as they develop moral, theological, and interpretative virtues within the context of the church's practices and as participants in Scripture's ongoing story of God and his people. Chief among the requisite virtues and practices are humility as the recognition of one's own finitude and imperfection, wisdom to discern and practice fitting readings, charity that allows for plurality in interpretation, faith in God, consistent prayer, and communal formation through catechesis and social engagement. However, apart from a few somewhat ambiguous treatments of the Spirit's leading, there is little emphasis in this group on that which primarily defines the hermeneutical situation, and thus the reader: God's prior action on behalf of his people. Hence, in light of these two polarities in the current conversation regarding readers of Scripture, further ways need to be sought to bring together the concerns of both groups.

Thesis and Argument: A Royal Priesthood of Readers

As some of the above proposals have at least suggested, the two polarities need not be mutually exclusive. In agreement with Trevor Hart, these perspectives are not incompatible yet, as he notes, "they are differences of emphasis that could ultimately lead in significantly different directions."[64] This study, therefore, aims to correct and corroborate both groups through the deployment of a biblical-theological

---

trasts academic, "Proustian," and "Victorine" modes of reading, arguing that Christian theological schools must give serious attention to what mode is most essential to the formation of students. He favors the Victorine option since it has moral transformation as an important end (Griffiths, "Reading as a Spiritual Discipline," 32–47), and his *Religious Reading*, for a detailed and enlightening account of different types of reading among various religious groups. Other, less detailed proposals have been offered by Francis Watson. For example, he appeals to eleven principles derived from Augustine's *On Christian Teaching* to help govern what would make a good interpreter, such as a personal orientation toward holiness and the fear of God (Watson, "Authors, Readers, Hermeneutics," 122–23). Elsewhere he takes up the cause of defending the three unpopular ideas of single determinate meaning, the role of readers as receiving not creating meaning, and the possibility of adjudicating between interpretations. Although indirect, his defense serves as a way of repositioning the reader rightly (see *Text and Truth*, 95–126). See also Peterson, "Caveat Lector," 2–12 and idem, "Eat This Book," 5–17.

64. Hart, "Tradition," 202. Christopher Spinks' recent publication attempts to offer a middle way between (roughly) these two polarities, focusing on the issue of "meaning" in the proposals of Vanhoozer and Fowl (see Spinks, *The Bible and the Crisis of Meaning*).

motif: royal priesthood. I argue that the designation of Israel and the church as a royal priesthood, conditioned and informed by the related Israelite offices of king and priest, carries with it themes that frame the hermeneutical situation in such a way that both divine agency and human responsibility are given due weight in the depiction of readers of Scripture. This study provides a biblical-theological lens through which to see the unity of both poles—theological *and* ethical accounts of readers. Moreover, along with bringing together these apparently divergent streams, this project has another concern: to give biblical theology a seat at the hermeneutical table.[65] At the risk of being simplistic, it must be said that Scripture should have its say on how to read Scripture—even if we must bring this into interaction with a wider set of considerations. Though the above proposals present cogent Christian efforts to reinstate a relationship between Scripture and readers that is appropriate to the nature and functions of the Bible, with the exception of exegesis done by Fowl, Briggs, and a few authors on select portions of Scripture, it seems that biblical theology has not received extensive engagement, nor have its key themes been leveraged, to present a more comprehensive picture of Bible readers and their situation—one that accounts compellingly for both divine agency and human response.[66] This study intends to help fill

---

65. What I have in mind is a theologically interested and informed version of biblical theology—one that views the Bible as a unity centered on Christ. Moreover, I trace the canonical development of a particular theme. For a typology of biblical theologies and their relationship to the theological interpretation of Scripture, see Treier, "Biblical Theology," 16–31.

66. Calvin Seerveld does extensive exegesis of Numbers 22–24 and draws out implications for reading Scripture correctly in *How to Read the Bible to Hear God Speak*. Other significant exceptions might include Treier, *Virtue and the Voice of God*, chap. 3, where he undertakes a biblical theology of wisdom by interpreting Prov 3:13–18 within the context of Proverbs 1–9, the rest of the OT, and the NT. He further examines what the NT teaches regarding the founding and formation of wisdom and *phronesis*. In his *Introducing Theological Interpretation*, Treier throughout examines the image of God theme in the OT and NT as an example of the issues related to theological interpretation. Also see Moberly, *The Bible, Theology, and Faith*, which offers thick interpretations of Luke 24, Genesis 22, and Matthew's gospel on the way to arguing for a theologically (indeed Christologically) informed biblical hermeneutic. Somewhat related is Moberly's sequel to the aforementioned, *Prophecy and Discernment*, which examines key OT and NT texts to find ways to understand the nature of prophecy, as well as criteria for discerning prophetic voices. Vanhoozer presents Paul's letter to Philemon as a metaphor for right reading with Paul as author, Philemon as reader, and Onesimus the slave as the text that has no claims on Philemon (Vanhoozer, "Imprisoned or Free?," 89). Also, G. Venema's study of reading in the OT has some parallels to my work,

these gaps, not least by seeking to understand how biblical motifs such as covenant actually hold the relevant concepts together.

The study is broken into three parts. Part I is an exploration of royal priesthood as it relates to the Word of God in biblical theological perspective. Chapter 2 examines the motif of royal priesthood throughout the Old and New Testaments, focusing on Exod 19:4–6 and 1 Pet 2:4–9 as the programmatic texts, Isa 59–62, the book of Revelation, Hebrews, ultimately terminating in the Pauline corpus.[67] The goal of this chapter is to describe royal priesthood and the themes that help inform it, examine how this designation relates to the Word of God (broadly defined), and demonstrate that royal priesthood provides a biblical-theological depiction of how God's people are to "read" his Word.[68] Chief among these themes are divine initiative in electing and sanctifying God's people (and the privileges these afford), the institution of a covenant, the corresponding responsibility of the people to be holy through obedience to the law, and the resultant vocation of Israel and the church to proclaim God's Word.

The third chapter adds depth to the portrait of Israel (and the church) as royal priestly "readers" by presenting the ideal king of Israel as the ideal Israelite. As the ruler of the people, he played a key role in shaping Israel with respect to its self-understanding. This chapter contends that the Old Testament presents Israel's monarch, among other things, as the ideal *exemplarist* "reader" of God's Word—the one whose attitude toward, aims in "reading," and responses to torah are to be

---

though his emphasis is on the unifying purpose of torah reading narratives and not on the role of the reader (see Venema, *Reading Scripture in the Old Testament*). None of these exegetically grounded proposals, however, substantially address the polarity I wish to pursue in this study.

67. These texts represent the most explicit references to corporate priesthood. An account of the implicit references and themes is beyond the scope of this study.

68. By "reading" (particularly in quotation marks) this study refers to a variety of modes of engagement with God's Word in its many forms—as spoken, written, and/or symbolized. Thus, "reading" is to be seen as a multifaceted church practice, or a conglomeration of several practices, and includes hearing, ordinary reading, speaking, preaching, and many other acts. Part of the argument of the study is that reading must take many forms if it is to be faithful to the character and call of Scripture, and achieve all the goods internal to it (to borrow from MacIntyre, *After Virtue*, 187).

emulated by Israel.[69] He is the preeminent virtuous "reader."[70] He was the paradigmatic devotee to torah, whose spiritual success and shaping of the nation depended largely on his relationship to God and his law. This thesis regarding the king is developed by an examination of the OT depictions of the king-torah relationship found in Deuteronomy's kingship law, two narratives involving Israelite kings, and the Psalter.[71] What emerges from this exploration is that royal "reading" is virtuous reading, characterized, at the very least, by love for, openness to, submission under, and obedience to God's Word.

Chapter 4 examines the Old Testament presentation of the priesthood and its relationship to God's Word. I argue that as judges, teachers of the law, and cultic officials, the priests functioned as the paradigm for didactic Scripture reading in the OT, and that this is borne out in the legal, narrative, and prophetic material in the form of prescriptions, descriptions, and denouncements. As with the kingship, Israel's self-understanding as a royal *priesthood* was shaped by the priesthood of its experience. As a particular relation to the Word of God defines

---

69. In chapter 4 I will refer to the priests as ideal "didactic" readers of Scripture. The designation "exemplarist" denotes that, for the king, a primary purpose of reading torah was to inculcate and model personal piety and love for YHWH and his law, especially for the purpose of leading the people well. The term "didactic" seeks to convey that the priests' reading of torah was directed toward teaching the people in various forms. Although the terms "exemplarist" and "didactic" are used in this way, it is acknowledged that for the king there was also a public dimension to his reading and, for the priest, a responsibility to appropriate torah personally. Moreover, both had corporate piety as chief aims of their "reading." That being said, their key functions in relation to torah may still be accurately described as exemplarist and didactic, that is, piety as a public model (king) in contrast to public instruction (priest).

70. I will define *virtue* in this chapter by the use of three concepts: attitude/disposition, aim, and response. By *attitude/disposition* I refer to the reader's heart-orientation toward God's Word (e.g., humility, openness, love for, etc.); by *aims* I have in mind the reader's intended ends in reading (e.g., to become pure, to be fortified in abstaining from sin, to conform to God's will, etc.); by *responses* I speak of the enacted outcomes or results of reading (e.g., obedience, avoidance of evil influences, delight in God's ways, faith, etc.). Responses do sometimes become dispositions, and aims become responses. But the three categories are helpful in understanding how one's approach to each shapes the reading act in a specific way and renders it virtuous or not virtuous.

71. The texts selected in chapters 3 and 4 are largely representative examples from the biblical canon. Related to this, some historical nuance in the presentation of kingship and priesthood has been avoided for reasons of scope (e.g., the apparent hope for a fusion of both offices in the post-exilic period in Zechariah 6). What follows is largely a synchronic reading of those texts.

the professional priesthood, so it does the universal priesthood. What we discover is that "reading" for the priesthood involves the following: teaching torah; distinguishing between sacred and profane, clean and unclean; instructing the people on such matters; judging difficult civil cases according to the wisdom gained from torah; and pronouncing identity-forming blessings on Israel. In the end, the priest is to interpret torah faithfully *for others* and apply it to the difficult and changing circumstances of Israel's community life.[72] This chapter begins to address the issues of the ecclesial use and appropriation of Scripture, the interrelationship between well-functioning public reading practices and communal piety, and the dynamism of reading acts, among other matters.

Part II is a bridge between the biblical theology of Part I and the theological synthesis of the final chapters. In the fifth chapter, Jesus Christ is presented as the obedient King, faithful High Priest, and the fulfillment of Israel's corporate call as a royal priesthood. I contend that he fulfills these callings significantly *by* being the supreme "reader" of God's Word. In his person and work he demonstrates that to be king, priest, and Israel-as-royal priesthood, is to be oriented to the Word of God in a particular way that reflects OT expectations of torah fidelity but transcends them. I contend, first, that traditional construals of Christ's threefold office do not adequately take account of the centrality of the Word of God to each of the offices. Consequently, it will be demonstrated that the Mediator's offices are logocentric and are united by this focus on the Word of God. In the end, to be "Christ" is to exemplify the type of relationship to God's Word that remained unrealized in the OT. This chapter establishes this picture of Christ as Word-centered King, Priest, and Israel-as-royal priesthood by examining the Gospels' portrayals of his life and ministry. The chapter concludes by offering three episodes of Jesus' "reading" of torah in Mark's Gospel in order to provide concrete examples of Jesus as the ideal royal-priestly reader of Scripture. Ultimately this chapter lays the groundwork for viewing Scripture reading covenantally: Jesus as the Mediator and embodiment of the covenant accomplishes his work through his "reading" of the Word. He is the sub-

---

72. It is worth acknowledging that there may have been some development over time of the nature and function of priesthood in Israel. For a brief discussion of different views regarding this possible development of priestly functions, see Betts, *Ezekiel the Priest*, 5–9.

ject matter of Scripture and the standard for proper reading practices. Reading is covenantal, and covenantal reading is Christological.[73]

Chapter 6 details Martin Luther's theology of the priesthood of believers and presents it as a fruitful and concrete, though underdeveloped, attempt to integrate royal priesthood with the reading of the Word of God. Luther is important because he brings together many of the central biblical-theological themes related to royal priesthood, offers some of the clearest arguments for universal priesthood, ties royal priesthood to the Word of God in rich ways, and broadens our understanding of the Word of God by prioritizing its oral and sacramental forms. In the end, he argues that all believers share the privilege of royal priesthood, and their common principal calling is to "proclaim" the Word in its many forms. Through Luther, I develop further the case that revitalizing a vision for royal priesthood, or the priesthood of all believers, may open up the way for the greater transformation of the church's life and mission by the Word.

Part III brings together the results of the study by foregrounding the major theological and ethical themes that attend royal priesthood, and suggests how these contribute to a depiction of readers and their situation that draws from both poles of current hermeneutical discussions. Chapter 7 deals with the place of divine agency—in the forms of election and sanctification—in situating readers of Scripture biblically as a royal priesthood. Chapter 8 addresses the place of human response in depicting readers, focusing on some interpretive "virtues" as well as reading practices that flow most directly from the study of the biblical material and attend a royal-priestly relationship with the Word of God. At the center of these poles is the covenant—the nexus of divine and human relations—and Jesus Christ as the embodiment of reading in light of the covenant. Through open engagement with and guided reflection on the biblical material, this study aims to help make contemporary

---

73. In the OT and NT sections, the question may be raised as to why the prophetic office was left out of this treatment. With respect to the *munus triplex* of Christ I simply contend that, though Christ fulfilled all three offices, it is not clear in Scripture that he fulfilled a teaching role mainly *as prophet* (as is taught traditionally). For formal or heuristic purposes it is appropriate to divide his offices and the functions peculiar to each. However, in the OT, all three offices had teaching functions, though I argue that the priest was the primary expositor of torah. Jesus as the fulfillment of all offices performed the functions most proper to those offices, while giving full expression to the fact that in the OT the functions were sometimes blurred.

theological interpretation further conversant with biblical theology, as well as Christology, soteriology, theological anthropology, and ecclesiology, that these conversations would yield more fruitful and faithful readers of Scripture, the *viva vox Dei*.

PART ONE

Royal Priesthood and "Reading" in Biblical-Theological Perspective

2

Royal Priesthood Meets the Word of God

A Biblical-Theological Sketch

The distinctiveness of the people of God in the Old and New Testaments is summed up well in the epithet "royal priesthood." That Israel and the church are bestowed a particular dignity and calling is without question, but the specific character of these benefits requires some elaboration. For our purposes, does the royal priestly privilege and vocation of God's people have any connection to the Word of God or any bearing on how they are to approach it? The goal of this chapter is to (1) outline the biblical theme of royal priesthood by looking at the most explicit references to it in Scripture, giving special attention to Exod 19:1–6 and 1 Pet 2:4–9 as the central texts in the OT and NT respectively, (2) highlight key connections between royal priesthood and God's Word, and (3) demonstrate that royal priesthood and the theological themes that accompany and comprise it—election, sanctification, obedience, holiness, suffering, and vocation—provide a biblical and theological depiction of God's people as readers of his Word. Ultimately, these themes help to bring together, at least preliminarily, the two poles in the hermeneutical conversation by depicting readers and the reading of Scripture in both theological and practical-ethical terms. What follows are the basic elements upon which subsequent chapters will expand in various ways. We begin our exploration at the base of Mount Sinai, where the call of God's people as a royal priesthood is programmatically articulated.

Israel as a Royal Priesthood

The Programmatic Text: Exodus 19:1–6

After YHWH's mighty deliverance of Israel from the Egyptian forces (Exod 14), his miraculous provision of water (15:22–27; 17:1–7), manna (16:1–7), and quail (16:8–21), and the defeat of the Amalekites (17:8–16), the people arrive at Sinai (19:1–2). Exodus 19:1–24:11 is the second of three Sinai theophanies (cf. 3:1–4:17 and 32:1–34:35) and opens the entire Sinai narrative, taking up the most important elements of the ensuing narrative—history, law, covenant, and cult.[1] Exodus 19:1–8 provides the introduction and explanation to the subsequent section (Exod 19:9–24:11).[2]

Shortly upon arrival at Sinai, Moses ascends the mountain to meet with God (19:3a). YHWH speaks to him from the mountain and prescribes the words he is to bring to Israel (19:3b). The Lord's words begin with a reminder of his past dealings with Israel. "What I did to the Egyptians" (19:4a) refers to the totality of the plagues on Egypt and Israel's deliverance through the Red Sea. No Israelite should deny that God's gracious presence is with him, since all have witnessed these events. They also beheld how he "bore them on eagles' wings" (19:4b)—an image that speaks of Israel's complete dependence on YHWH and his tender and protective care.[3] Finally, the people have seen how he "brought them to himself" (19:4c), that is, to Sinai, the mountain of his special presence, so that they might worship him.[4] Thus, by the use of three "I" statements ("what *I* did to the Egyptians," "*I* brought you to myself," and "*I* lifted you up on eagles' wings), verse 4 underscores absolute divine initiative—a theme that reverberates throughout this passage—and the associated privilege and calling of God's people.

The Lord's commands to Israel are structured as a conditional clause, with the protasis ("If you will obey my voice . . . and covenant") beginning in 19:5a and the apodosis ("then you will be . . .") consisting of verses 5b–6a. Some debate surrounds the nature and logic of this conditional sentence. It is typically viewed as either a pure condition or a

---

1. Dohmen, *Exodus 19–40*, 43.
2. Wells, *God's Holy People*, 33.
3. Durham, *Exodus*, 262.
4. Ibid.

definitional condition. The first view sees the apodosis as entirely dependent upon the fulfillment of the protasis. In the latter view, which is preferable, the protasis defines the nature of the appellations in the apodosis. As Davies observes: "The emphasis on this [latter] reading falls on the divine initiative, not on a *quid-pro-quo* arrangement. The relationship already exists and is the basis for the appeal for (continued) loyalty."[5] The protasis and apodosis are a proclamation, a declaration of YHWH's favor, calling for a response of covenant obedience.[6] This reading is confirmed by parallel passages in Deuteronomy. For example, Deut 7:6–11 first highlights Israel's privileged position as God's holy people (קדוש עם) and treasured possession (סגלה), God's election (בחר), his covenant (ברית) and, only then, Israel's duty to keep (שמר) the covenant.[7] Should they keep YHWH's covenant by obeying his voice, they would *continue* to be a special, covenant people to the Lord and thus fulfill their calling. Divine favor primarily determines their privileged status.[8] To be God's people is to accept the privileges and responsibilities involved in keeping his covenant. Therefore, the joint themes of divine initiative and Israel's election are primary and function as the context within which a particular relationship to the covenant stipulations is expected.

The apodosis expresses the privilege afforded to Israel by the use of three images. The first is "treasured possession" (סגלה) (19:5b), a term sometimes used in Scripture to refer to personal property and, specifically, the treasure of kings (1 Chr 29:3; Eccl 2:8). Its primary use in the

---

5. Davies, *A Royal Priesthood*, 43.

6. Patrick paraphrases the conditional sentence: "Being Yahweh's own possession, his holy nation and kingdom of priests, entails submitting to his will." He goes on to argue that the people's acceptance, not their proven obedience, was enough to activate the covenant (Exod 19:8–9) (Patrick, "The Covenant Code Source," 45–57).

7. The parallels with Deut 26:18–19 are also telling: "The LORD has today declared you to be His people, a treasured possession, as He promised you, and that you should keep all His commands; and that He will set you high above all nations which He has made, for praise, fame, and honor; and that you shall be a consecrated people to the LORD your God, as He has spoken" (NASB). See Davies, *Royal Priesthood*, 44.

8. It is most preferable to see this "covenant" as referring to that which is about to be stipulated at Sinai (e.g., Cassuto, *Exodus*, 227). Some view the aforementioned covenant as referring to the Abrahamic or patriarchal covenants (see, e.g., Dumbrell, *Covenant and Creation*, 86; Enns, *Exodus*, 387). Either/or statements may be avoided if we follow Fretheim who underscores the continuity of both covenants and concludes that the "covenant at Sinai is a specific covenant within the context of the Abrahamic covenant . . . an already existing covenant with an elected, redeemed, believing, worshiping community" (Fretheim, *Exodus*, 209).

OT is metaphorical, designating the special status of Israel in relation to God (Deut 7:6; 14:2; 26:18; Ps 135:4; Mal 3:17), thus connoting divine/royal favor and implying a context of election and covenant. There is also a connection in the biblical literature between being a special possession and filial servitude.⁹ Malachi 3:17, for example, states: "They shall be mine, says the Lord of hosts, my special possession (סגלה) on the day when I act, and I will spare them as parents spare their children (בן) who serve (עבד) them."¹⁰ Therefore, when Israel is described as God's סגלה, this expresses their gracious election, royal dignity in distinction from the other nations, covenant relationship with YHWH, and their responsibility to serve him as a consecrated and obedient people. God's electing love and the requisite holiness (as obedience) of the people are held together.

The second and third images are closely related to the first. The people are to be a ממלכת כהנים and a גוי קדש (19:6a). The latter phrase is less perplexing: Israel is set apart from other nations for the worship and service of YHWH. What is striking about this appellation is the use of קדש in reference to Israel, which occurs here for the first time in the Pentateuch. Most other references to קדש are tied to the sanctuary, the place of God's presence.¹¹ As Wells points out, one implication of the notable use of this term for Israel is that the characteristic of holiness—both God's definitive sanctification of them and their continuance therein—is made an identifying marker of Israel as YHWH's elect.¹² Furthermore, the term גוי ("nation") denotes a group that is founded, thus assuming a founder. Israel is not just a עם, a given ethnic reality, but a nation established by the Lord and joined together by a common relationship to him. Inherent in their establishment as a people is the call to remain YHWH's

---

9. Davies, *Royal Priesthood*, 53–54.

10. Not insignificant is the context of this quotation, namely, that of priestly malfunction. When God takes the people again as his special possession (Mal 3:17) the people will learn what it means to serve God truly (3:18), something the priests failed to model. Therefore, Israel's priestly service is tied to the Levites' service, and all of this is connected to them being YHWH's special possession.

11. Other occurrences of קדש prior to Exodus 19 are applied to Sabbath (Gen 2:3; Exod 16:23), ground (Exod 3:5), and the mountain (Exod 15:17) (Wells, *God's Holy People*, 27 n. 2).

12. Ibid., 27. See Wells' fine volume for a thorough analysis of the theme of holiness in biblical-theological perspective.

consecrated ones through obedience to his commands. Thus, election, sanctification, obedience, and holiness are closely linked.

The former image, our main concern—ממלכת כהנים—is more difficult to interpret and is subject to a few different interpretations.[13] The first view sees ממלכת as a construct noun meaning "kingdom" or "kingship." Thus ממלכת כהנים is interpreted as a body of people (or a realm) consisting of or characterized by "priests"—priesthood being the more important, defining term—and ruled by YHWH the King.[14] The second view interprets ממלכת not as a group of subjects, but as the exercise of royal authority. ממלכת may be an absolute form, thus making כהנים and ממלכת stand in apposition as two ways of characterizing a segment of Israel (i.e., as an active kingship or royalty who are also priests). However, if ממלכת כהנים is taken as a construct chain, then כהנים would be a subjective genitive, yielding "a reigning group of priests." Whichever way the terms are taken, in this view the referent is an elite group or ruling class in Israel.[15] A third view resembles the second view, but applies ממלכת corporately to all Israel. Whether taken as an absolute or taking כהנים as an appositional or subjective genitive, ממלכת is a metaphorical and honorific designation for Israel as those who have royal attributes.[16] Israel is a "kingship, priests" to God. This reading makes the most sense of how later translators variously rendered ממלכת כהנים (as "kings, priests" in Jub 16:18, Rev 1:6, Philo, Targums; as "royal priesthood" in Exod 19:6 LXX, 1 Pet 2:9; and as those who will reign in Rev 5:10, 20:6; cf. Symmachus, Theodotion, Peshitta, Syro-hexapla).[17] In addition, it best preserves the theme of bestowed honor and dignity, and applies these not only to a select group but to the whole people in the same way

---

13. For a fine presentation of the three ensuing interpretations, see Davies, *Royal Priesthood*, 70–86.

14. E.g., Childs, *Exodus*, 367; Fretheim, *Exodus*, 212.

15. E.g., Lohfink, *Studien zur biblischen Theologie*, 192 n. 102; Moran, "A Kingdom of Priests," 7–20.

16. E.g., Dumbrell, *Search for Order*, 43–46.

17. See Davies, *Royal Priesthood*, 63–66, for a list of versions and citations of Exod 19:6 in ancient texts. The material from early and later Judaism views Israel as both royal and priestly. The primary emphasis of the appellation "royal priesthood" is on Israel's dignity as a people chosen by God to be his holy servants. Their calling as priests extends even to Gentiles who will be gathered into Israel in the last days. Election, consecration, ongoing holiness, and service are thus the themes that occupy discussions of Exod 19:4–6 in the Jewish literature.

as the other epithets in this passage. Therefore, it is preferable to translate ממלכת כהנים as something like "kings/royalty, priests/priesthood" or "royal priesthood," highlighting both the royal and priestly dignity and calling of Israel as God's people.

How is one to understand כהנים? How might readers of Exodus have understood Israel's calling as priests? It seems probable that what is less familiar (i.e., the notion of a universal priesthood) would have been read in light of what is more familiar (i.e., a professional priesthood). "The reader of Exodus 19," Davies writes, "is assumed to have knowledge of some form of institutional priesthood (vv. 22, 24). It is difficult to believe, then, that Israelite readers were not to make a conceptual connection between כהן in Exod 19.6 and the priesthood of their experience, or with the other occurrences of the word in the same document."[18] If this is so, then Sarna is correct when he writes, "The priest's place and function within society must serve as the ideal model for Israel's self-understanding of its role among the nations. The priest is set apart by a distinctive way of life consecrated to the service of God and dedicated to ministering to the needs of the people."[19] As priests to YHWH, Israel's vocation, therefore, has both vertical and horizontal dimensions. On the one hand, they are consecrated by the Lord and called to remain set apart from the surrounding nations by obeying YHWH's commands, which no other nation on earth has been so privileged to receive (Deut 4:8). They are to display *coram Deo* their privileged identity as his holy and elect ones. On the other hand, each member of the community is responsible for the collective holiness of the people and of the nations.[20]

---

18. Davies, *Royal Priesthood*, 89. Elliot, on the contrary, writes: "Insofar as this Exodus pericope derives from a period far earlier than the establishment of the Levitical priesthood, it appears inadvisable to derive the significance of the phrase 'kingdom of priests' from a comparison with [the] later cultic institution" (Elliot, *Elect and the Holy*, 57–58). This argument is unpersuasive since regardless of the dates of the events, the composition of Exodus likely occurred with full knowledge of the Levitical priesthood or some other established concept of priesthood.

19. Sarna, *Exodus*, 104.

20. One need not debate whether priesthood is seen in primarily ontological *or* functional categories. Elliot, for example, holds that royal priesthood is simply "a concrete example of the quality of holiness" (*Elect and the Holy*, 55–56). See also Schüssler Fiorenza, *Priester für Gott*, 142, who views "priesthood" functioning as an adjective synonymous with "holy." Among those who hold to a "functional" view (or both) are Cassuto, *Exodus*, 227; Durham, *Exodus*, 263; Merrill, *Kingdom of Priests*, 80. There is, however, no reason why the notion of dignity or distinctiveness could not be wedded

As the prior images ("treasured possession" and "holy nation") stress election and the call to holiness and obedience, so ממלכת כהנים emphasizes Israel's unique relationship to YHWH and duty to be holy, not only *before* him but *for* the community and the nations. Generally, God's people are to function as priests in ways similar to the Levitical priesthood. "Royal priesthood" expresses the privileges and duties granted to all Israel.[21]

Royal Priesthood and "Reading" the Covenant Stipulations

We must now give particular attention to the function of the laws stipulated in Exod 20:1—23:33 (as well as those outlined in the remainder of the Pentateuch). On this, two related questions should be answered. First, what is the relationship of the laws to the surrounding narrative material? Second, what is the overall function of the laws, particularly in relation to the unconditionality/conditionality of the covenant?

Given the considerable amount of space devoted to the covenant laws in the Pentateuch, it is difficult to view them as merely auxiliary.[22]

---

with the various functions the priest performed to give an account of the nature of Israelite priesthood. For instance, Dumbrell combines the two by noting that Israel was to "serve the world by her separateness, just as a priest served his society by being removed from it." It is by her difference that Israel would lead the nations (Dumbrell, *Search for Order*, 45).

21. In this light, the lengthy prescriptions for the tabernacle and professional priesthood that span from Exod 25:1 to Lev 16:34 need not be seen as antithetical to the primacy of Israel's corporate priesthood. The stipulations of Exod 19:7–24:18, which stress the people's priestly calling, might be seen as forming an *inclusio* with Lev 17:1ff., which also largely underscores the requisite holiness of the people. The requirements for the Levitical priesthood and cultus are enfolded by the more important emphasis on the people's special status and holiness before God. This literary portrayal of Aaron and his sons "serves to flesh out for the reader something of what is meant by the image of Israel's corporate royal priesthood." Thus, the special priesthood of Aaron is presented as subordinate to and supportive of the central theme of Israel's priesthood.

22. Sailhamer, for instance, argues that the function of the laws within the narrative is to provide examples of an incorrect basis for a relationship with YHWH. The laws, according to him, are a foil for faith (Sailhamer, *Pentateuch as Narrative*, 59–78). Cf. Schmitt, "Redaktion des Pentateuch," 188–89, who likewise sees the Pentateuch, Prophets, and NT as emphasizing the same relationship between faith and law. It is doubtful, however, that such copious material is intended simply to present a principle the narrator wants the people to avoid (see Davies, *Royal Priesthood*, 113). Moreover, it is not entirely clear why the Pentateuch could not simultaneously emphasize faith as the proper basis for a relationship with YHWH and keeping of the law as an expression of that faith. This appears to be the case in Deut 6:1–9, where the people are called to

Davies proposes that the function of the laws within the narrative is to describe what life in the land—the land as a new creation of sorts—would be like. The Sabbath law, for example, directs the reader back to Gen 2:2–3, where the creation enjoys rest in an ideal state. Davies goes on to say: "If the land of Canaan is to be a new 'garden of Yhwh' (Gen. 13.10), then presumably the people of Israel, as God's 'special treasure', that is, his 'royal priesthood and holy nation'—are to take the place in that restored sanctuary of the primal man."[23] The laws, then, represent the ways of the new creation. They are something to be lived out as an expression of the people's calling as a royal priesthood.

The question of the unconditionality versus conditionality of the covenant should naturally be raised. If obedience to the covenant stipulations does not determine the covenant, what is the ongoing role of these laws? Davies compares the Sinai covenant to a land grant, wherein the royal figure by his own initiative bestows favor upon a subject and in turn expects continued loyalty.[24] In this case, the Divine King bestows on Israel the dignity of royalty and the privilege of priesthood with the expectation that the people would continue to walk in loyalty by obeying his commands. Failure to keep the law would result in expulsion from the land, their place of blessing and service. They would (temporarily?) forfeit their royal priesthood by not living up to that which defines it. Therefore, it may be best to view the Sinai covenant as a substantially unconditional covenant with elements of conditionality.

The point of emphasis, for our purposes, is that God's gracious and free election of Israel forms the primary context within which Israel is to relate to the covenant stipulations. YHWH furthermore sets the people apart as holy—he sanctifies them—in order that they would continue to live holy lives before him and the nations. Hence the objective sanctification of the people provides another important setting within which

---

love YHWH by means of keeping his commands. Surely to love the Lord with one's heart includes having faith in him. Hence, "law-keeping" done correctly is the appropriate expression of faith in God. Sailhamer points to the new covenant promises in the Prophets as evidence that the law was problematic (Sailhamer, *Pentateuch as Narrative*, 77–78). However, the promise of the law being written on hearts does not necessarily mean that two principles are being opposed—law and faith. Rather, the new covenant promises get to the point of the matter, namely, the need for renewed hearts that follow YHWH with faith, love, and obedience.

23. Davies, *Royal Priesthood*, 113.

24. Ibid., 178.

obedience to the law—active holiness—is to occur. Finally, at the risk of stating the obvious, Israel's obedience to the covenant stipulations is predicated on the existence of a covenant relationship. No covenant, no laws. This suggests that the "reading" of torah is intended primarily to occur in a covenantal context. In the end, then, initiation into royal priesthood is initiation into a particular type of relationship with God's law.

The Renewed Promise of Royal Priesthood: Isaiah 59–62

Isaiah 61:6 is the most explicit intertextual reference to Exod 19:6 in the OT. It is embedded in a unit (Isa 59–62) that focuses on the restoration of Israel, and develops the theme of Israel's corporate priesthood. Among the many promised blessings are the return of YHWH in Zion (59:20; 60:2b), a renewed covenant (59:21), the rebuilding of ruined cities (61:4), the subservience of foreign peoples (61:5), attainment of the wealth of the nations (60:5–17; 61:6b), safety (60:18), "everlasting joy" (61:7), and glory (60:3, 9; 62:2). As in the Exodus narrative, the emphasis in these chapters is on God's initiative and decision to act for his helpless people.[25] Some of the imagery used to depict Israel's restoration is royal and priestly (cf. Isa 59:17; 60:16, 21; 61:10; 62:3, 12), the clearest being 61:6a. After promising the servitude of foreigners (Isa 61:5), Isa 61:6a announces: "But you shall be called priests of the Lord, you shall be named ministers of our God." In the broader context of covenant renewal (or a new covenant) (59:21), Israel's royal priesthood is reaffirmed. This situation is reminiscent of Exod 19:5–6, where God initiates a covenant that grants Israel the status of royal priesthood. What does their priesthood in Isa 61:6a entail? It appears that the essence of priesthood here has to do with the privilege of being YHWH's servants at a time when his presence is restored to his people. The author contrasts the desolation and ruin of former times, as well as the subjugation of "strangers," with the promise of priesthood. The Lord says in effect: "They will serve you, *but you* will serve *me*." Primarily in view here is Israel's honored position before God, as is evidenced by the many blessings bestowed upon her.

---

25. This is especially clear if one recognizes the pervasive Exodus and Promised Land imagery employed throughout Isaiah 40–66. In Exod 19:1–3, the recurrent note struck is that YHWH initiated and accomplished the deliverance of his people. Likewise, here in Isaiah a second exodus and re-entry into the Promised Land will have divine initiative and action as their cause.

Israel's service is rendered first to YHWH. It is also probable that this service to God has a horizontal dimension. The purpose of the nations marveling at YHWH's favor toward his people (61:9) is that they would stream to Zion to worship him (cf. Isa 2:2). As a priesthood Israel was not to rule over foreigners, but to mediate between God and humanity, serving the latter by assisting them in the worship of YHWH, blessing them, and teaching his ways (as priests are commanded to do throughout Scripture; see Lev 10:9–11; Num 6:22–27; Deut 10:8; Deut 31:9–13; Deut 33:10a).[26] This mediatorial or priestly understanding of Israel's vocation is expressed throughout Isaiah from as early as chapter 2. John Oswalt writes: "The nations have come, and will come, to Israel . . . to give themselves to the God who is revealed through Israel's experience and through the revelation that has been given to Israel. Whenever 'Israel' fails to fulfill its priesthood, failing to make it possible for the nations to call Israel's God *our God*, 'Israel' has missed its calling and failed to fulfill the function of its servanthood."[27] In the future, however, Israel will carry out its vocation—as the fulfillment of Exod 19:6—by the work of God himself. Thus the themes of Exod 19:5–6 reemerge, namely, Israel's election, special covenant relationship, and the vertical and horizontal dimensions of priesthood.

Furthermore, the broader context suggests that the renewed priesthood of Israel will involve a new relationship to the Word of God. In emphatic terms, YHWH promises his Servant that the spirit and word in him will also "not depart from the mouths of [his] offspring . . . from now on and forever" (Isa 59:21). The "spirit" refers to the power of YHWH to bring justice and righteousness, particularly through the proclaimed Word.[28] "Word" refers to the Lord's truth, particularly the ministry of the Word or the gift of communicating the will of God in human speech—the prophetic word.[29] The phrase "the word will not depart . . ." is an allusion to Josh 1:9, and suggests in the present context that the tradition of Moses and Joshua would be continued by the Servant and his "offspring." The phrase further speaks of the fact that the Word would remain "a continuing mark" of the Servant and subsequent generations, and that the people would speak the Word and meditate on

---

26. Oswalt, *Isaiah 40–66*, 571–72.
27. Ibid., 572.
28. Ibid., 564.
29. See Motyer, *Isaiah*, 493; Blenkinsopp, *Isaiah 56–66*, 201.

it continually.³⁰ If, then, the figure in 59:21 is the Anointed of 61:1–3 and the offspring of the former are the restored "servants" of 61:6, then in the same way as the relationship to YHWH's "word" is passed on to his offspring in 59:21, so the ministry of the Anointed would be passed on to the "priests" of 61:6. Part of the task of the restored priesthood is to "proclaim" the "good news" in a ministry similar to that of the Anointed.³¹

Within the promise of a restored kingdom and priesthood is found the guarantee of a renewed relationship to God's Word. As priests, Israel would be a "people of the word" who emulate the work of the Anointed by loving God's Word, meditating on it, orienting their lives around it, and proclaiming it as gospel to the oppressed (61:1–3). As we turn to the New Testament, this very notion of God's people as a royal priesthood who are devoted to his Word is forcefully rearticulated in Peter's first letter, to which we turn.

The Royal Priesthood of the Church

The theological themes that frame the relationship between royal priesthood and "reading" pervade 1 Peter and are present in the particular section with which we are concerned: God's election of Christ and the believers (1:1, 20; 2:4–6, 9), the objective sanctification (1:2; 2:9) and subjective holiness of the church (1:14–16, 22; 2:1, 5, 11; 3:1–11; 4:1–6), and encouragement to perseverance through suffering and trials (1:1, 6–7; 2:4, 12–25; 3:13–22; 4:12–19). The structure of the letter is fairly straightforward: 1:1–2 forms the introductory greeting; 1:3–2:10 highlights and affirms the dignity and identity of the recipients as God's elect exiles, chosen by his grace; 2:11—4:11 prescribes the appropriate conduct for this elect people; 4:12—5:11 provides comfort to a suffering flock; 5:12–14 is the letter's conclusion.³² Our central text (1 Pet 2:9) is situated within the section of the letter that primarily stresses the believers' identity as God's chosen ones and takes up all the above-stated central themes.

---

30. Motyer, *Isaiah*, 493; Woudstra, *Joshua*, 63.

31. Those who see the figures as identical include Motyer, *Isaiah*, 493, and Oswalt, *Isaiah 40–66*, 564.

32. See, e.g., Jobes, *1 Peter*, 56–57; Schreiner, *1, 2 Peter, Jude*, 19.

An Elect and Holy Priesthood: 1 Peter 2:4–9

The early verses of 1 Peter 2 announce a central theme, particularly Christ as the rejected but chosen stone (2:4) and the people as elect and holy (2:5), while the subsequent verses expand on them (2:6–8 and 2:9–10 respectively).[33] Christ is described as the "living stone" (λίθον ζῶντα) (2:4a), which refers to his resurrection from the dead and subsequent life-giving ability.[34] This living stone is rejected by humans (in their rejection of the gospel), but is nevertheless elect (ἐκλεκτόν) and precious (ἔντιμον) to God (2:4b). Christians, who are themselves "living stones" (λίθοι ζῶντες) (2:5a) by virtue of their connection to the true Living Stone, may find comfort in their suffering, because as Christ was vindicated after rejection, so they will be as well.[35] The living stones metaphor is carried further when believers are referred to as "being built up" (οἰκοδομεῖσθε) and as "a spiritual house" or "house of the Spirit" (οἶκος πνευματικός) (2:5b), both alluding to the temple.[36] The term οἶκος may also refer to the people that inhabit and/or make up the house (e.g., "house of David," "household of faith," "house of Jacob").[37] This understanding is borne out as the metaphor shifts from temple to priesthood. The purpose (εἰς) of their building up is that they would be a "holy priesthood" (ἱεράτευμα ἅγιον) that offers "spiritual sacrifices" (πνευματικὰς θυσίας) acceptable to God through Jesus Christ (2:5c). The emphasis of the former phrase is on the collective nature of the priesthood, namely, that believers are a body or community of priests who, by virtue of God's election and the sanctifying work of the Spirit, together share the benefit of direct access to God.[38] By implication, of course, this refers also to the individuals that make up the priestly body.[39] The latter phrase lays stress on the idea that the multitudinous sacrifices offered by this priesthood are motivated or wrought by the Holy Spirit, thus

---

33. Achtemeier, *1 Peter*, 150.

34. Ibid., 154. Cf. Elliot, *Elect and the Holy*, 34. Others simply see the participle "living" as referring to the basic life and life-giving capacity of the "stone." See, for example, Bénétreau, *Pierre*, 119–20; Spicq, *Pierre*, 82.

35. Achtemeier, *1 Peter*, 154; Spicq, *Pierre*, 83.

36. Schreiner, *1 Peter*, 105.

37. Achtemeier, *1 Peter*, 155; Elliot, *I Peter*, 414–18.

38. Elliot, *I Peter*, 420. Cf. Spicq, *Pierre*, 84–85.

39. Schreiner, *1, 2 Peter, Jude*, 106–7.

making them acceptable to God.[40] Hence, through Christ, believers are being formed into a community of sanctified priests whose purpose is to worship God in the Spirit, particularly amidst the trying circumstances they face. The church's priesthood is informed, even reified and illuminated, by suffering.

The author validates his claims about Christ and the church by citing Isa 28:16 and claiming that Christ is the chosen (ἐκλεκτόν) and precious (ἔντιμον) cornerstone God promised to lay in Zion (1 Pet 2:6a).[41] He is the foundation of God's building project announced in verse 5.[42] Although the letter's addressees were experiencing hardships because of their faith in Christ, they would ultimately "not be put to shame" (Isa 28:16; 1 Pet 2:6b), that is, they would receive the same vindication as the chief cornerstone upon whom they are being built. The author elucidates this promise by picking up on terminology used in the previous verse and applying it to his audience. The ἔντιμον ("precious") and the ὁ πιστεύων ("the one who believes") of 2:6 are taken up in the ἡ τιμή ("the honor") and ὑμῖν ... τοῖς πιστεύουσιν ("to the ones who believe") of 2:7a. Only those who trust in the stone are honored (the positive side of not being put to shame).[43] Conversely, those who do not believe in the stone (2:7b), namely, those who disobey the gospel (2:8), will face shame. The author applies Ps 118:22 and Isa 8:14 to describe the situation of the recipients' opponents, who reject the important foundation stone and consequently face ultimate destruction. By the use of the same verb, the author contrasts Christ's elect status with that of the rejecters. Christ is the precious Stone appointed (τίθημι) by God (1 Pet 2:7) and the unbelievers are appointed or destined (ἐτέθησαν) for destruction through unbelief (2:8b). The audience may draw comfort in their suf-

---

40. Elliot, *I Peter*, 422; idem, *Elect and the Holy*, 197; Goppelt, *I Peter*, 142; Schelke, *Die Petrusbriefe—Der Judasbrief*, 58–59; Schreiner, *1, 2 Peter, Jude*, 107.

41. In Isaiah 28, the laying of the stone in Zion is part of God's judgment on Israel's arrogant rulers who take refuge in lies and not YHWH.

42. Jobes, *1 Peter*, 151.

43. Achtemeier, *1 Peter*, 160–61; Calloud and Genuyt, *Pierre*, 128; Jobes, *1 Peter*, 152; Spicq, *Pierre*, 88. Spicq notes that the use of the article before timh, has the value of a demonstrative, so that it may be translated as "this honor," that is, the specific honor given to the stone and those who trust in him in verse 6 (*Pierre*, 88). Others, like Norbert Brox, follow the common translation/interpretation of the honor or esteem being given to Christ by believers (Brox, *Petrusbrief*, 101).

ferings from the truth that they instead face a promising future as God's elect and dearly loved ones who are allied with the elect Stone.

The central verse, for our purposes (2:9), recapitulates and further elaborates on the themes of 2:5—the election, vocation, and sanctification of the letter's recipients. The opening phrase (ὑμεῖς δε) (2:9a) emphasizes the stark contrast between the rejecters and the church. The disobedient are consigned to destruction but believers are a "chosen people" (γένος ἐκλεκτόν, 2:9a), a phrase taken from the LXX of Isa 43:20.[44] The context of the OT passage is that of God's promise of deliverance to Israel from the Babylonian exile. Peter identifies his audience in some way with the remnant of Israel who would be delivered by YHWH. The church is a "chosen race" of Jews and Gentiles.[45] Along with ὑμεῖς δε, the subsequent phrases, "royal priesthood, holy nation" (βασίλειον ἱεράτευμα, ἔθνος ἅγιον, 2:9b, c) are taken from the LXX of Exod 19:6 and further draw attention to the privilege of Israel's election and covenant relationship with YHWH.[46] As Israel experienced a great act of deliverance from Egypt and awaited settlement in the Promised Land, so these believers in Jesus have been rescued from pending destruction and await final salvation (cf. 1 Pet 1:9). The final epithet, "a people for [his] special possession" (λαὸς εἰς περιποίησιν, 2:9d), is taken from both Exod 19:5 and Isa 43:20–21, and likewise underlines God's electing, saving, and consecrating a people for himself out of the nations of the world.[47] Indeed, all four appellations for Israel are now applied to the multiethnic church and recall the gracious initiative of YHWH on behalf of his people. In Christ, sufferers are royal priests who live out their calling with one eye to their hardships and the other to their dignity.

---

44. Isa 43:20b (LXX): "... ἔδωκα ἐν τῇ ἐρήμῳ ὕδωρ καὶ ποταμοὺς ἐν τῇ ἀνύδρῳ ποτίσαι τὸ γένος μου τὸ ἐκλεκτόν."

45. On the ethnic makeup of the congregations, see Elliot, *Conflict, Community, and Honor*, 16, who observes that the material in 1 Peter itself makes reference to both Israelite tradition (i.e., frequent citations of the OT; contrast with the prophets, 1:10–12; the titles given the church, 2:4–10; references to models of faith, 3:5–6, 20) and former Gentile ways of behavior (1:14, 18; 4:3–4), thus suggesting recipients of a mixed ethnic makeup. Cf. Goppelt, *I Peter*, 6; Jobes, *1 Peter*, 23–41; Spicq, *Pierre*, 12–13, 40–41.

46. Exod 19:6 LXX: "ὑμεῖς δὲ ἔσεσθέ μοι βασίλειον ἱεράτευμα καὶ ἔθνος ἅγιον."

47. Exod 19:5 LXX: "... ἔσεσθέ μοι λαὸς περιούσιος ἀπὸ πάντων τῶν ἐθνῶν"; Isa 43:21 (LXX): "λαόν μου ὃν περιεποιησάμην τὰς ἀρετάς μου διηγεῖσθαι."

Royal Priesthood and the Word of God in 1 Peter

In trying to tie the above exposition further to our theme, it is important to note the purpose clause of 1 Pet 2:9e: "... in order that you may proclaim the mighty acts of him who called you out of darkness into his marvelous light." The *raison d'être* of the royal priesthood of believers is that they would declare God's ἀρετάς (virtues, mighty acts, praises)—a likely reference to Isa 43:20–21 LXX where those delivered from Babylonian exile would declare τὰς ἀρετάς of God.[48] As "worship" and "evangelism," the Lord's delivered ones proclaim—even celebrate—the ἀρετάς of God, particularly those relating to the fulfillment of his promises.[49] Royal priesthood is tied to the declaration of God's Word, in that God's promises (inscripturated or otherwise), and the fulfillment thereof, form the basis of the church's joyful proclamation. Any announcement of the Lord's praises is at once a proclamation of his salvation *and* the Word that promised that salvation.

If we expand our gaze not far beyond the immediate context, we find the author's admonition of believers to love one another as those born anew by the gospel, the Word of God (1:22–25). This good news is the message that God's promises to Israel of a return from exile have been fulfilled in the church (cf. Isa 40:9). The gospel brings into existence a new community that is to relate to one another as those who have been made new. This group is comprised of those later declared to be a royal priesthood (1 Pet 2:9b). Furthermore, believers are to crave pure, "spiritual (λογικόν) milk" so that they might grow in their salvation (2:2). The milk they are to long for is the Word of God.[50] Therefore, it is fair to say that the gospel begets and in some sense defines royal priesthood. To be

---

48. Isa 43:20b–21 LXX: "τὸ γένος μου τὸ ἐκλεκτόν λαόν μου ὃν περιεποιησάμην τὰς ἀρετάς μου διηγεῖσθαι..." Cf. Jobes, *1 Peter*, 163.

49. Schreiner, *1, 2 Peter, Jude*, 116. cf. Elliot, *Elect and the Holy*, 197. Those who only see reference to worship here include Michaels, *1 Peter*, 110.

50. Λογικόν is often translated as "milk of the word" because it recalls lo,goj of 1:23. Since it only occurs once elsewhere in the NT it is difficult to translate, and we must rely on the present context to understand its meaning. Therefore, identifying the milk as the word of God or the gospel is quite reasonable (See Bigg, *St. Peter and St. Jude*, 126–27; Brox, *Petrusbrief*, 91–93; Elliot, *1 Peter*, 394, 399; Kistemaker, *Peter and Jude*, 81; Schreiner, *1, 2 Peter, Jude*, 116). Calvin provides somewhat of a mediating position, viewing "spiritual milk" as that sustenance which is fitting for the new life in Christ, and may include God's Word (Calvin, *Commentaries on the Catholic Epistles*, 61). Cf. Jobes, *1 Peter*, 130–41.

a priesthood before God is to be a people of the gospel; it is to live out the new life by loving others, striving for holiness of character and conduct, and craving the Word of God as that which brings growth and maturity.

Royal priesthood carries with it the expectation that one should relate to the Word of God in particular ways. The explicit *telos* of royal priesthood, according to 1 Pet 2:9, is the declaration of the mighty acts of God promised by the prophets in the Scriptures. Furthermore, new birth by the Word of God into this priestly community entails a life of holiness, obedience, and love in keeping with the commands of God. The new life, however, is predicated on the election, covenant, and redemption wrought by God himself. To be a royal priesthood means living in accordance with that calling (1:22–23; cf. 1 Pet 2:1–3), but also presupposes the ability to do so—an ability granted to those who have been born anew through the gospel of Jesus Christ. Thus, again, the primacy of God's work on behalf of his people forms the context and foundation for engagement with his Word.

Readers as Martyrs: Royal Priesthood in the Book of Revelation

The book of Revelation contains three explicit references to the kingly priesthood of God's people. The first, Rev 1:6, is found amidst a doxology that praises Christ for three particular benefits: his love for us, his liberating us from our sins by his blood (1:5b), and his "[making] us to be a kingdom and priests to serve his God and Father" (1:6a). The last consolation is taken from Exod 19:6 and applied to the church as those who fulfill the pledge of royal priesthood. Christ's death and resurrection not only established him as "ruler of the kings of the earth" and priest (cf. Rev 1:13–18), but also instituted a twofold office for his people. Suffering believers are not merely subjects of his kingdom, but are deemed kings and priests together with him (cf. 1:9a). The church reigns presently as royal priests, sharing in Christ's authority.[51]

---

51. Beale offers several convincing arguments for the *present* rule of believers, including (1) the verb evpoi,hsen (or evqpoi,hsen) carrying the sense of being *installed into an office*; (2) in addition to Rev 1:6, 9 and 5:10, basilei,a occurring six times in the book, five of which refer to active reigning, and (3) in Rev 1:9 the phrase "fellow partaker" (NASB) or "companion" (NIV) in the "persecution and kingdom and patient endurance" implying involvement in three activities and not simply existence in three realms (see Beale, *Revelation*, 194–96). Cf. Schüssler Fiorenza, *Priester für Gott*, 70–71.

Revelation 5:9–10 echoes the refrain of 1:6. The Lamb is praised for the accomplishment of two works: (1) redeeming people from every tribe and nation and (2) making them to be a "kingdom and priests" to serve God and reign on the earth. In addition to Exod 19:6, the text builds on Dan 7:22b, 27a LXX, which speaks of the church as those who are given a kingdom.[52] Here they are *made* a kingdom and given reign on the earth. Moreover, as priests their calling is to serve God. If this text is indeed repeating the thought of 1:5b–6a and is the fulfillment of Daniel 7, then the believers' reign is exercised presently as in the former passage (Rev 1) and is the inaugurated fulfillment of the latter (Dan 7).[53]

Finally, Rev 20:4, 6 speak of the saints as reigning for a thousand years with Christ. They will also be priests to God and Christ during that time. It appears from the use of the future verb, ἔσονται, that a *future* reign and ministry are in view.[54]

Exactly how believers exercise these functions is not made explicit in these passages. Beale, however, argues that believers exercise priesthood and kingship in a manner similar to Christ, who as priest reveals God's truth "through his sacrificial death and uncompromising 'faithful witness' to the world (1:5a)" and reigns as king by defeating death and sin through his shed blood and resurrection (1:5). The church fulfills the same offices by following Christ's model, particularly by being faithful witnesses to the world of Christ's absolute kingship and priesthood. It could be argued that the rest of the book of Revelation is an explanation of how the church carries out its royal priestly ministry amidst persecution.[55] For our purposes, being a kingship and priesthood involves hearing and heeding the words of John's prophecy (1:3; 22:7, 9), "keeping" (τηρέω) Christ's word and not denying him (3:8, 10), holding to the truth of God's Word even to the point of death (6:9; 20:4), proclaiming the "testimony of Jesus" (19:10), and overcoming by the word of that

---

52. Beale outlines four shared features between Rev 5:10 and Dan 7:22b, 27a LXX, demonstrating that the former reflects the influence of the latter, such as the giving of a kingdom to the saints in the end time and the giving of sovereign authority to a divine figure (Beale, *Revelation*, 361).

53. Beale also notes that the "present" reading of this passage is more difficult, thus making it the more likely original reading (ibid., 362).

54. Apart from these explicit references to kingship and priesthood, priestly themes occur throughout the book (for example, Rev 7:15; 22:3, where the saints "serve" God) (Osborne, *Revelation*, 709).

55. Beale, *Revelation*, 193.

same "testimony" (12:11). It is those who keep God's commandments (12:17), endure in faith (13:10; 14:12), and are not cowardly (21:8) who will reign with Christ as priests and kings. Thus, the function of ruling and serving as king-priests has much to do with "reading" the words, promises, commandments, and prohibitions of Christ, especially within the context of adversity. According to Revelation, those who orient their lives around God's Word truly are (and will be) a royal priesthood to God.

Universal Priesthood in Hebrews

Apart from the explicit quotations in 1 Peter and Revelation, it is the epistle to the Hebrews that speaks most of the priesthood of the church. From a number of passages we will take up only three.

By virtue of Christ's high priestly mediatorial work, believers are encouraged to "approach" or "draw near to" (προσερχώμεθα) the "throne of grace" in bold and confident prayer (Heb 4:16).[56] The verb προσέρχομαι, in the LXX and elsewhere in Hebrews, is a cultic term, usually referring to priestly access to the sanctuary for the purpose of ministering to the people.[57] The "throne of grace" refers to the location where God dwells in the most holy place of the tabernacle. Under the Mosaic covenant, it was only the high priest who was permitted once a year to "approach" the altar of the most holy place. Here, the "right of priestly approach," as Westcott notes, "is now extended to all Christians."[58] Implicitly, then, believers are called into a priesthood through the preeminent priesthood of Christ.[59] Finally, the purpose of priestly access to God is that they would "receive mercy and find grace to help in time of need" (4:16b). Therefore, the priesthood of believers is rooted in Christ's priesthood and expressed in prayerful dependence on a merciful and gracious God.

---

56. For an extensive argument for why drawing near in this context refers to prayer, see Scholer, *Proleptic Priests*, 107–12. Cf. Koester, *Hebrews*, 295; Lane, *Hebrews 1–8*, 115.

57. For an in-depth study of the use of προσέρχομαι in the LXX and Hebrews, see Scholer, *Proleptic Priests*, 91–149.

58. Westcott, *Hebrews*, 108.

59. Many scholars observe the cultic connections and the unprecedented access granted believers in the passage but do not make reference to the *priesthood* of Christians. See, for example, Bénétreau, *Hebreux 1*, 200; Bruce, *Hebrews*, 86; Koester, *Hebrews*, 295; Lane, *Hebrews 1–8*, 115–16.

It is the priesthood of Christ that opens up the way into the priesthood for his followers (10:19–21). Believers enter the "holy place" (10:19) and the "house of God" (10:21) through the "veil" of Christ's flesh (10:20). As those baptized and consecrated into a priesthood (10:22a), believers are exhorted to (1) "draw near" (προσερχώμεθα; 10:22b), (2) "hold fast their confession of hope" (10:23), and (3) "stimulate one another to love and good deeds" (10:24–25).[60] A context of adversity or trial may be discerned from these activities. The connection between these various activities suggests that they constitute different dimensions of the priestly calling of believers.[61] The first duty was addressed above (see Heb 4:16). The "hope" of verse 23 refers to the basis for Christians' hope, namely, Christ's priestly sacrifice.[62] As priests, believers perform their second duty as they patiently and unwaveringly rest in the work of *the* Priest. Finally, believer-priests are called to serve their Christian brothers and sisters by provoking them to live according to their calling as those cleansed and sanctified. Stimulation to "love and good deeds" occurs in the context of communal Christian worship (10:25a) and involves exhortation (παρακαλοῦντες, 10:25b). A teaching function analogous to OT priests may be discerned by the use of παρακαλοῦντες. It might be for this reason that some were rebuked for not being mature enough to teach (5:12).[63] Whatever the case, the church is called to communicate God's words of warning, lest any fall away amid their trials on account of unbelief (cf. Heb 3:7—4:13). In sum, believers are invited into a priesthood by Christ's work, initiated through baptism, and called to carry out a variety of functions—such as proclaiming God's Word—as part of their service to the house of God, that is, the church.

The priestly calling is, moreover, to express itself in service and a holy lifestyle. Believers are to love one another (Heb 13:1), show hospitality (13:2), and visit those languishing in prison (13:3). They are to keep the marriage bed pure (13:4), be free from the love of money (13:5), and not be swayed by false teaching (13:9). Why? For the "altar" Christians have surpasses that of the old covenant, as Christ's blood surpasses that of animals (13:10–12). Since the sacrifice of Jesus accomplished a last-

---

60. For arguments regarding the priestly consecration and Christian baptism parallel, see Leithart, *The Priesthood of the Plebs*, 100–102.

61. See Floor, "General Priesthood," 76–80.

62. Lane, *Hebrews 1–8*, 288.

63. Floor, "General Priesthood," 79.

ing result, the church is encouraged instead to offer "sacrifices," through Christ, of praise and thanksgiving to God (13:15) and sacrifices of kindness and generosity to their fellow creatures (13:16a). The phrase, "the fruit of lips that confess his name" (13:15b), is taken from Hosea and refers to worship, preaching, and witness.[64] Thus, it appears that priestly service extends to every domain of life. Christians are priests and all they do in response to Christ's high priestly work—exhorting each other, praising God, giving money, showing hospitality, retaining pure doctrine, or living holy lives—constitutes their service to God.

Although more passages could have been surveyed,[65] the preceding are enough to establish that (1) Hebrews speaks of believers as a priesthood, (2) general priesthood is rooted in Christ's priestly sacrifice, (3) priesthood brings with it the privilege of access to God (especially in prayer) and service to the church, and (4) this ministry is largely "reading," involving exhortation, teaching, fellowship, and practicing holiness and obedience. As a priesthood definitively consecrated by Christ, they are to live in the grace and mercy of God, rendering faithful service in the midst of suffering, with an eye to their eschatological hope.

Other NT References to the Church's Priestly Calling

We round out our discussion of royal priesthood by examining a few Pauline references to the priestly calling of the church. Our focus will be on four passages—two from Romans and two from Philippians.

Romans 12:1–2 begins with the exhortation that believers, in light of the mercies of God in Christ, should present their bodies as living, holy, pleasing sacrifices to God (12:1). Instead of priests offering animals on the altar, believers are to offer themselves—the totality of their being—to God as a sacrifice. Like Christ and in response to his work, they are both priest and sacrificial victim.[66] Their "spiritual worship" (λογικὴν λατρείαν) is a response to God's mercies, that is, his saving work, forbearance with Israel, gracious inclusion of Gentiles among his

---

64. Bénétreau, *Hebreux 2*, 227, notes that there are two aspects of this "sacrifice of praise": "La reconnaissance pour le salut réalisé par la mort et la résurrection du Christ, et la louange-confession du nom de Dieu, comprise comme accueil de la parole du Christ qui révèle Dieu." Cf. Floor, "General Priesthood," 78; Spicq, *Hebreux 2*, 430.

65. Scholer, for example, includes Heb 7:19, 25; 11:6; 12:18–24 (Scholer, *Proleptic Priests*, 113–48).

66. Best, "Spiritual Sacrifice," 287.

people, election, and covenant fidelity. The priestly service of believers, as spelled out in verse 2, involves eschewing the sinful patterns of the world and being transformed for the purpose of "testing and approving" (δοκιμάζειν) the will of God. The renewed mind of the believer enables her both to discern and to put into practice that which is good and pleasing to God.[67] The offering of ourselves in worship, therefore, is tied to our moral/spiritual transformation, so that both victim and priest take on the characteristics of the new age, as delineated throughout Scripture and especially in Romans. Thus, again there is an implicit connection between God's Word and the priestly service of believers.

In speaking of his ministry, the Apostle Paul refers to himself as a "minister" (λειτουργόν) of Jesus Christ in the priestly service (ἱερουργοῦντα) of the gospel of God, with the goal of presenting the Gentiles as a pleasing sacrifice to God (Rom 15:16). Given the sacrificial and cultic imagery of the passage ("offering," "acceptable," "sanctified") and the explicit priestly reference (ἱερουργοῦντα), it would seem that λειτουργόν should be rendered "priest." Paul is a priest who uses the gospel as a means of offering Gentile converts to God as an acceptable sacrifice.[68] The apostle likely saw his ministry as a fulfillment of Isa 66:18–20, where the glory of God is proclaimed to the nations and "kindred from all the nations" are presented as an offering to YHWH.[69] Although Paul's priestly service may primarily refer to his evangelistic preaching, it may legitimately extend to his entire ministry of teaching and equipping. All of these tasks are for the purpose of presenting Christians as pleasing to God (cf. Col 1:28). Furthermore, though Paul's ministry was unique in many ways, the apostolic task of declaring the good news, establishing churches, and gathering the nations to Christ is ongoing in the church today. Thus, all Christians, and particularly those engaged in these enterprises, are performing a priestly service to God.[70] The priesthood of Christians involves serving God by proclaiming the gospel in and with

---

67. Morris observes that δοκιμάζειν contains elements of "testing" and doing, since what Paul has in mind is not just the knowing of God's will but the performance of it (Morris, *Romans*, 436).

68. See Moo, *Romans*, 889–90. Cf. Schreiner, *Romans*, 766. Contra Morris who only sees it as referring to general service to God (*Romans*, 510–11) and Jewett who views the term as referring to Paul's ambassadorial rather than priestly role (Jewett, *Romans*, 906–7).

69. Schreiner, *Romans*, 767.

70. So Peterson, *Engaging with God*, 181–82.

the power of the Holy Spirit, with the aim that the nations would serve God through Jesus Christ (Rom 15:17–19).

Philippians 2:17 is laced with cultic imagery. Paul, as he suffers for the gospel, is pictured as the "drink offering" poured out (σπένδομαι) on the "sacrificial service" (τῇ θυσίᾳ καὶ λειτουργίᾳ) of the Philippians' faith. The image is one of the Levitical priest, whose "service" involved offering a sacrificial animal accompanied by a drink offering of wine (Num 28:7).[71] Hence the Philippians are presented as priests who serve by offering sacrifices that have something to do with their faith. What seems to be in view is their sacrificial partnership in the gospel that springs from their faith.[72] Priesthood takes place in the midst of suffering, particularly that on behalf of the gospel, and involves the giving of oneself wholly for the cause of advancing the Word of God.[73] In a similar way, Philippians 4:18 speaks of the Philippians' financial gifts as "a fragrant offering, a sacrifice acceptable and pleasing to God." The service of this new priesthood is to offer financial resources for the purpose of Paul's work and the gospel's advancement.

In sum, Romans and Philippians broaden our understanding of what universal priesthood entails in the NT. In Romans, conformity to the will of God and proclamation of the Word of God are the central features of priestly ministry. In Philippians, any service rendered in faith and on behalf of the gospel is taken as a pleasing offering to God. Underlying all accounts of priesthood is the grace of God revealed in the work of Jesus Christ. On the basis of God's mercies believers carry out their varied ministries in service of the Word of God.

---

71. Fee, *Philippians*, 251.

72. Thus "faith" is taken as a subjective genitive. This seems like the best reading in light of future references to the Philippians' gifts as λειτουργία (Phil 2:30) and an "acceptable sacrifice" (4:18); see Silva, *Philippians*, 129; cf. Hawthorne, *Philippians*, 105. O'Brien, on the contrary, sees faith itself as the sacrifice (*Philippians*, 310). It is difficult, however, to understand what it means to offer faith as a sacrifice. Even if "life of faith" is meant, this does not appear so dissimilar to the meaning rendered by taking τῆς πίστεως ὑμῶν as a subjective genitive.

73. Note that Epaphroditus in his service to Paul is also a λειτουργόν, thus referring to the former's ministry in priestly/cultic terms.

Conclusion: From Biblical Motif to Theological-Ethical Context

This chapter began with a threefold purpose: to offer a brief outline of the theme of royal priesthood, to draw connections between royal priesthood and God's Word, and to identify the surrounding theological themes in Scripture that shape an understanding of royal priesthood and provide a theological and ethical context for construing readers of the Word of God. We examined Exodus 19, which provides the foundational account of the relationship between God's commands and royal priesthood, highlighting that keeping God's covenant stipulations is predicated on the existence of a divinely initiated covenant relationship with YHWH. Isaiah 59–62 places emphasis on the "reading" function of proclamation, that is, declaring to the nations the ways of YHWH. The promise of eschatological restoration is accompanied by the pledge of a renewed relationship to God's laws and promises. First Peter 2:4–10 and its surrounding context similarly connects royal priesthood to the declaration of God's virtues, underlining that this proclamation is performed by a suffering priesthood. The Book of Revelation stresses that securing present and eschatological kingship and priesthood requires holding to, proclaiming, and obeying the Word of God, again amidst adverse circumstances. Hebrews, less directly, connects universal priesthood and the Word of God, speaking of the priestly duties of teaching and exhortation. Finally, the rest of the NT underscores the priestly duty of proclaiming the gospel and enabling such proclamation by sacrificial giving.

Throughout the Scriptures, royal priesthood has to do primarily with the people's dignity before God, by virtue of their gracious election and sanctification. In turn they are called to live in holiness by keeping the law of YHWH. When we come to the NT, issues of Christology are brought clearly into focus. Jesus Christ as *the* High Priest initiates others into his priesthood by his death and resurrection (and believers' subsequent baptism). Union with Christ determines the church's priesthood in the NT age. Therefore, "reading" God's Word in light of royal priesthood means relating to it (indeed, to *him*) as those graciously chosen by God, consecrated definitively as priests, invited into covenant with him, called to maintain and display holiness in often difficult situations, and all of this through the work of Jesus Christ. The interweaving of these theological themes with the manifold relationship of royal priesthood and the Word of God helps us to understand, at least preliminarily, what it means for royal priesthood to function as a theological and ethical context for reading Scripture, and thus begin to mediate between apparently divergent proposals in the theological interpretation of Scripture. In the next two chapters we move from this panoramic and primarily theological portrayal of readers, and turn our attention to the requisite character and practices of readers as modeled by the two main sanctioned readers in the OT—the king and priest respectively.

3

Virtuous Royal Reading

The King as the Ideal "Exemplarist" Reader of Scripture

The people of God are a kingly people. What this means and how this reality plays out are tied to how Israel and the church relate to God's Word. While the previous chapter provided a biblical-theological overview of the relationship between royal priesthood and the "reading" of the Word of God, this chapter begins to fill out this picture by examining in detail what the royal relationship with torah was to be. Israelite kingship was to be a vivid picture and reminder of the people's royal dignity. Israel's monarch was an image of election, bestowed dignity, and separateness, but was also to be a picture of devotion to God's Word. As his identity and function are determined by torah and his relationship to it, so Israel's corporate "kingship" is determined by the same. This chapter argues, consequently, that through both positive and negative portrayals, the Old Testament presents the king of Israel as the ideal virtuous "exemplarist" reader of God's Word—the one whose attitude toward, aims in reading, and responses to torah are to be emulated by Israel. As the ruler of the people, the king had a primary role to play in shaping Israel's self-understanding—politically, morally, and religiously. How he shaped the nation depended largely on his relationship to God and his torah. In what follows, we will (1) explore the OT depictions of the king-torah relationship found in the law, narrative, and Psalms, with an eye to (2) identifying how royal reading might shape an account of the interpretive virtues. The early sections concerning the law and kingship narratives center on (though not exclusively) the issue *that* the king is the ideal reader, while the last section dealing with the Psalter focuses on *how* (though not exclusively) one should read in light of the kingly exemplar. Our examination begins, however, with a brief description of interpretive virtues as they relate to the concerns of this study.

The Virtues and Royal Reading

A preliminary definition of virtue vis-à-vis reading might help us grasp what it means for the king to function as the paragon of virtuous reading practices. MacIntyre defines virtue generally as "an acquired human quality the possession and exercise of which tends to enable us to achieve those goods which are internal to practices and the lack of which effectively prevents us from achieving any such goods."[1] Virtue, first, is an acquired human quality that one possesses and exercises. It denotes a *disposition* or *attitude* that one embodies in the performance of whatever practice. Second, virtue enables one to achieve certain "goods" intrinsic to that practice. Thus, virtue is teleologically defined—it has an *aim* toward which purposeful action is directed. These characteristic features of virtue in general can be translated in the realm of interpretative ethics to render what are often called "interpretive virtues." Definitions and descriptions of interpretive virtues abound. Vanhoozer, for example, defines an interpretive virtue as "a disposition of the mind and heart that arises from the motivation for understanding, for cognitive contact with the meaning of the text."[2] An interpretive virtue is an intellectual and affective disposition that has understanding as a chief aim. Thus, according to these two definitions, virtue in the practice of "reading" Scripture has to do with embodying certain characteristics that enable one to achieve goods that are internal to Scripture "reading," such as understanding. Dispositions and aims are central concepts. However, faithfulness or virtue in the sphere of Scripture reading requires a further quality: responsive action. Stephen Fowl helpfully defines the virtues as "habits of seeing, feeling, thinking, and acting that, when exercised in the right ways and at the right times, will enhance one's prospects of both recognizing, moving toward, and attaining one's proper end." If applied to Scripture reading, this definition accounts for what Fowl

---

1. MacIntyre, *After Virtue*, 191.

2. Vanhoozer, *Is There a Meaning*, 376. This non-exhaustive definition is circumscribed by the concerns of his particular study.

describes as "virtue *in* interpretation" and "virtue *through* interpretation," that is, the dispositions, aims, *and* responses requisite for faithful reading.³ Indeed, if interpretive virtue arises from a desire to make contact with meaning (so Vanhoozer), and meaning may be expanded to include Scripture's implied practices, then virtue involves the carrying out of those practices—for that is part of making contact with Scripture's meaning.⁴ Virtue arises from a desire to follow Scripture; it is consummated by the following itself. Thus, interpretive virtue in this study is described as *a disposition of the heart and mind that arises from and contributes to appropriate aims, and results in appropriate action.* For the king to be the ideal reader, he must embody the right attitudes, aims, and responses regarding Scripture. The remainder of this chapter provides a biblical description of what interpretive virtue might look like in royal perspective, beginning with the kingship law.

The King and Torah in the Kingship Law

Israelite kingship was established and legislated in an ANE milieu in which kings were often viewed as semi-divine priestly figures who mediated between the gods and the people and whose actions had universal significance.⁵ However, as we will observe, what is most striking about the prescription for Israel's kingship is the disjunction between it and the ideologies of monarchy among the surrounding nations. The only law in the OT governing Israelite kingship is found in Deuteronomy 17:14–20, which, together with the law of the prophets (18:9–22), stands at the structural center of the book of Deuteronomy, as a frame around the law of the Levitical priests (18:1–8). "This fact," Duane Christensen notes, "suggests that a primary concern of the book of Deuteronomy, and perhaps the Pentateuch as a whole, is [the] matter of leadership of the people of God."⁶ But, for our purposes, one of the most notewor-

---

3. Fowl, "Virtue," 838.

4. This expanded notion of meaning roughly parallels Spinks, *Bible and the Crisis of Meaning*, chap. 4.

5. Whether Israel was primarily influenced by Egyptian, Mesopotamian, or Canaanite conceptions of kingship is difficult to determine. It may be most helpful to discuss the "common cognitive environments" of Israel and its neighbors, allowing for a variety of relationships (influence, coincidence, borrowing, or otherwise). For a helpful discussion of these issues, see Walton, *Ancient Near Eastern Thought*, 15–40.

6. Christensen, *Deuteronomy 1:1—21:9*, 381.

thy features of this section of Scripture is the radical de-emphasis on the priority of the king compared to the other authorities. Tigay writes: "Whereas the laws about judges, priests, and prophets allude to their rights and authority as well as their duties, and require obedience to the high court and the prophets, the law about the king says nothing about his rights or authority or obeying him or about governmental functions performed by him."[7] In the ANE, as Tigay observes, "The king was the lawgiver. He was inspired by the gods with the wisdom to make laws, but the laws themselves were his. In Egypt, the king was believed to be a god, and he *was* the law. These ideas had few echoes in Israel."[8] Although Israel's neighbors would provide the natural source for a model of monarchy, her kingship would not be distinguished by its political acumen, but by its religious character, as the following exposition of the law of the king will make clear.[9]

By a reaffirmation of YHWH's right and ability to provide a land for the people, the kingship law begins with a stress upon divine priority and the covenantal character of all of Israel's affairs (Deut 17:14a). It goes on to foresee a time when Israel will ask for a king (17:14b), a time realized during the days of Samuel (1 Sam 8:5, 20).[10] The people would request a king like the other nations, a desire that is not here viewed negatively (as in 1 Sam 8:5), but reluctantly. Accommodating this request, Moses's work, stated well by Brueggemann, "is to provide a monarchy that will maintain the distinctiveness of Israel as YHWH's chosen people, that is, a monarchy 'like all the nations' for a people that is to be *unlike* all the nations."[11] The initial requirements enjoined upon Israel in selecting a king are two. First, he must be one whom YHWH has chosen (Deut 17:15a). The "choosing" formula employed here (". . . that/whom the LORD your God chooses") is used only for the place of worship (12:5) and the king.[12] Thus, the office of the king would not be dependent upon

---

7. Tigay, *Deuteronomy*, 166.

8. Ibid.

9. Craigie, *Deuteronomy*, 254.

10. Daniel Block argues that although this request may catch the reader by surprise, the notion of an Israelite kingship was certainly not entirely new in the preceding sections of the Pentateuch. He argues, for example, that God promised on three occasions that Israel's ancestors would have kings among their descendants (Gen 17:6, 16; 35:11) ("The Burden of Leadership," 261–62).

11. Brueggemann, *Deuteronomy*, 184.

12. McConville, *Deuteronomy*, 293.

popularity or military might, but on the express approval of God.[13] He would be the "elect" of God. Here, as in the corporate calling of Israel, it is the election of God that is determinative. Second, he is to be chosen from among the Israelites and not from among foreigners (17:15b). This legislation was designed primarily to preserve the integrity of Israelite religion. Foreigners who attain to high positions, such as Abimelech (Judg 8:29–10:1), posed a serious threat to Israel's covenant fidelity.[14]

Military, political, and economic restraints are next placed on the king (17:16–17). First, he is not to multiply horses and chariots for his cavalry, which represents military might, but is to trust the Lord to fight Israel's battles (17:16a). For the Israelite king to amass horses betrayed dependence on the military tactics of Israel's enemies, against whom their principal strength was YHWH himself.[15] A related injunction comes next in the form of a prohibition against causing the people to "return to Egypt to multiply horses" (17:16b). This uncertain phrase is best understood, not as a physical sending of the people back to Egypt (as slaves or mercenary soldiers), but as a metaphorical return to Egypt by enslaving them, since the biblical witness does not attest to the actual practice of sending Israelites to Egypt as slaves or soldiers.[16] Next, the reference to multiplying wives has to do with consolidating political alliances, which in turn would bring the promise of increased wealth and national security (17:17a). Inordinate riches and misplaced political stability must not endanger the religious purity of the nation, as the king would likely adopt the worship of the strange gods of his foreign wives.[17] Finally, the king is prohibited from amassing excessive riches, likely through heavy taxation and trade. The primary concern here is the danger that wealth would produce the illusion of self-sufficiency on the part of the king.[18]

Until this point in the kingship law, Israelite monarchy has been defined mainly in negative terms, as a "no!" writ large or a series of pro-

---

13. Craigie, *Deuteronomy*, 254.

14. Ibid., 254–55. Cf. Daube, "One from Among Your Brethren," 480–81.

15. Craigie, *Deuteronomy*, 255.

16. Biddle, *Deuteronomy*, 289. Samuel's warning was that a king would take their resources and kin to fund and man his army (1 Sam 8:10–20). Furthermore, Solomon fulfilled these warnings (1 Kgs 10:26–29).

17. McConville, *Deuteronomy*, 294–95.

18. Tigay, *Deuteronomy*, 168.

hibitions enjoined upon Israel and its future king. We now arrive at the positive content of this legislation, namely, a description of the king's primary duties. What, then, is the king commanded to do? He is, first, to write a copy of the law for himself in the presence of the priests (17:18). In the ancient Near East, writing was often associated with kings. Royal inscriptions were one way by which kings hoped to perpetuate their names and receive a blessing from future generations. Monarchs also resorted to writing in order to publish their own legal stipulations.[19] Against this background, the remarkable character of the king's writing stands out. By divine command, the first order of business when he sits upon his throne is to write for himself a copy of YHWH's law.[20] At least two pertinent questions arise from this command: (1) what is "this law?" (2) what is the importance of writing in this injunction? Let us take up these issues in order.

Concerning the phrase "this law," there is no consensus among commentators as to its exact identity in this passage. Some view "this law" as referring only to the immediate passage (17:14–20), others to small sections of Deuteronomy, still others to the Sinai covenant (Exod 24:7).[21] Most commentators, however, understand "this law" to be referring to most or all of Deuteronomy.[22] Thus, the projection of the law into a distant future date along with its strong linkage to kingship serve

---

19. Sonnet, *Book within the Book*, 72–73. For example, in the epilogue to the Code of Hammurabi, the king variously remarks that he wrote "on my stela" his "precious words" and ordinances, which no one should transgress ("The Code of Hammurabi," translated by Meek [*ANET*, 177–80]).

20. Sonnet, *Book within the Book*, 73. It is the king himself, not the Levites, who is doing the writing. The phrase מלפני הכהנים הלוים is best translated as "*in the presence of* the Levitical priests" not as "at the dictation of" or "by" (see Christensen, *Deuteronomy*, 368; Driver, *Deuteronomy*, 212; McConville, *Deuteronomy*, 295; Tigay, *Deuteronomy*, 168). לפני can also be understood as "under the eyes of" or "in the keeping of" (Driver, *Deuteronomy*, 212 n. 18). Sonnet observes that no oral transmission by or instrumental mediation of the Levites in the act of copying is mentioned at all. He concludes: "The Levites rather appear as the ones from whom the standard copy emanates, the ones in charge of the *Urschrift*. This is in keeping with what is known up to now from the role of the Levites, divinely appointed as custodians of the *written* tablets in the ark" (Sonnet, *Book within the Book*, 74).

21. On the first, see Merrill, *Deuteronomy*, 266. For the second, see Tigay, *Deuteronomy*, 168. On the third, see Craigie, *Deuteronomy*, 256.

22. E.g., Christensen, *Deuteronomy*, 386–87; Driver, *Deuteronomy*, 212; McConville, *Deuteronomy*, 295; Nelson, *Deuteronomy*, 225.

to prophesy indirectly of the ongoing authority of the totality of Moses' commands over the kingship and people of Israel.

The significance of the king's writing may be seen in two ways. First, writing serves a basic devotional and pedagogical aim, namely, to make a more lasting impression than mere reading might accomplish.[23] As Philo remarks in his commentary on these verses: "[I]f he is writing they [the laws] are stamped upon his heart at leisure, and they take up their abode in the heart of each individual as his mind dwells upon each particular, and settles itself to the contemplation of it, and does not depart to any other object, till it has taken a firm hold of that which was previously submitted to it."[24] Second, the medium upon which the law is copied also proves significant. Just as the people were commanded to write Moses' words (6:4–9; 11:18–21), the king is commanded to do so as well (17:18). The people were to inscribe portions of the law onto amulets or surrounding architecture, while the king was to copy the *whole* law onto a *scroll* (ספר). This scroll was the most appropriate medium upon which the total law could be written and carried around by the king. Both in the case of the people and that of the king, the injunction to transcribe the law is meant to encourage allegiance to the covenant stipulations by having it physically permeate one's time and space.[25]

The king is further commanded to keep the torah with him at all times and read it all the days of his life (17:19a).[26] Some take this to mean that the king was to carry a copy of torah on his person at all times.[27] Moreover, the king was to read it continually. Up till this point in the Pentateuch, only Moses has been described in the act of reading (Exod 24:7). Israel's future king, therefore, is the first Israelite besides Moses to be associated with reading.[28] In this command, the king is to קרא (to call) torah, with the verb having the meaning of "read" in the

---

23. Tigay, *Deuteronomy*, 168.

24. Philo, *Spec. Laws* 4.160.

25. Sonnet, *Book within the Book*, 75.

26. Sonnet notes echoes of this command in the divine injunction to Joshua: "This book of the law shall not depart from your mouth, but you shall meditate on it day and night..." (Josh 1:8) (ibid., 76 n. 107).

27. Tigay notes the various explanations of how this could be physically possible. Some held that the king kept a miniature version of Torah, while others believed that he carried a full-sized scroll containing the whole of Deuteronomy or the Ten Commandments (Tigay, *Deuteronomy*, 168).

28. Sonnet, *Book within the Book*, 76 n. 108.

present context.²⁹ Since the act of silent reading was basically unknown in antiquity, the phrase וְקָרָא בוֹ ("and he shall read in it") connotes oral recitation. Reading, in some way, resurrected the "voice of the words," and here implies that parts of the written document are "activated" by the reader.³⁰ Royal reading is an oral and aural activity.

The aims of writing and reading torah were to inculcate reverence for YHWH and to learn how to properly obey his commandments (17:19b). Furthermore, the pious reading of the law was intended to teach the king not to think of himself as better than his fellow Israelites (17:20a), that is, it was expected to cultivate humility in the king. One could say, with Sonnet, that "the Deuteronomic law that 'dissociates' the royal ruler from his Israelite fellows aims to ensure the king's non-dissociation from the people."³¹ The king must learn to remain on God's straight path, not turning "to the right or the left" (17:20b). The result of this ideal torah obedience would be the preservation of a godly dynasty in Israel (17:20c).³²

Nowhere in the ANE apart from Israel is a ruler commanded to write "for himself" the laws that circumscribe his own exercise of power.³³ In one sense, the king is similar to all Israelites in having to allow torah to shape and govern his life. The point of this kingship law, however, is that, in a way not expected of prophets, judges, or even priests, he is to do so *par excellence*.³⁴ What we do not have is a "king reduced to a mere titular figurehead of the state," an "otiose" and impotent viceroy.³⁵ What we have, in outline form, is a portrait of the king as the "arch-

---

29. Ibid., 78.

30. Ibid., 77.

31. Ibid., 78.

32. Craigie notes: "Although the question whether or not kingship would be dynastic is not explicitly broached, the implications of v. 20 are conditionally dynastic. The true king would exercise his reign over the kingdom for a long time, as would his sons after him" (*Deuteronomy*, 257).

33. Peter Vogt puts it too strongly when he writes: "[N]owhere in the ANE is the power of the king limited by a written document" (*Deuteronomic Theology*, 218). Sonnet, however, cites both Hittite and Mesopotamian examples of such limitation by a written document in the ANE (*Book within the Book*, 77–78).

34. "The people are to follow the torah, to keep the torah, not to forget the torah, but the king is to *excel* in these areas ... [I]t seems that the king is being set apart as *an exemplar* of torah-piety for all the people in the awareness that his example would have an effect on the torah-obedience of the whole nation" (Grant, *The King as Exemplar*, 208).

35. So Levinson, *Deuteronomy and the Hermeneutics of Legal Innovation*, 141.

reader" of Scripture.[36] His *disposition* involves trust in the Lord and humble submission to his law. His chief *aims* are to know and embody this law. His enacted *response* will be steadfast obedience. The king, by submitting to God's commands, subordinates himself to the true King whose sovereign reality confronts him through the words of Moses. Far from being above the law, he will be its student. He will be the exemplar of virtue and obedience—the model Israelite and ideal reader of torah.

Rendering the Ideal in Narrative Form

What has been established to this point is *that* the king is intended to be the model reader of torah—the ideal Israelite—and we have caught brief glimpses into *how* he is to relate to torah, and thus how all Israel is to relate to it. In other words, what emerged in imperative form are the interpretive dispositions, aims, and responses the king is to embody as the paradigmatic reader of torah. This section builds on these conclusions through an examination of Old Testament narratives concerning the kings of Israel—specifically, Josiah and Jehoiakim—and their relationship to the law. The aim is to demonstrate further that the king was indeed to be the ideal reader of torah and to illustrate what shape his torah embodiment took, or did not take, in the narratives of the OT. We will, first, show that the narratives affirm the theology of the kingship law, and thus present the ideal king as a model reader of torah. Second, we will examine in some detail two representative episodes and figures in Israel's history that focus on the kings' relationships to torah, moving us closer to the issue of *how* one should, or should not, read Scripture.

The Kingship Law and the Old Testament Narrative

It is commonly acknowledged that the law of the king has some relationship (literary, chronological, conceptual, etc.) to the Old Testament narrative. This law and the foundational text for the Davidic dynasty (2 Sam 7:11b–16) may be viewed as "the poles of the dialogue about the nature of kingship in Israel that is played out between law and narrative."[37] On the one end, there is the law, severely limiting the powers of the king. On the other, the narrative presents David as unconditionally promised a

---

36. A phrase taken from Sonnet, *Book within the Book*, 78.
37. McConville, "King and Messiah," 271.

prosperous dynasty. If the law is negative toward kingship, but the narrative is positive (at least in 2 Sam 7), are they not in contradiction? Moreover, what does one make of the circumscription of the king's powers in Deuteronomy in light of the seemingly endless freedoms enjoyed by Israelite kings in practice? Does the OT narrative, then, promote, refine, or contradict the Deuteronomic vision?

Scholars have sought to resolve this perceived tension in a number of ways.[38] The best attempt, in my estimation, is that of Baruch Halpern, who seeks to establish a strong link between the law and the kingship narratives. He, first, addresses the issue of the law's origin. Against those who posit that the law was "resurrected" and reformulated during the time of Josiah to promote his reforms, he argues that it is unlikely that Josiah would "saddle" himself with the restrictions of Deuteronomy. "The impulse toward the limitation," he writes, "must therefore have been a popular or sacral one."[39] Furthermore, since succession and kingship are taken for granted in Israel and Judah, it would be strange, in a law originating at a later time, to find kingship portrayed as an option not a given.[40] Against the view that the kingship law originated among a group (during Josiah's time) that opposed the excesses of Solomon, he argues that since the DtrH is not entirely anti-Solomonic, it is unlikely that the law was written as a polemic against the king.[41] Finally, he contends that the kingship law, far from being anti-monarchic, embraces the same conditional understanding of dynasty held in the DtrH and Psalm 132.[42] Thus, not only are the narratives of the kingship preceded by the law of the king, but they share the same concept of the king "under torah" found in that law. By taking seriously the likely chronological relation of the kingship law to the inception of the kingship, reckoning

---

38. Bernard Levinson, for example, argues that the DtrH completely departs from the kingship law, showing that in exercising judicial authority, presiding over cultic matters, and leading in war, etc., the view of kingship reflected in the DtrH is incompatible with the "utopian manifesto" of Deuteronomy (Levinson, "The Reconceptualization of Kingship," 524–34). For other representative views, see Boecker, *Die Beurteilung der Anfange des Konigtums*, 89–92, and Knoppers, "The Deuteronomist and the Deuteronomistic Law," 344–45.

39. Halpern, *The Constitution of the Monarchy*, 226.

40. Ibid., 228.

41. Ibid., 227.

42. He even goes on to hint that David himself was aware of the law and followed it (ibid., 230–31).

with the conditional aspects of the Davidic dynasty, and dealing fairly with both the negative and positive narrative appraisals of kingship without jettisoning one or the other, Halpern comes closest to offering a satisfying "solution" to the relationship between the kingship law and narratives.

Another critical element in helping to discern the interplay between law and narrative is the importance of the cultural setting, namely, the ancient Near East and its lofty ideologies of kingship. We saw earlier that Deuteronomy 17 was a deconstruction of ANE views of kingship. The OT narrative (e.g., Samuel's warnings about kingship and 1 King's disapproval of Solomon's dissolute life) should be viewed as having the same purpose, that is, to demonstrate what happens when kings are given or arrogate to themselves too much power.[43] The narratives show that the history of kingship, even in its heroes like David, Solomon, and Josiah, departs from the Deuteronomic ideal. "[Even] the glories of Josiah," writes McConville, "if they issue in Jehoiakim and ultimately Nebuchadnezzar, take on a paler hue."[44] The central criterion for judging the king is his faithfulness to and embodiment of torah—as in the kingship law.

A Tale of Two Readings

If we allow that the kingship law somehow influenced the telling of the OT narrative, we must now look specifically at how the narrators evaluated the kings' performances and, more importantly, their respective relationships with Scripture. In what follows, we will examine two representative accounts of kings vis-à-vis God's Word—one positive and one negative—that highlight their faithfulness or unfaithfulness to the Deuteronomic ideal of a monarch who meditates on and lives out torah. In so doing, we will catch a glimpse of what exemplary reading practices might entail. We will first examine the narrative of Josiah (2 Kgs 22–23), whom we argue is presented as one of the (if not *the*) greatest kings in Judah's history because of his virtuous relationship with the "book of the law." Second, we look at the account of Jehoiakim's burning of the scroll of Jeremiah (Jer 36), as this represents one of the lowest points in the history of Israel's kings and their appropriation of the Word of God.

43. McConville, "King and Messiah," 290.
44. Ibid., 293.

The Discovery of the Book: 2 Kings 22–23

Josiah was eight years old when he began to rule over Judah (2 Kgs 22:1). Contrary to his father and grandfather before him, he walked uprightly before YHWH (22:2a). This commendation is expressed in two important ways. First, the passage notes that "he walked in all the ways of his father David" (22:2b), praise which, up until this point in Kings, only Hezekiah has drawn. David's piety is put forward here, and throughout Kings, as the ideal against which the actions of the kings of Judah are measured.[45] Second, it is said that Josiah did not "turn aside to the right or to the left" (22:2c), a phrase not used for any other king. Outside of the books of Kings the only place this phrase is found in relation to a king is in Deuteronomy's kingship law (Deut 17:20).[46] Therefore, already in the introduction, Josiah is linked with the law of Moses and, in anticipation of the rest of this account, is presented as the ideal of torah-piety.

In the eighteenth year of his reign, Josiah commissioned the repair of the temple (2 Kgs 22:3–7). This aspect of the account provides "character background" for Josiah, presenting him as one with deep piety, even before the book is found.[47] In the next verse, the story takes a turn, shifting focus from money and temple repairs to the "book of the torah" found by Hilkiah in the temple (22:8a). In a subtle way, a book has been substituted for the temple in a story that seemed to be all about the temple and its restoration.[48] What is this book of the torah? According to most scholars, it can be nothing but the book of Deuteronomy or significant parts of it.[49] Shaphan then reads the book (22:8b) and returns to the king to report on the temple project (22:9). At this point in the story the tension is heightened, as the question is raised of how the king will react when the book is read to him. The focus has now shifted from the book itself to the reading of the book.[50]

---

45. Venema, *Reading Scripture*, 63.

46. Ibid., 63–64.

47. Nelson, *First and Second Kings*, 255. Cf. Venema, *Reading Scripture*, 66.

48. Venema, *Reading Scripture*, 68.

49. Numerous reasons can be given for this conclusion. Cogan and Tadmor, for example, offer at least two: (1) Josiah's mournful reaction to the book points to Deuteronomy's maledictions, which warn all violators of the covenant; (2) no other book of the Pentateuch besides Deuteronomy requires cultic centralization in YHWH's chosen place (Cogan and Tadmor, *II Kings*, 294).

50. Venema, *Reading Scripture*, 75.

At the end of his report, Shaphan mentions the book that was given to him by Hilkiah and reads it to Josiah (22:10). The king does not know what this book is, though the readers are aware that it is the book of the law. "This," according to Venema, "makes his reaction all the more telling, and a fitting climax to the end of the pericope." As soon as the king hears the words that Shaphan is reading (ויקראהו), he tears his clothes (ויקרע), an alliteration meant to highlight his dramatic response of repentance and humility (22:11).[51] "Josiah's response," observes Brueggemann, "suggests that the Torah he hears is threatening and deeply unsettling to him. That is in part a comment on the nature of the scroll, and in part a comment on the king's readiness to hear."[52] Indeed, "hearing" implies obedience or the willingness to act on what one hears. In light of the theology of Deuteronomy that is operative in this text, Josiah is presented as the model reader, one who is ever ready to submit to God's law.[53]

The king immediately sends his royal advisors to inquire of YHWH what exactly these words mean for him and Judah (2 Kgs 22:12–13). His concern is that he, his people, and the fathers had not obeyed this book and were, therefore, in danger of experiencing God's fierce wrath. Of special note is Josiah's recognition that the fathers were familiar with the book that was found. The point of the narrative is to show how Josiah, as compared to the fathers, reacts to the book.[54] The prophetess Huldah confirms Josiah's fears, informing his advisors that the Lord's anger against his people will not be assuaged because of their continued disobedience to his commands (22:14–17). The king, however, will receive favor from YHWH because "his heart was tender," he humbled himself, he tore his clothes in repentance, and wept before God (22:18–20a). In other words, his disposition toward the scroll and his responses upon hearing it were pleasing to the Lord. Huldah's prophecy, it seems, is not about the future of the city or the land, but a positive judgment on Josiah.

Upon receiving the prophetess' words, Josiah initiates a national covenant renewal ceremony, wherein he reads in the hearing of the people the entire book of the law (23:1–3). The king (and the people after him) covenants to keep YHWH's commands with "all *his* heart and

---

51. Ibid.
52. Brueggemann, *1 & 2 Kings*, 545–46.
53. Ibid., 546.
54. Venema, *Reading Scripture*, 78.

all *his* soul" and to put them into practice (23:3). The language echoes that of Deuteronomy (Deut 6:5, 17) and, in light of his covenant renewal, functions to present Josiah as a new Moses or Joshua figure.[55] As part of his program, the king orders that all false worship be done away with in Judah (2 Kgs 23:4–20, 24). In obedience to the book of the law, the reform culminates in a renewal of Passover (23:21–23). The narrator comments that the Passover had not been celebrated since the days of the judges, a fact meant to demonstrate the stark contrast between Josiah and the rulers of the past. Josiah's reading of the "book of the covenant" in the temple ends in both the termination of idol worship and the commemoration of the Exodus from Egypt.

Finally, the author's evaluation of Josiah is summed up in these words: "Before him there was no king like him, who turned to the Lord with all his heart, with all his soul, and with all his might, according to all the law of Moses; nor did any like him arise after him" (23:25). This verse is the only place in the OT other than Deut 6:4–5 in which the phrase "with all his heart and with all his soul and with all his might" is used.[56] In no stronger way could Josiah be portrayed as the model king-reader. He appears to be the ideal king of Deuteronomy 17, whose hearing of Scripture cut to his heart and shaped his behavior. He was open to the book of the law, submitted himself to it, quickly obeyed its commands, and called the people to do the same. In all his ways toward the law—particularly his disposition and response—he was an ideal reader of Scripture and a model for Judah to follow.

The Burning of the Book: Jeremiah 36:1–32

In the fourth year of the reign of Jehoiakim, descendant of Josiah, the Word of YHWH came to Jeremiah (Jer 36:1). The timing of this prophecy is notable because of the important defeat of Egypt at Carchemish by Babylon, which gave a sense that the region would soon be in the control of the latter.[57] Jeremiah is commanded to write on a scroll all that the Lord had spoken to him and to present these to the people with the hope they would repent and avoid the impending disaster (36:2–3). Jeremiah dictates these words to Baruch the scribe and commands him to read these words to the people in the temple (36:4–7). Baruch carries

---

55. Hobbs, *2 Kings*, 332.
56. Venema, *Reading Scripture*, 93.
57. Keown, Scalise, and Smothers, *Jeremiah*, 205.

out the prophet's orders during a fast day in the fifth year of Jehoiakim's reign (36:8–10). At this point in the account, three things are worth noting. First, outside of Jeremiah, King Josiah is not mentioned anywhere frequently, while in this small section he is mentioned three times (36:1, 2, 9).[58] As will be expanded on later, this is a deliberate move to connect this narrative with that of Josiah's reform (2 Kgs 22–23). Second, the scroll is read from the "room of Gemariah son of Shaphan" (Jer 36:10), one of Josiah's officials, which intimates that he was sympathetic to Jeremiah, as his relative Shaphan was to Josiah and his reforms.[59] Third, the narrator uses the phrases "the words of YHWH" (36:8) and "the words of Jeremiah" (36:10) interchangeably, thereby identifying one with the other.[60] Thus the purpose of these words is not simply to provide information, "but to authorize, energize, and evoke a transformed life that will avoid and deter the coming evil."[61]

In the next sequence, the words of YHWH are read to the king's aides (36:11–15). Upon hearing the words of judgment, the officials immediately realize that they must report what they have heard to the king (36:16). Until now, the king is the only person of importance that has not read the scroll. After reassuring themselves that the words are indeed from the prophet Jeremiah, they command Baruch (along with Jeremiah) to hide himself, hide the scroll, and brace themselves to report their findings to the king (36:17–20a). That the royal officials would have to hide the scroll from the king reveals that he was not a Josiah, one receptive and responsive to the Word of God. The tension is indeed high. How will the king respond?

The officials report everything to the king (36:20b), who then sends for the scroll (36:21a), which is subsequently read (36:21b). Everything depends on Jehoiakim's reaction. At this decisive moment, the king responds by burning the scroll. The burning is described graphically to highlight its atrociousness, noting that as soon as a section of it was read, Jehoiakim tore it and threw it into the fire, until nothing was left. There are some noteworthy points of contrast with the Josiah narrative. First,

---

58. Venema, *Reading Scripture*, 100.

59. Keown, Scalise, and Smothers, *Jeremiah*, 206. Cf. Bright, *Jeremiah*, 182, argues that many of the officials were sympathetic to Jeremiah's words because they or their relatives were positive toward the Josianic reforms.

60. Venema, *Reading Scripture*, 116.

61. Brueggemann, *To Build, To Plant*, 130.

it is said that upon hearing the words of the scroll Jehoiakim tore (קָרַע) not his clothing, like Josiah (קָרַע, 2 Kgs 22:11), but the scroll (Jer 36:23). The narrator puts the contrast in these striking terms: "Yet the king and all his servants who heard all these words were not afraid, nor did they rend their garments" (36:24). Second, whereas King Josiah immediately obeys the law and unites the people in covenant renewal (2 Kgs 23:1–3), Jehoiakim rejects the words of the scroll and persists in disobedience.[62] "The king wants to be and is 'scroll-less' because he imagines he is autonomous and need give no answer," writes Brueggemann. He does not respond in great fear like his royal advisors (Jer 36:16, 25), a contrast that suggests that the king has reached the limit of defiance, being utterly cynical and in opposition to the scroll and to the God who speaks therein.[63] "The burning of the scroll," writes Else Holt, "is the theological centerpiece of the narrative, where all important aspects meet."[64] First of all, by burning the scroll, which is the ultimate rejection of the Word of God, the king is marked as a villain. Second, as the king serves as the representative of all the inhabitants of the land, his rejection of the divine Word thus represents the people's rejection.[65]

After comments about the king's treatment of the prophet (36:26), Jeremiah is commanded to produce another scroll (36:27–28), upon which he is to add the punishment to be exacted on Jehoiakim for his destruction of the previous scroll. The penalty would go beyond the calamity to come upon the land (36:31), including the guarantee that none of the king's descendants would ever take the throne and the promise that he would suffer an undignified death and burial (36:30). Finally, at the dictation of the prophet, Baruch records the second scroll with additional content (36:32). In this section, the king's irreverent response to God's words is underlined as the narrator mentions four times that the first scroll was burned by Jehoiakim (36:27–29, 32). Moreover, a parallel should be noticed between this "rewriting" and its predecessor, the tablets of the law, which were broken and rewritten by Moses (Exod 32:18–19; 34:1–35).[66] In both accounts, it is covenant infidelity expressed through

---

62. Numerous other similarities between this narrative and that of 2 Kings 22–23 have been detected. For an illuminating study of the stylistic similarities, see Isbell, "2 Kings 22:3–23:24 and Jeremiah 36," 33–45.

63. Brueggemann, *To Build, To Plant*, 135.

64. Holt, "Word of Jeremiah," 184.

65. Ibid.

66. Ibid., 185.

disobedience to God's Word that results in the destruction and rewriting of the texts. The Moses narrative lends authority to the Jeremiah narrative and, therefore, to the scroll of the prophet.[67] God's Word will always be the authority over Judah and its kings. Brueggemann sums up the point well when he writes: "God will generate as many scrolls as necessary to override the king's zeal for autonomy. The king cannot finally sustain a world where he need not listen. The king's life consists in listening to the reality of the scroll."[68] As we approach the nadir of the OT narrative, however, we encounter the failure of the king as the preeminent Scripture reader to secure Israel's piety and joyous future.

The OT evaluation of Josiah and Jehoiakim is clear. Josiah, when he heard the newly discovered book of the law, mourned, turned to the Lord, and afterward recommitted the nation to the Lord and his law. Jehoiakim, who ruled shortly after Josiah, demonstrated the ultimate contempt for God and his words. These narratives, ultimately, highlight a number of virtuous reading practices as embodied by or absent in Israel's kings: humility, fear, readiness to submit to the law, and quick obedience. The royal interpretive virtues are, however, more often implied than spelled out in this history. It is in the Psalter that we find the clearest expression of the king as ideal reader.

The Psalter: A Royal Doxological Guide for Reading Torah

The final strand of our presentation of the king as paradigmatic reader of Scripture leads to the Psalms. In the previous two sections, our primary aim was to establish *that* the king is presented as the ideal reader of Scripture, while offering a few observations about *how* kings were supposed to and actually did read torah. In this section, although we will still attempt to establish that the king is the ideal reader in the Psalms, we shift our emphasis to offer specific insights into *how* he (and all of Israel as a *royal* priesthood) was to approach torah. The central argument is twofold. First, the Psalms present a theology of the king-torah relationship similar to that of Deut 17:14–20 and the OT narrative, as presented above. Against this very backdrop, the Psalms repristinate the ideal picture of that king-torah relationship. Second, the Psalms give concrete examples of how the king was to (and sometimes did) approach

67. Ibid., 186.
68. Brueggemann, *To Build, To Plant*, 135.

Scripture, providing a clear picture of the interpretive virtues in royal priestly perspective, and thereby offering a model for future readers. In this light, the Psalter may be viewed as a manual for reading torah, particularly when read with the king in mind as its primary subject, model, and/or author. We begin with a discussion of the importance of royal and torah themes to the Psalms, on the way to making a brief case for the king as exemplary reader, before examining the particulars of the king's relationship to the Word of God.

The Psalms as Royal

Before the rise of modern criticism, it was commonly believed that most of the psalms had a royal connection, with King David as the primary author. As the critical approach gained prominence, the Psalms began to be dated after the demise of the monarchy, and the belief in Davidic authorship seemed untenable. Consequently, the individual who speaks in the Psalms came to represent a collective, as the personification of the nation or a pious group therein. Even psalms in which royal themes were pervasive were given this collective interpretation. John Eaton's *Kingship and the Psalms* confronts this issue and builds a case for a more extensive royal interpretation of the "psalms of the individual" and the Psalter as a whole.[69] His general arguments include: (1) seventy-three psalms begin with the heading *l^edāwīd*, denoting at the very least a royal link;[70] (2) this superscription, translated as "by David," makes most sense in light of what we know of David from other OT literature, apocryphal writings, Josephus, and the NT witness;[71] (3) the only situation that has really been attested in the "psalms of the individual" is that of the king; (4) the psalms in which "I" and "we" alternate (e.g., Pss 9–10; 22; 44) can be explained best by the representative nature of the king; and (5) throughout the "psalms of the individual" there are at least twenty-four motifs or expressions that are royal or especially appropriate for the king.[72] The royal interpretation makes the most sense of the Psalms and presents

---

69. Eaton, *Kingship and the Psalms*, 1. Eaton both builds on and refutes prior work by Hermann Gunkel (see, e.g., Gunkel and Begrich, *Introduction to Psalms*, 99). For a brief but fine overview of the work of Gunkel and Eaton, see Grant, "Psalms and the King," 103–4.

70. Eaton, *Kingship*, 20.

71. Ibid., 21. Cf. Waltke and Yu, *An Old Testament Theology*, 873–74.

72. Eaton, *Kingship*, 23–24.

them as a deeply meaningful and consistent unity. Eaton, as a result, expands the number of royal psalms from eleven to sixty-five. Although not every scholar agrees with the extensiveness of Eaton's conclusions, his argument has proven strong because it takes Davidic superscriptions seriously and allows the content of the psalms of the individual to speak.[73]

In addition, Gerald Wilson makes the case that the placement of royal psalms at the "seams" of the Psalter (Psalm 2 at the beginning of Book 1, Psalm 72 at the beginning of Book 2, and Psalm 89 at the end of Book 3) demonstrates that kingship was central to at least Books 1–3.[74] Royalty is also important to Books 4 and 5 since they highlight, for example, the return of the Davidic king in Psalms 101–103, the eschatological presentation of the Davidic king in Psalm 110, and the Davidic monarch as the last voice heard in the Psalter before the concluding doxology (Ps 145).[75] These facts suggest that the whole of the Psalms in its final form holds kingship to be a central and unifying theme.

Psalms and Torah

Our second step in arguing that the Psalms are concerned with the king as torah-reader is to demonstrate the importance of torah to the Psalms as a whole. To accomplish this, we will show that the Psalms reflect the language and theology of Deuteronomy, highlight the significance of the placement of torah psalms (Psalms 1, 19, 119) in the final form of the Psalter, and discuss the pervasiveness of torah themes in non-torah psalms.

The influence of Deuteronomy on the whole OT is so strong that it would be a surprise to find that it had no effect on the Psalms. Indeed, in the first psalm, one finds that the "law of the Lord" is that upon which the righteous person meditates. This phrase "meditate on the law day

---

73. Grant, "Psalms and the King," 106. Steven Croft, for example, offers a helpful evaluation of Eaton's classifications. Though he does not agree with every classification, he is largely affirming of Eaton's corrective. See Croft, *Identity of the Individual*, 73–132.

74. Wilson mainly argues that the emphasis of the editor(s) in Books 4 and 5 was to answer the problem of the failed Davidic kingship presented in the previous three books. He suggests that Books 1–3 were primarily concerned with highlighting the Davidic dynasty and were, therefore, more directly royalty-themed books. Books 4 and 5 are more focused on YHWH as king and his torah (Wilson, *Editing of the Hebrew Psalter*, 214–15, 227; cf. idem, "Shaping the Psalter," 74).

75. Grant, "Psalms and the King," 109.

and night" is found in only two places in the OT: Ps 1:2 and Josh 1:8. In the latter, it is clear that the law being referred to is that which the king was to write and upon which he was to meditate (Deut 17:18, 19). Joshua is told to "do" in accordance with all that is written in the book of the law by not turning from it "to the right or to the left" (Josh 1:7; cf. Deut 17:20) and, in so doing, his way would be made prosperous. This promise is echoed in Psalm 1.[76] Next, in all three torah psalms as well as other non-torah psalms, meditation and recitation of torah are prevalent, which also reflects a similarity to Deuteronomy (e.g., Pss 119:97; 104:34; cf. Deut 17:19).[77] Finally, the goal of both books is to teach the fear of the Lord. For example, when the psalmist writes, "Come, O children, listen to me; I will teach you the fear of the Lord your God" (Ps 34:11), he echoes the whole tenor of Moses' teaching in Deuteronomy (e.g., Deut 6:1–2; 31:12–13).[78] These factors should lead one to conclude that the "law" in Psalms is primarily Deuteronomy and, therefore, that the Psalms have torah as somewhat of a focus.[79]

When the canonical shape of the Psalter is taken into account, the three torah psalms are elevated from a position of relatively minor importance to one of central significance. Both Psalms 19 and 119 are placed at the center of their respective books. The former is the center of chiasm composed of Psalms 15–24, located at the center of Book One, while the latter is transparently the major psalm of the Book Five.[80] The most significant placement of a torah psalm, however, is that of Psalm 1. Placed at the beginning of the Psalter, it functions as half of the two-part introduction to the whole songbook. The psalm in its introductory role sets the entire tone for the Psalter and shows that Israel's songbook is concerned with fostering torah-piety, while simultaneously suggesting that torah-piety is essential to approaching the Psalter itself.[81] It is not only the Mosaic Torah that is to be heeded as Scripture, but also the book of Psalms, as sort of a "Davidic Torah," which responds and corresponds to the Mosaic.[82] Finally, when coupled with the most grandiose

---

76. Miller, "Deuteronomy and Psalms," 11.
77. Ibid., 12–13.
78. Ibid., 15.
79. On the "law" as Deuteronomy, see ibid., 11. Cf. Childs, *Introduction*, 513.
80. Grant, *King as Exemplar*, 24.
81. Mays, *The Lord Reigns*, 129.
82. Mays notes that the fivefold division of the Psalms corresponds to the fivefold

of psalms (Ps 119) as a sort of *inclusio*, the first psalm's placement is evidence that there is a focus on torah from the beginning to the end of the Psalter.[83]

The pervasiveness of torah themes in non-torah psalms further demonstrates the importance of torah to the book of Psalms. At least fourteen other psalms scattered throughout the Psalter speak of the torah of the Lord.[84] For example, at the end of Book 3 (Ps 89:30–33) we find David's sons being enjoined to keep torah (ordinances, statutes, and commandments). In addition, after historical recounting of God's relations with Israel, the psalmist closes by declaring that YHWH blessing the people was so that they would "keep his statutes and observe his laws" (105:45). Here, near the end of Book 4, torah is again of fundamental interest. We may conclude that, when this argument is taken with the previous two (i.e., the Deuteronomic nature of the Psalms and the significant positions of torah psalms), it becomes clear that the Psalter is indeed very concerned with one's relationship to God's Word.

The King as the Paradigmatic Reader of Torah

In order to establish that the king is presented as the ideal reader of torah in the Psalms, it is not enough to show that the Psalms are concerned with royal and torah themes taken separately. It is also necessary to show a connection between the two themes within the Psalter. The chief argument for this is that the deliberate juxtaposition of royal psalms (Pss 2; 18; 20; 21; 118) alongside torah psalms (Pss 1; 19; 119) is meant to reflect the theology of Deuteronomy's kingship law.[85] In other words, the central concerns of the kingship law are presented when psalms in which the king expresses dependence on YHWH are placed beside psalms that encourage love for and obedience to torah. The reader is, therefore, intended to imagine the words of the torah psalms as being spoken and lived out by the ideal king himself.[86]

---

division of the Mosaic Torah, thus giving another reason for identifying the Psalter with Torah (ibid., 122). Cf. Childs, *Introduction*, 513.

83. Claus Westermann argued that an original collection of psalms had Psalms 1 and 119 as the opening and closing hymns respectively (see *Praise and Lament*, 253). Cf. Wilson, "Structure of the Psalms," 236.

84. Psalms 18, 25, 33, 78, 89, 93, 94, 99, 103, 105, 111, 112, 147, 148.

85. This is the thesis of Jamie Grant's *The King as Exemplar*. I am heavily indebted to this work.

86. Perhaps it should be noted that although some of these psalms may be attrib-

Psalms 1–2

It is now common to see Psalms 1 and 2 as forming a two-part introduction since there are significant lexical and thematic similarities between the two psalms.[87] These connections are intended to establish two themes in the minds of worshipers—the priority of torah and the importance of the Davidic kingship. How are these two psalms related to the kingship law? We can identify at least three areas where the kingship law is reflected in this grouping as well as the others. First, that the king was to be chosen by God (Deut 17:15) is reflected in Psalm 2 by the terms "anointed one" (2:2), "my king" (2:6), and "my son" (2:7). Second, the kingship law's emphasis on the king's dependence upon YHWH shines throughout all of Psalm 2, where the king looks to the Lord, not his military might, to vanquish his enemies (2:4–9; cf. Deut 17:16). Third, and most importantly, the king's torah-piety is brought to the fore. If Psalms 1 and 2 are indeed linked, then the king is the blessed man of Ps 1:1, the one who delights in the law of YHWH and meditates on it regularly (1:2). He fulfills the express mandate of the kingship law (Deut 17:18–20).[88] Thus, the placement of these psalms, the common themes between them, and their commonalities with the kingship law indicate that the ideals of torah were more than a slight concern for the editors of the Psalter. The king is the elect and set apart covenant partner who in the dignity of his calling rightly responds to the Word of God. Every Israelite was to practice torah faithfully, but God's anointed would supremely embody the law as the ideal king and reader.

Psalm 1, then, is our first example of *how* the king was to express devotion to torah. It begins by pronouncing a certain type of person as "blessed" (אַשְׁרֵי: 1:1), which refers not to a state of emotional happiness, but to the favor of God freely granted to those who cling to him. The blessed person avoids "wicked" (רְשָׁעִים), "sinners" (חַטָּאִים), and "scoffers" (לֵצִים)—those who have no regard for God and his commands. "By the 'wicked', 'sinners', and 'scoffers,'" Eaton writes, "is meant those hardened in defiance of God and of all that is good; arrogant and unscrupu-

---

uted to David, it need not follow that David himself is the ideal reader. Rather, the ideal king—who indeed shares much with and is foreshadowed by David—is the ideal reader.

87. See, e.g., Auffret, *Literary Structure of Psalm 2*; Bullock, *Encountering the Book of Psalms*, 59–60; Miller, "Beginning of the Psalter," 83–92; Wilson, *Editing of the Hebrew Psalter*, 205–6.

88. Grant, *King as Exemplar*, 215–19.

lous, they would be god to themselves, attempting to procure their own gain."[89] The righteous person is he who decidedly turns from these and pursues a different path.

Instead, the righteous one finds his delight in the torah of the Lord (1:2a).[90] God's instruction is the source of joy for the righteous. It is his chief desire and that which he loves above all else. This delight in the law, then, leads to constant "meditation" (הגה) upon it (1:2b). The verb "meditate" denotes vocal recitation rather than silent reflection and may involve any of the following in Psalm 1:2: (1) *reciting* something memorized; (2) *reading aloud* something written; (3) *sounding* inarticulate groans, sobs, murmurs in the midst of deeply emotional thoughts; (4) *singing* in private contemplation.[91] Since הגה may refer to varied vocal activities, it is likely that none of these activities alone captures the fullness of the term. Nonetheless, when הגה is used in place of another speech verb, it highlights the speaker's wholehearted feelings toward the object. It refers to the deep affections of the human soul, and may mean that a man is "lost in his religion" and "filled with thoughts of God's deeds or his will."[92] In other words, on its own, הגה denotes a certain *quality* of speech and not simply a particular *kind*. In Psalm 1, therefore, "meditation" refers to a range of vocal acts as well as to the wholehearted quality of the activity.[93] Finally, this act of meditation occurs "day and night" (1:2b), which denotes the continual, ongoing, and habitual rehearsal of God's words. It is not necessarily a setting aside of special time for personal devotions, but the reading, singing, crying out, and reciting of God's law in the course of one's daily activities.[94]

The blessed person, the ideal royal-reader, delights in torah more than in his own arrogance, autonomy, and sinful pleasure. His greatest

---

89. Eaton, *Psalms*, 62.

90. In light of our previous discussion of the Deuteronomic nature of the first psalm, torah here likely refers to the entirety of God's revelation to Israel embodied in the five books of Moses (especially Deuteronomy) (LeFebvre, "Torah-Meditation," 220–21).

91. Ibid., 218–19.

92. Negoiță and Ringgren, "*hāghāh*," *TDOT*, 3:323.

93. Lefebvre, "Torah-Meditation," 219.

94. VanGemeren, *Psalms*, 55. Also note the similarities between the blessed man and the king in Deut 17:18–20. The king, we are reminded, is to meditate on torah all the days of his life and, as a result, his dynasty would be perpetually prolonged. The pattern of meditation, obedience, and blessing is repeated (cf. Ps 1:3 for blessing).

joy is found in being in conformity with the law of the Lord. As a result, he vocally reads, sings, rejoices in, prays, recites, and thinks on torah throughout the course of his day. He makes reading an overwhelmingly oral activity—the Word of God as a true "word" must be revivified by speech and brought to the hearing of the reader. The living character of the law must repeatedly be brought to bear on the reader or hearer. Here we have the virtuous reader, whose *attitude* toward torah is delight, love, and reverence; whose primary *aim* is to be in conformity to God's ways; whose *response* is obedience, as evidenced by the avoidance of corrupting influences. By placing this psalm at the beginning of the Psalter, this ideal Israelite reader shows that all of one's life is to be measured by how one relates to God's Word, and that one cannot make any progress in the worship of YHWH if his or her life is not oriented to torah as the *viva vox Dei*.

Psalms 18–21

We can discern similar themes and relations in Psalms 18–21 and indeed a great degree of continuity with Psalms 1–2. Beginning with Psalm 18 we find at least five similar themes: (1) the use of an *inclusio* to emphasize YHWH as a refuge to the one who trusts in him (18:3 and 18:47; cf. 1:1 and 2:12); (2) delight in and obedience to torah (18:21–22; cf. 1:2); (3) a theology of the two ways (18:20–27; cf. all of Psalms 1–2); (4) the king's universal dominion (18:37–50; cf. 2:8–12); (5) reference to YHWH's anointed, here for the first time since Psalm 2 (18:50; cf. 2:2).[95] Therefore, the linguistic and theological parallels between this psalm and those in the introduction suggest a common concern, namely, the wedding of torah and ideal kingship.

It is not difficult to see that Psalm 19 reflects the theology of Psalm 1 in one obvious way: its emphasis on delighting in torah. It expands on the torah theme of the first psalm by providing a more detailed example of what delight in torah looks like. Furthermore, the awareness of the psalmist that following the way of righteousness leads to great reward (19:11; cf. 1:3, 6b), the emphasis on proper meditation (19:14; cf. 1:2), the acknowledgement that wisdom comes from torah (19:7; cf. 2:10–11),

---

95. Grant, *King as Exemplar*, 86–89.

and the Davidic superscription suggesting that Psalm 19 is a royal hymn point, again, to a theology that is shared with the introductory psalms.[96]

There are also significant theological links between Psalms 20 and 21 and the introduction, particularly when taken together with Psalm 18. The most noteworthy connection, for our purposes, is that of the torah-kingship theme. The prayer *of* the king (Ps 18) and the prayers *for* the king (Pss 20–21) surround the central psalm (Ps 19). Miller is correct, it appears, to conclude: "In the midst of the explicitly royal psalms lies Yahweh's torah. God's Word through the torah and God's rule through the king are bound together. The witness to that single torah-shaped rule is the voice of the king here at the center."[97] As the introduction unmistakably joins torah (Ps 1) and Davidic kingship (Ps 2), so this group of psalms does likewise.[98] As in the introductory psalms, the king is the exemplar of one who delights in torah and experiences the blessedness of following in the ways of YHWH.

Psalm 19 then provides our second hymnic presentation of how the king exemplifies torah-piety. It begins with a presentation of the works of God in creation and what these reveal of him (19:1–6), moves on to praise the wonders of God found in his Word (19:7–11), and ends in a response of prayer (19:12–14). The heavens—sun, moon, stars, and vast expanse—continuously declare the glory and wisdom of God the Creator (19:1). In their own "speech" they give the knowledge of God to all peoples in all places (19:2–4b). The sun is portrayed as a bridegroom arising from his tent and as a champion running his course with vigor (19:4c–6a)—illustrating God's joy, glory, power, and wisdom. No words are necessary since, as the psalmist writes, "nothing is hidden from its heat" (19:6b).

From the glory of God in the heavens, the psalmist moves to the goodness of YHWH (hwhy) expressed in torah. He elaborates on six praiseworthy characteristics of torah, namely, its perfection (or comprehensiveness) (19:7a), dependability (19:7b), uprightness (19:8a), clarity (19:8b), purity (19:9a), and truthfulness (19:9b).[99] The words of YHWH

---

96. Ibid., 99–101.

97. Miller, "Kingship, Torah Obedience, and Prayer," 128.

98. For other common threads between these and the intro psalms, see Grant, *King as Exemplar*, 113.

99. For a helpful examination of each of these attributes, see Eddleman, "Word Pictures," 413–24. Cf. Craigie, *Psalms 1–50*, 181–83; Kraus, *Psalms 1–59*, 273–75.

are more valuable and beautiful than all that creation could offer (19:10) and in obeying them there is great reward (19:11). The psalmist portrays the revelation of God given in torah as vastly superior to that given in the cosmos. The six-fold repetition of the personal covenant name for God, YHWH, emphasizes that in torah God has drawn near and revealed himself to his people in an intimate way. Ross Wagner writes: "The dialogue of the heavens was speech about God; torah embodies YHWH's own speech with which he performs such actions as instructing and commanding."[100] Thus, from verses 1–11, we see a progression in the psalm from the "word" of creation given to all humankind to torah given to YHWH's people alongside a move from God (אל) the Creator to God the covenant Lord (יהוה).

The speaker's response to the wonderful revelation of God in creation and torah is found in verses 12–14. Faced with the beauty, wisdom, goodness, and power of God disclosed in his works and Word, the speaker is aware that he is insignificant and unworthy of such blessing because of his sins (19:12). He pleads that YHWH would restrain him from committing presumptuous sins, recognizing that continuous sins have the potential to rule over him (19:13a). With the Lord's help, the psalmist will be blameless and innocent of grievous sin against his Master (19:13b). He asks that the meditation of his heart would be blameless and bring joy to his faithful Redeemer's heart (19:14). Wagner writes:

> In this prayer the psalmist draws together various strands from every part of the psalm and weaves them together into a simple, yet elegant, petition which captures the intent of Psalm 19 as a whole. The poet here mentions speech for the first time since vv. 2–5, thus stitching the opening and closing of the psalm tightly together. Awed by the heavens' unceasing adulation of God, the psalmist longs to join in their praise.[101]

Thus, the psalm reaches its climactic point with the psalmist's final prayer.

---

100. Wagner, "From the Heavens to the Heart," 255. David Clines has furthermore argued that each of the benefits of torah (19:8–10) alludes to the tree of knowledge in Genesis 2–3, suggesting that the wisdom proceeding from torah is superior to that from the tree of knowledge (Clines, "The Tree of Knowledge," 8–14).

101. Ibid., 259–60.

Virtuous Royal Reading

In sum, the virtuous reader's *attitude* includes delight, awe, and humility before the revelation of God's majesty and goodness in his Word. His primary *aim* is to become conformed to God's will. His *responses* include praise and thankfulness for torah, confession of sins, prayer, and trust in YHWH. Also implied is the response of continued obedience to torah, which brings great reward. Here, again, we hear the voice of the ideal king modeling torah-piety for Israel.

Psalms 118–119

Our final pairing, Psalms 118–119, also confirms the argument of this section. Due largely to the lack of a Davidic superscription, some scholars view Psalm 118 as part of an Egyptian Hallel and therefore associated with exodus themes, not royal ones.[102] It is, however, clear to a number of commentators that the voice in the psalm is that of the king leading the people in a public celebration of God's faithfulness to Israel.[103] There are indeed some specific reasons to acknowledge this psalm as royal, such as (1) the praise ascribed to YHWH for military victory suggests that the speaker is he who leads the people in battle, namely, the king; (2) the speaker refuses to trust in "princes" (118:9), which is a likely reference to foreign alliances that only a king could make; (3) the representative nature of the speaker means that he must fulfill an official function on behalf of the people—the best explanation for the alternating "I" and "we" statements.[104] It is safe to conclude that Psalm 118 is a royal psalm. The significant placement of this psalm beside Psalm 119 may now be highlighted.

There are canonical and theological reasons for viewing Psalms 118 and 119 as being intentionally juxtaposed. Among the canonical reasons we find that (1) they are positioned between two larger groups of psalms, the hallelujah psalms on one side and the Songs of Ascent on the other and (2) they both lack a superscription.[105] On the first point, Grant writes: "Psalm 118 is dislocated from the surrounding psalm groupings and therefore is associated with its neighbouring work which also cannot reasonably be adjoined to either of the bracketing groups of

---

102. For example, see Goulder, *Psalms of the Return*, 191; Kraus, *Psalms 60–150*.

103. See, for example, Allen, *Psalms 101–150*, 123–25; Croft, *Identity*, 104; Eaton, *Psalms*, 404–6; Mays, *Psalms*, 379; Terrien, *Psalms*, 787; VanGemeren, *Psalms*, 729.

104. Grant, *King as Exemplar*, 127–28 n. 11. Cf. Eaton, *Kingship*, 20–26, 61–63.

105. Grant, *King as Exemplar*, 175–76.

psalms."[106] On the second point, the rarity of psalms lacking superscriptions in Book 5 of the Psalter is significant in light of the pairing of two such psalms.[107] Among the lexical connections are shared word, such as: חסד (steadfast love: Pss 118:1–4; 119:41, 64, 76), ירא (fear: 118:4, 6; 119:63, 74, 79), ישׁועה (salvation: 118:14–15, 21; 119:123, 155), היה (living: 118:17; 119:17, 25, 40, 93, 144, 159, 175), אשׁרי / ברך (blessing or blessedness: 118:26; 119:1–2), and אור (to enlighten: 118:27; 119:105, 130, 135). "The significance of the juxtaposition of two poems using these words," writes Grant, "is not necessarily found in the number of times that these words are repeated but rather in the centrality of the concepts which they express."[108] Finally, among the theological links are included themes such as dependence on YHWH for salvation, the two ways, and the importance of proper piety before YHWH.[109]

How, then, do these two psalms relate to those already discussed? To avoid unnecessary repetition, the pertinent similarities include: (1) emphasis on torah-piety; (2) the importance of meditation on torah; (3) the result of torah meditation and obedience as blessedness and prosperity; and (4) dependence upon YHWH as per the kingship law.[110] Thus, the juxtaposition of Psalms 118 and 119 reflects the theology of Deuteronomy, particularly bringing the kingship law to the forefront of the Psalter's call to torah-piety.

Psalm 119 presents our final and most developed expression of devotion to God's Word. This longest work in the Psalter is a very intricate hymn with two overriding structural components. The first is its acrostic form: each stanza is headed by a successive letter of the Hebrew alphabet and each line begins with that particular letter. The deployment of an acrostic structure was likely for aesthetic reasons, with the ultimate aim of exalting torah and showing its magnificence and beauty.[111] The

106. Ibid., 176.

107. Ibid. Only Psalms 107, 118, 119, 136, and 137 lack superscriptions in Book 5 of the Psalter.

108. Ibid., 176–80.

109. Ibid.

110. Ibid., 181–87.

111. Will Soll counters with the view that the structure was meant to aid in memorizing the contents of the psalm (Soll, *Psalm 119*, 32–34). His argument seems unlikely, particularly in light of the length of the psalm as well as the fact that each line of a stanza began with the same letter. Both factors seem more of an impediment than an aid to memory.

second component is the eight terms deployed to describe torah. In each stanza, the psalmist uses a combination of these eight terms (laws, statutes, commandments, judgments, ordinances, words, testimonies, and precepts) as synonyms of torah. "The overall impression," writes Grant, "is not that the psalmist is trying to subtly distinguish between the various torah terms, rather that he uses them interchangeably to reflect the totality of God's revelation."[112] Thus, by the use of an extremely difficult form and structure, the author is able to expound ideal torah-piety with great passion, concentration, and beauty.

As with Psalms 1 and 19, it is the king who prays this extensive 176 verse song.[113] What is the content of his torah devotion? Due to the length of this psalm, no attempt will be made to provide a detailed exposition of its contents and, thus, the king's piety. Instead, I will simply outline some of the exemplary attitudes, aims, and responses to torah of the speaker throughout this hymn.[114]

The speaker expresses his devotion to torah, first, in his disposition toward YHWH and his law. For example, he approaches torah with fear and trembling (119:120), treasures it (119:11a, 72), recognizes his need for God to open his eyes so that he might truly understand his Word (119:18, 27, 34, 73, 125, 144, 169), longs for the law (119:5, 20, 40), delights in it (119:24, 35, 47, 77, 92, 103, 111, 143, 162), stands in awe of the words of God (119:161), has a heart geared toward obedience (119:112), praises God for the law (119:163), and recognizes that the law cannot be separated from YHWH the lawgiver (119:4, 126). On this last point, David Freedman concludes that the psalmist grants to torah "virtually the status of a divine hypostasis." He continues: "Neither *tôrâ* nor *hokmâ* can be separated from Yahweh, who created them; yet each embodies an essential aspect of Yahweh that nevertheless can be addressed,

---

112. Grant, *King as Exemplar*, 158.

113. Soll offers a number of arguments in favor of this view. For example, in Deuteronomy, the OT history, and the Psalms, "the king emerges as the individual with the greatest cause for preoccupation with Torah due to the role Torah plays in the royal ideology." Also, the emphases on "meditation," "teachers," and the privileged relationship with YHWH enjoyed by the speaker, are most intelligible if the king is the subject (Soll, *Psalm 119*, 135–42).

114. Admittedly, it is difficult at times to distinguish attitudes, aims, and responses in this psalm. The recognition of purpose clauses, for example, is helpful in showing what is an aim and not simply a disposition of the heart. However, sometimes responses are attitudes that one brings into subsequent interactions with torah, and attitudes are responses to previous readings. In one sense, the whole psalm is a response to torah.

invoked, and appealed to itself as the object of devotion. Each has the power to order and bless the worshiper's life."[115] Indeed, for the speaker, an encounter with the torah is an encounter with YHWH himself, which requires all due reverence, humility, delight, and obedience.

The aims of the speaker can be summed up by one of the earliest lines in the hymn, where he writes: "How can a young man keep his way pure? By guarding it according to your word" (119:9 ESV). This sentiment is echoed elsewhere, as he seeks to avoid sinning against God (119:11b) and pursues his own holiness (119:133). He also prays so that he might keep the law (119:88), and seeks wisdom (119:98), insight (119:99), and understanding (119:18, 27, 34, 73, 100, 125, 144, 169). He restrains himself so that he might keep the law (119:101) and longs for obedience (119:117, 134, 145, 146).

Finally, his responses include the following: He gladly proclaims the law to others (119:13, 46), rejoices in it (119:14, 16), joyfully sings the statutes (119:54, 172), gives thanks for the law (119:62), hopes and waits expectantly for the fulfillment of its promises (119:49, 81, 114, 123, 131, 147), and observes them because he sees their greatness (119:129). On top of these, one might venture to say that the fitting response to torah is the psalm itself. Often lost amid much technical analysis is the fact that this psalm is a prayer from start to finish (except, possibly, the first two verses). Prayer, then, is also the appropriate response of the psalmist to the law of God—prayers of praise, thanksgiving, dependence, and expectancy. Surely prayer in turn nurtures a more able and sensitive reading of the Scriptures. These prayers may be spontaneous and informal, well-crafted and formal; they may be personal or public or both. Moreover, it should not go unnoticed that affliction is the context of much of this prayerful reading (e.g., 119:67, 71, 87, 92, 153). Exemplary reading of Scripture is not performed in a vacuum. Rather, it is shaped and informed by very real, unresolved suffering. The ideal reader responds to torah faithfully, particularly when circumstances are difficult and bewildering.[116]

---

115. Freedman, *Psalm 119*, 89–90.

116. It is notable that Luther develops his triadic formula for the study of theology—*Oratio, Meditatio, Tentatio*—from this psalm (see Luther, "Preface to the Wittenburg Edition," 72–74). These themes of prayer and suffering will be expanded upon in the final chapters of this study.

What we find in the three torah psalms is a comprehensive description of what devotion to and the ideal reading of torah entails. The one who would approach God's Word rightly must fear the Lord, be humble, and delight in the law as coming from the mouth of the Lord. One's primary aim must be conformity to its ways, which leads to obedience, prayer, praise, and proclamation. This is the piety of the ideal king and should be that of every covenant member.

Conclusion: Ideal King as the Virtuous Reader

In many genres of the OT witness the ideal king is presented as the paradigmatic reader of Scripture. The kingship law mandates that the king is to be the model Israelite and ideal reader of torah. The narrative presentation of the actual kings of Israel and Judah and their relationship with the law left the sense that, even at their best, they fell short of being effective paragons of love and obedience to torah, which was a key concern in these narratives. Finally, the Psalter proved to be a rich handbook for reading torah, for in it we observe the highest devotion to torah, manifested in particular attitudes, aims, and responses—interpretive virtues—"modeled" by the ideal king for all God's people to follow. Chief among the characteristics of the ideal reader were the fear of God, humility, delight in the Word, dependence on YHWH, and the orientation toward and response of obedience. It is by emulating the commitment to God's Word of the king, both as the representative Israelite and as the royalty of its lived experience, that God's people would demonstrate its faithfulness to YHWH, procure the blessed life, and in part fulfill its calling as a royal priesthood to God. In the final chapter we will examine some of these royal priestly interpretive virtues in some detail. But for now we turn our attention from ideal royal reading virtues to ideal priestly reading practices.

4

Reading *Pro Ecclesia*

The Priest As the Ideal "Didactic" Reader of Scripture

In the last chapter, we examined how the king of Israel was to be the paradigmatic exemplarist reader of Scripture. In his "personal" life and, ultimately, his office, he was to show a devotion to torah that would be emulated by the people. In so doing, he would ensure the good of the nation for generations to come. In this chapter, we examine the Old Testament presentation of the priesthood and its relationship to torah. It is argued that as preachers and teachers of the law, the priests function as the paradigm for didactic Scripture reading in the OT, and that this is borne out in the legal, narrative, and prophetic material. Israel's self-understanding as a priesthood, then, was shaped by this depiction of its professional priesthood. As the latter is defined by a certain relation to the Word of God, so is the former. Therefore, this chapter (1) cursorily defines priesthood vis-à-vis the Word of God, (2) presents an overview of the various priestly "reading" practices—distinguishing between holy and profane, teaching, judging legal matters, public reading, and pronouncing blessing—and (3) provides two "case studies" in priestly reading practices in order to catch a glimpse of these forms of public reading in action. As a result of this exploration, we will gain a sense of the varied "priestly" practices that contribute to a proper "reading" of Scripture among God's people.

What Is a Priest? Priesthood and the Word

The Hebrew term כהן is used to designate Israelite priests of YHWH as well as those of its neighbors, whether Egyptian (Gen 41:45), Phoenician (2 Kgs 10:19), or Philistine (1 Sam 5:5).[1] Though its etymology is uncertain, its use indicates that it generally denotes those who performed some sort of mediatorial function between God (or the gods) and the general populace. To be called a "priest" was to be bestowed with an honorific title, on the level of kings and nobles. Like royalty, the *sin qua non* of priesthood was that the priest be chosen by God himself (cf. Deut 17:15)—it is a matter of divine grant and election (Num 16:5, 7; 17:20; 1 Sam 2:28; Ps 105:26; cf. Heb 5:4).[2] In fact, one author argues that the general concept of the election of Israel derives from such special concepts of election.[3] Priests are consequently consecrated—sanctified—for service to the community. Indeed, privilege and responsibility are interwoven into the fabric of priesthood. Election and sanctification, which affords the priest continual access to the presence of the Lord in the sanctuary, is accompanied by the communal responsibilities of offering sacrifices for the people, helping them discern holy from profane and clean from unclean, teaching torah, applying its stipulations to the varying circumstances of Israel's life, and blessing the people in YHWH's name. The overarching rationale for this depiction of the priesthood is summed up well by Davies:

---

1. Sabourin, *Priesthood*, 98–99. For other detailed studies of priesthood in Israel, consult the following works along with Sabourin: Blenkinsopp, *Religious and Intellectual Leadership*, 66–114; Cody, *A History of Old Testament Priesthood*; de Vaux, *Ancient Israel*, 345–405; Grabbe, *Priests, Prophets, Diviners, Sages*, 41–65; Nelson, *Raising Up a Faithful Priest*.

2. Davies, *Royal Priesthood*, 155.

3. Johann Maier writes: "For them [the priests], the concept of election had the significance of a special election restricted (1) to the place of worship . . . and (2) to the descendants of Levi and Aaron, and within the priestly group sometimes even referring to the election of Pinhas and Zadok and their descendants as the leading priestly clan, the Zadokites. This point of view presupposes a restriction, a narrower concept of election, claiming for the priestly group a central role within Israel and for Israel, corresponding to and competing with the likewise restricted concept of election according to Davidic dynasty theology" (Maier, "Self-Definition," 145–46). While I do not hold to a theory of "competition" between David and Levi, the main point that the priests' election is both example and provision for Israel is helpful in spelling out the relationship between "ordained" and "universal" priesthood.

> If the sanctuary is בית יהוה ("the home of Yhwh," Exod. 23.19), then the priest is at least a regular visitor to that divine abode, a welcome and honoured beneficiary of the divine hospitality. The priest belongs in two worlds. While his everyday life is among his fellow Israelites, when he dons his vestments and crosses the threshold he becomes a participant in the heavenly or ideal world.[4]

The priest is the ideal man who represents the people before YHWH in the sanctuary. He holds up the ideal and reaffirms the prospect of Israel's royal and priestly dignity, while simultaneously providing for their holy calling through the cult and the various activities associated with it. He is both the model and provision for Israel's royal priesthood.[5]

For our purposes, the term "priest," moreover, designates one who has to do with the Word of God, whether oracular or codified.[6] T. F. Torrance brings out the significance of this connection, arguing that the priest is concerned primarily with the tabernacle, the Holy of Holies (דביר), as the place in which the Word (דבר) resided in the form of the Ten Words and book of the law. "All that the priest does," writes Torrance, "all liturgical action, answers to the Word given to the priest who bears that Word and mediates it to man, and only in relation to that primary function does he have the other functions of oblation and sacrifice."[7] Priestly work is Word work as both a mediation of the divine commands and a witness to God's revealed will. On the most basic level, the priest (as we will see) instructs the people in God's law. However, even the priest's task of bearing the iniquity of the people was simultaneously a witness to God's saving will and an obedient response to the Word that initiated the priestly service of atonement. This service furthermore resulted in the confirmation of God's gracious Word in the form of the benediction or blessing.[8] Thus, it is difficult to conceive of the nature and role of priesthood in Israel apart from its connection to the Word of YHWH. Indeed, a priest *is* a minister of the Word. God's

---

4. Davies, *Royal Priesthood*, 164.

5. Ibid., 166. Cf. Cheung, "Priest as the Redeemed Man," 265–75, who likewise presents the priest as the ideal man.

6. Schrenk, "ἱερεύς," *TDNT*, 3:260.

7. Torrance, *Royal Priesthood*, 1.

8. Ibid., 3–4.

people as a priesthood are also people of the Word. The shape of this relationship to the Word occupies the next section.

Priestly "Reading" Practices in the OT

As a minister of the Word, one of the priest's primary tasks is to "read" torah, and this reading involves diverse practices that are found throughout OT corpus, whether as legislated or as elaborated by narrative descriptions and prophetic indictments. This section examines five "reading" practices—distinguishing, teaching, judging, reading, and blessing—with the intention that these would inform the universal priesthood's practices as well.[9]

Distinguishing the Holy

As with the kingship, we find legislation for the priesthood in the Pentateuch. After Aaron's two sons are destroyed by YHWH for profaning his altar, the LORD speaks to Aaron and prescribes his primary responsibilities as a priest to Israel (Lev 10:8–11). First is the duty of distinguishing between the holy and profane (or common), and the clean and unclean. Persons or objects can exist in one of four possible states: sacred, common, clean, and unclean. To be holy is to be separated to God and separated from the common, in the same way that God sanctified the Sabbath (Gen 2:3; Exod 20:10–11), the priesthood (Exod 22:9), and his people (22:32).[10] The term "common" refers to everything that is not holy, and can be divided into two groups: clean and unclean. The "normal" state of most things/people is to be clean.[11] Holy or sacred things (e.g., the temple) must remain pure at all times. If they become defiled they must be purged immediately or the community would suffer bitter punishment from the LORD. The unclean and the holy should never come together.[12] The first duty of the priest is to respond to the

---

9. For a recent examination of the teaching ministry of the priests, see Betts, *Ezekiel the Priest*, chap. 2.

10. Milgrom, *Leviticus 1–16*, 615.

11. Wenham, *Leviticus*, 19.

12. Milgrom, *Leviticus 1–16*, 616. The relationships may be viewed as such: clean things become holy when they are sanctified; unclean things cannot be sanctified; clean things can be made unclean; holy items may become defiled and become common, possibly unclean. When clean, one may enter the sanctuary. Otherwise, that person must

needs of the people by making the proper distinctions that the law requires between these categories of objects.¹³

In Ezek 22:26, we find YHWH's charges against Israel's priesthood in very clear terms:

> Its priests have done violence to my teaching and have profaned my holy things; they have made no distinction between the holy and the common, neither have they taught the difference between the unclean and the clean, and they have disregarded my sabbaths, so that I am profaned among them.

This indictment is a virtual cataloguing of most of the central functions of the priesthood. First, the priests did violence to YHWH's torah. The phrase "do violence to torah" (חמס תורה) is found only twice in the OT (cf. Zeph 3:4) and underlines the priests' utter contempt for the law, both its ceremonial and moral stipulations.¹⁴ This wrong treatment of torah may have involved deliberate misinterpretation and misrepresentation or requiring payment for instruction or both.¹⁵ Second, they profaned the holy things (קדשׁים), which in Ezekiel refer to both sacred objects and donations.¹⁶ Third, they failed to distinguish for the people between sacred and profane objects. By this neglect, profane objects were allowed to be used for the worship of the Lord. Fourth, they did not instruct the people concerning ceremonial cleanness and uncleanness, thus allowing them to go their own way with reference to hygiene, diet, and other health-related practices.¹⁷ This negligence on the priests' part no doubt led many to desecrate the temple and the worship of God. Fifth, they "turned a blind eye" to Sabbath violations by disregarding their duty to uphold the Sabbath before the people by prosecuting those who

---

be excluded then purified before reentering worship with God's people (see Wenham, *Leviticus*, 19–20; cf. Hartley, *Leviticus*, 135).

13. "The making of distinctions is the essence of the priestly function" (Milgrom, *Leviticus 1–16*, 615).

14. Block, *Ezekiel 1–24*, 725. Some commentators hold that Ezekiel was dependent on Zech 3:4. Whether that is the case or not, since the passages are so similar, the fuller Ezekiel passage will only be treated.

15. Blenkinsopp, *Ezekiel*, 98. A similar charge is brought against the priests in Mic 3:11, which states: "Her leaders pronounce judgment for a bribe, her priests instruct for a price."

16. Block, *Ezekiel 1–24*, 725.

17. Ibid., 726.

desecrated it.[18] As a result of the priests' many sins, YHWH's name is defiled by the very ones charged with guarding his holiness (cf. Lev 10:3; 21:6) and the whole nation is hindered from following his ways. In this passage, the importance of the priest's duty to distinguish and preserve the holy is powerfully reaffirmed.

Teaching the Truth

The second and related responsibility of the priesthood was to "teach" Israel all the statutes that YHWH had given to Moses (Lev 10:11). This instruction involved the explication of the laws of Moses and not simply making the above distinctions.[19] In Moses' blessing of the tribe of Levi, he pronounces as much: "They shall teach Your ordinances to Jacob, and Your law to Israel" (Deut 33:10a). Situated as it is in a blessing, it becomes even clearer that the ongoing mandate for the priesthood of Israel is that they would instruct the people in torah and, in that way, help to preserve positive covenantal relations between YHWH and Israel.

This function is affirmed in Jeremiah. Sandwiched between poetic words of judgment, Jer 18:18 recites the words of the prophet's opponents: "Then they said, 'Come, let us make plots against Jeremiah—for instruction shall not perish from the priest, nor counsel from the wise, nor the word from the prophet. Come, let us bring charges against him, and let us not heed any of his words.'" Jeremiah's opponents—likely the priests, sages, and prophets of Israel—are "the power structure, the knowledge industry, and the religious authority of the establishment."[20] In their minds, no matter how much judgment the prophet announces, torah, counsel, and prophecy will never be taken away from the people, for these are the very modes of authority that ordered community life.[21] For our purposes, what is noteworthy is the confidence with which these leaders asserted the permanence of the priests' teaching office. As long as Israel stood, there would be priests teaching the law of God. According

---

18. In Lev 20:4, the phrase "turned a blind eye" expresses the people's refusal to prosecute a Molech worshipper (Greenberg, *Ezekiel 21–37*, 462–63).

19. Milgrom, *Leviticus 1–16*, 617. Milgrom cites Philo, *Laws* 1.100, as implying a broader teaching function for the priests.

20. Brueggemann, *Jeremiah*, 171. Cf. Lundbom, *Jeremiah 1–20*, 826.

21. Brueggemann, *Jeremiah*, 171.

to Jeremiah this was a patently false assumption. Only a faithful priesthood would continue to teach God's people.[22]

Indeed, it is the quality of the priestly teaching (and conduct) that is at issue in much of the prophets. In Jeremiah 6, we encounter a nation that does not want to hear the Word of the Lord (6:10) and people from every strata of society—poor, wealthy, and powerful—who are making a profit by violent means, including the religious leaders (6:13a; cf. 8:10).[23] Concerning the religious leaders, Jeremiah proclaims: "From the prophet even to the priest, everyone deals falsely. They have healed the brokenness of My people superficially, saying, 'Peace, peace,' but there is no peace" (6:13b–14 NASB; cf. 8:10b–11). Not only are prophet and priest benefiting from violence and injustice, they also "commit falsehood" both by false teaching and deceptive behavior.[24] Instead of performing the necessary "surgery" by condemning sin and teaching the people the law of God, both prophet and priest give a false sense of security. They proclaim, "Peace (שׁלם), peace (שׁלם)," which means not only that the community will be free from conflict, but that its well-being is assured.[25] Calvin captures these leaders well:

> They were like the unskilful who by rashly applying false remedies, cause inflammation, even when the disease is not serious; or like those who are only bent on easing pain, and cause the increase of the disease within, which is the more dangerous as it is more hidden. This is not to heal, but to kill.[26]

Those who should be most concerned about the holiness and righteousness of the people fail in this most fundamental charge. Their neglect of teaching the *truth* was a fundamental failure of the priesthood.

Finally, Mal 1:6—2:9 condemns the quality of priesthood's teaching, while highlighting indirectly the nature of faithful instruction. YHWH's central charge is that the priests have "despised" his name, not showing him the honor they would show to earthly fathers and masters (1:6). For

---

22. Ezra is a noteworthy example of such a faithful priest (Ezra 7:1–5). He is upright (Ezra 7:10), skilled in the law (7:6), blessed by YHWH (7:9b), intent on teaching the people (7:11–12), successful in discharging his duty (Neh 8:1–18).

23. Lundbom, *Jeremiah 1–20*, 430. Jeremiah 5 contains similar condemnations of the priesthood.

24. Ibid.

25. Ibid., 431.

26. Calvin, *Jeremiah and the Lamentations 1*, 337.

this reason, they will be severely punished (1:14–2:3). The Lord then recollects the covenant he made with Levi and how the priests used to walk faithfully and reverently before him (2:4–7), saying:

> True instruction was in his mouth, and no wrong was found on his lips. He walked with me in integrity and uprightness, and he turned many from iniquity. For the lips of a priest should guard knowledge, and people should seek instruction from his mouth, for he is the messenger of the Lord of hosts (Mal 2:6–7).

The faithful priests of old, in contrast to their descendants, were trustworthy teachers of the law, because their instruction was characterized by righteousness, reliability, and adherence to the intent of the law ("reliable instruction": תורת אמת) (2:6a).[27] The exemplary life of the former priests is expressed by the simple phrase "he walked with me in peace and uprightness" (2:6b), which denotes a right relationship and intimate fellowship.[28] By carrying out their duties faithfully, they turned many of the "lay members" of the religious community from their iniquitous paths (2:6c). The role of the priest is further emphasized by the conjunction כי, which should probably be rendered "indeed," "surely," or "truly" (2:7).[29] Indeed, "the lips of a priest," namely, his pedagogical duties of teaching torah to Israel, should preserve knowledge (2:7a). By carefully maintaining and faithfully transmitting the received tradition about YHWH—torah—the priest "guards" the knowledge of God.[30] This being the case, people should and would seek (and find) reliable instruction from him (2:7b). The priest is "the messenger of the Lord of hosts" when he faithfully carries out his responsibilities (2:7c). He does not replace prophets or angels as God's messengers (מלאך), but plays a complementary role. As prophets and angels proclaim the Lord's will on specific occasions, so the priests regularly proclaim the same through their teaching ministry.[31] The priests in Malachi's time, however, were far from circumspect. Instead of walking with YHWH "in peace and uprightness" (2:6), they have turned aside from the way (2:8a). Instead of turning "many from sin" (2:6), their teaching caused many to "stumble"

---

27. Verhoef, *Haggai and Malachi*, 247–48.
28. Hill, *Malachi*, 209.
29. So Verhoef, *Haggai and Malachi*, 249–50; cf. Hill, *Malachi*, 210.
30. Hill, *Malachi*, 211.
31. Ibid., 212–13; Verhoef, *Haggai and Malachi*, 250.

(2:8b) by showing partiality (2:9b).³² By providing false or inadequate instruction concerning sin and its dangers, they were responsible for the downfall of many. Instead of standing in awe of YHWH's name (2:5), the priests "corrupted the covenant with Levi" (2:8c), that is, rendered it inoperative and useless.³³ Thus they receive the Lord's just judgment (2:9a). Though the priests often failed, they were called to be faithful readers as teachers of torah's truth and wisdom, and this for the sake of the community's fidelity to the covenant.

Judging Legal Matters

Deuteronomy 17:8-13, especially verses 9 and 10, prescribes the legal procedures in cases too difficult for local authorities to handle, thus requiring more competent experts, particularly the priests at the sanctuary. McConville points out that "fine judgment" may be required for a number of biblical laws, which makes it plausible that legal expertise would of necessity have to be sought in certain instances. He lists, for example, the issues of distinguishing between murder and manslaughter (Exod 21:12-14), pronouncing on the seriousness of an assault or theft (21:18-21), or deciding when negligence becomes culpable (21:28-29).³⁴ As authorities in the law, the priests would explain its stipulations to the parties involved and render the verdict (Deut 17:11a). The decision, announced by the high priest, would then be binding on all parties with the threat of death for disobedience (17:11b-13). Thus, priests also functioned as judges, teaching and applying the law to difficult civil matters (cf. 21:5).

This understanding of the priestly vocation is echoed in Isa 28:1-13, where the prophet condemns the priests and prophets of Israel, saying:

> And these also reel with wine and stagger from strong drink: the priest and the prophet reel with strong drink, they are confused by wine, they stagger from strong drink; they reel while having visions, they totter *when rendering* judgment. For all the tables are full of filthy vomit, without a *single clean* place (Isa 28:7-8 NASB).

---

32. "Stumbling" in Scripture often refers to the disastrous effects from sin's failure and is an ever-present danger to those who follow wicked ways (Taylor and Clendenen, *Haggai-Malachi*, 316).

33. Ibid., 316-17.

34. McConville, *Deuteronomy*, 291.

The wickedness of the people was evident also among the religious leadership of the day. Contrary to the command in Lev 10:8–10, which prohibited drinking wine when performing their duties, the priests not only drank but were overwhelmingly intoxicated. The debauchery of the nation's religious leaders overflowed into the performance of their religious and civil functions. The prophets "reel" when giving visions and the priests "totter" when rendering decisions on legal and cultic matters. Both of these officials could have been instrumental in directing the people to YHWH in Israel's last days. "The priests," Oswalt writes, "could make the difficult judgments which would alienate many but might perhaps restore to the nation a sense of right and wrong, or they could make those decisions which would placate the poor and gratify the rich."[35] Nevertheless, poor judgments come easily when one is drunk or experiencing a hangover. By their character, the priests were poor models and, by their drunken decision-making, they failed in their duty to apply torah rightly to the lives of the God's people. Rendering faithful judgments was to be an ongoing practice of the priesthood that would help keep the people faithful to the Lord amidst communal strife.

Communal Torah Reading

In Moses' parting speech to the children of Israel, he puts in place the necessary pieces for the ongoing success of the nation as they enter the Promised Land, and these include instructions to the priests (Deut 31:9–13). He commands that every seven years, at the Feast of Booths, the priests are to assemble the people, and the law is to be ceremonially read before all of Israel. The purpose of this practice is to inculcate the fear of the Lord and obedience to his law in every generation. In giving torah to the priests, Moses delegates responsibility for the preservation and transmission of his teaching to future generations. The priests function as those who are responsible for building the law into the worship life of Israel in perpetuity, so that those "who have not known" (31:13) will do so no longer.

This practice is affirmed after the exile and following the rebuilding of Jerusalem's wall (Neh 1–7), when the people gathered together and Ezra was summoned to bring the law of Moses before them (8:1–2). At the time, the narrator writes, "He read from it before the square which

---

35. Oswalt, *Isaiah 1–39*, 510–11.

was in front of the Water Gate from early morning until midday, in the presence of men and women" (8:3). For half a day, Ezra read portions of the Pentateuch to the people.[36] Since we will examine this passage in some detail later, the point here is simply that Ezra read the law of Moses to all Israel and was expected to do so. Further on the passage describes the other priests and Levites coming to Ezra seeking insight into the law (8:13). As the exemplar of holy priesthood, Ezra was also a model reader and interpreter of Scripture who, by this practice of public reading, wove torah into the fabric of the peoples' post-exilic life.

Blessing the People

A final reading function required of the priests is that of pronouncing blessing on Israel: "At that time the Lord set apart the tribe of Levi to carry the ark of the covenant of the Lord, to stand before the Lord to minister to him, *and to bless in his name*, to this day" (Deut 10:8; cf. 21:5, italics added). The life setting of blessing was normally the sanctuary and worship service, wherein the priest would give the benediction to the people as they entered and, more commonly, as they departed the service.[37]

Many scholars agree that Num 6:22–27 presents this priestly blessing in its programmatic form, for not only does the passage command the recitation of a blessing, it also prescribes, as authoritative torah, the shape the recitation should take.[38] Indeed, the blessing spells out the precise ways in which YHWH would be among his people.[39] The general structure of the passage is straightforward. Verses 22–23 represent the introduction and verse 27 the conclusion. The blessing itself occurs in verses 24–26, in which each verse contains one or two specific petitions/promises:

36. Fensham, *Ezra and Nehemiah*, 216.
37. Miller, "The Blessing of God," 242.
38. See, e.g., Budd, *Numbers*, 76; Knierim and Coats, *Numbers*, 94; Milgrom, *Numbers*, 51.
39. The form and content of the blessing influenced later biblical literature. Psalm 67:1, for example, employs almost identical terminology in invoking the favor of YHWH on his people. Moreover, the Songs of Ascent (Psalms 120–134) display the influence of Num 6:24–26 in that they constantly make use of four key terms in the priestly blessing ("bless," "keep," "be gracious," and "peace") and can be shown to be an elaboration of these terms and, therefore, the blessing itself (see Liebreich, "The Songs of Ascent," 33–36; cf. Ashley, *Numbers*, 151).

> The Lord bless you and keep you;
> the Lord make his face to shine upon you, and be gracious to you;
> the Lord lift up his countenance upon you, and give you peace.

The first verse contains the all-inclusive petition that YHWH would "bless" the people (6:24a), which refers to the provision of abundance and fruitfulness in every area of the community's life.[40] The second clause (6:24b) asks that God "keep" (שׁמר) his people. In the OT, God is the only one who keeps or preserves persons. He alone has the power to guard and protect his people no matter what circumstances, whether in battle or amidst life's ongoing vicissitudes.[41] The next verse "requests" that the Lord "make his face shine upon" Israel (6:25a). The face of YHWH "shining" depicts anthropomorphically his positive presence for favor and help, his friendship and nearness to his servants, and the gracious turning of almighty God toward human beings, which is also what the second clause (6:25b) emphasizes when it speaks of God's graciousness.[42] The graciousness of God often refers to the bestowal of mercy and favor, forgiveness of sins, and deliverance from affliction (cf. Pss 4:1; 41:4).[43] The first clause of verse 26 repeats that of the previous verse (Num 6:26a; cf. 6:25a). The second clause, however, asks that the people be granted "peace" (שׁלום), or wholeness and universal well-being (6:26b). Thus, in different ways, each verse "gives expression to God's commitment to Israel—a commitment which promises earthly security, prosperity, and general well-being."[44]

Contrary to some scholars, the blessing is not a magic formula or a typical prayer to God, but lies somewhere in between.[45] It is directed toward the people (second person plural) by the priest, but, through the threefold use of the name YHWH, emphasizes that it is he who is the source of blessing, not the priest. As Knierem and Coats put it: "The

---

40. Ashley, *Numbers*, 152.
41. Ibid. Cf. Miller, "The Blessing of God," 245.
42. Miller, "The Blessing of God," 245.
43. Ibid.
44. Budd, *Numbers*, 77.
45. Nelson, for example, writes: "In Israel, a blessing was more than just a pious wish, but an effective and power-laden formula, especially when spoken by a priest (1 Chron. 23:13). It was what we call 'performative speech'; it did what it said in the very act of saying it. God worked to bless Israel through the words spoken by the priests. Their words gave effect to Yahweh's will to bless" (Nelson, *Raising Up a Faithful Priest*, 45).

priest is the reciting agent, Yahweh the blessing agent."[46] The blessing is intended to assure the assembled congregation of YHWH's promises and strengthen their hope that the blessings of the formula already experienced in sanctuary worship will extend into its day-to-day life after the worship. Miller, furthermore, describes God's "blessing" as "the ongoing, steady, regular work of God to provide and care for life."[47] Put theologically, God's blessing is his favorable providence. How does this relate to "reading"? When the same blessing is repeated over and over again in changing times and situations, it functions as a pronouncement of God's will and promise, expressed throughout Torah, to bless his covenant people perpetually, especially as they walk faithfully before him. Uttered in its prescribed form (which itself is torah), it bestows God's gracious care upon his people, not because it possesses some innate power, but because a gracious God enacts it according to his promise. In the blessing, reading becomes the promise, reminder, and bestowal of God's providential care.

The priesthood is assigned a number of logocentric tasks: distinguishing the holy from the profane, teaching torah, applying the law to legal pronouncements, publicly reading the law, and blessing the people. The common feature of all of these acts is their clear public or didactic orientation. Priests "read" chiefly for others. It was their duty to bring the Word of the Lord to bear on the entirety of Israel's existence, whether mundane or sacred, legal or cultic. Priests were to be heralds of the will of YHWH as disclosed in his law. They interpreted the Word for the people and applied it to the difficult and varying circumstances of Israel's community life. These priestly reading practices contribute in different ways to forming a covenantally faithful people by constantly directing the gaze of the community to the very Word that formed it.[48]

Case Studies in Priestly Reading

The priest's performance as an interpreter of torah is often stated, but rarely illustrated in the OT. However, there are two post-exilic episodes

46. Knierem and Coats, *Numbers*, 94.

47. Miller, "The Blessing of God," 248. Cf. Westermann, "Creation and History," 11–38.

48. Chapter 6 explores how cognates of some of these practices are taken up by Luther and applied to the universal priesthood, while chapter 8 develops this chapter's as well as Luther's contributions.

in which some of the priesthood's reading functions are put on display. In the first, Nehemiah 8, it is the priests' reading, translation, and exposition that are highlighted, while in the second, Haggai 2, it is their cultic judging or "directing" function that is underscored.[49] The following "case studies" are intended to elucidate what has already been established in the previous section by giving concrete examples of priestly interpretative practices. What they demonstrate is the interplay between fidelity and dynamism—faithfulness to the law, and flexibility and creativity with regard to its use and application—that characterizes priestly reading practices. Thus these examples may help illustrate what practices the church, as a priesthood, might embody.

Elucidation and Reinterpretation: Nehemiah 8:1–18

The occasion of the gathering in Nehemiah 8 is the celebration of the Feast of Booths. All the people—men, women, and children—gather for one purpose: to hear "the book of the law of Moses" (Neh 8:1). Immediately one is reminded of Deut 31:10–13 where Moses commands the priests to gather the people together every seven years, at the Festival of Booths, to hear the book of torah and learn to fear YHWH. In summary fashion we are told that Ezra reads from the book and the people listen attentively (Neh 8:2–3), while verses 4–8 expand the summary statement of verse 3. A number of features stand out in this account. First, Ezra is accompanied by a number of unknown men, probably laypeople since only their names are mentioned (8:4b).[50] Second, he blessed God to the approval of the people (8:6). Third, Ezra is aided by thirteen Levites who "explained" (בין, 8:7), "read" (קרא), "elucidated" (פרשׁ),[51] and "gave the sense" (בין) of the law so that the people could understand (בין) it (8:8). The verb בין has thus far been used four times in the brief narrative, suggesting that a proximate aim of the "reading," led by Ezra and assisted

---

49. The term "directing" is taken from Budd, "Priestly Instruction," 4–7, referring to the practice of distinguishing holy from profane and applying torah to difficult religious matters.

50. Venema, *Reading Scripture*, 167; Blenkinsopp, *Ezra-Nehemiah*, 286; Fensham, *Ezra and Nehemiah*, 216–17.

51. The exact translation of this word is difficult to pin down. It may be rendered "explain," "translate," or "elucidate" (see Venema, *Reading Scripture*, 169 for an explanation of the options).

by the Levites, is that the people would *understand* torah.⁵² Thus, if 8:4–8 is viewed as an expansion of the previous section, then all the various activities of Ezra and his associates comprise the whole act "reading" torah.⁵³ Priestly reading is an oral-aural, communal, doxological, and educational enterprise.

The people wept in response to the reading of the law (8:9b), probably because of their failures in keeping it and the threats imposed for such failure (cf. 2 Kgs 22:11). Ezra, Nehemiah, and the Levites taught, however, that the appropriate response was not weeping but rejoicing, because the day was set apart to the Lord for that express purpose (Neh 8:9a, 10–12).⁵⁴ The people then went away and celebrated with joy *because* they "understood" (בין) (8:12). This fifth and final use of בין underscores that the ultimate goal of reading torah was finally reached, namely, understanding manifested in joy *and* obedient action.⁵⁵

The second account of reading involves only the priests, Levites, and leaders of the people, who go to Ezra to "gain insight into the words of the law" concerning the Feast of Booths and how they are to conduct themselves in its light (8:13–14). Presumably as a result of their conference, they execute the commands of torah vis-à-vis the Festival (8:15–17). Lastly, the proceedings are summarized (8:18).

Four features of the law's implementation deserve mention as examples of the interpretation of torah, both by the characters in the story and the narrator himself. First, in the law the people are told to take "the fruit of majestic trees, branches of palm trees, boughs of leafy trees, and willows of the brook; and you shall rejoice before the Lord your God for seven days" (Lev 23:40). The law does not prescribe what exactly to do with this foliage, but since it later mentions that the Israelites are to live in booths (Lev 23:42), it appears that the contingent of leaders in Ezra's time inferred that the branches be used to construct or cover booths.⁵⁶ Thus, we observe further specificity brought to the interpretation of the

---

52. Ibid., 170.

53. Ibid., 167.

54. This point is driven home by the parallel structure of the passage. Ezra prohibits grief and enjoins rejoicing (8:9–10). His prohibition is repeated by the words of the Levites (8:11) and the actions of the people (8:12) (see Throntveit, *Ezra-Nehemiah*, 97).

55. Venema, *Reading Scripture*, 173. The themes of joy/delight and obedience in reading are developed in the final chapter of this study.

56. Blenkinsopp, *Ezra-Nehemiah*, 291–92.

law for the people of the post-exilic period. Second, the types of foliage used to construct the booths in Nehemiah differ from those mentioned in Lev 23:40. This apparent difference may suggest further interpretation and application of the unspecific legislation (e.g., "leafy trees") for the present context. Third, the reading of torah occurred every day in the Nehemiah account (Neh 8:18), whereas there is no clear indication that this daily reading was part of the Mosaic regulations.[57] This possible innovation may represent interpretative freedom exercised by Ezra for the purpose of resituating torah at the center of Israel's worship life, particularly at this crucial juncture in its history (i.e., the reconstitution and recommitment of the people). Finally, this suggestion is confirmed by the narrator's own interpretation of the events of the restoration as a "second exodus." Like Israel liberated from Egyptian bondage, Ezra's generation are those who "returned from captivity" (8:17a). The author states that "from the days of Joshua son of Nun until that day, the Israelites had not celebrated it like this" (Neh 8:17b NIV), a further connection to the Exodus generation and entry into the Promised Land. Historically, this statement is inaccurate, since the Festival was celebrated in the days of Solomon (2 Chr 7:8–10; 8:13) and Hosea (Hos 12:9).[58] The emphasis of the comparison, however, is on the purpose for which the ceremonies were celebrated. Prior to Ezra's (and the leaders') reinterpretation of the law, the Festival was connected to harvest celebrations. Now, again, the events are linked to covenant renewal as the people are "invited to focus on the festival's earlier emphasis: the effective presence and nurturing care of God toward the small community that had been so graciously redeemed and mercifully preserved."[59] Moreover, the narrator interprets and presents Ezra as a second Moses or Joshua because of his role in placing torah at the center of the life of the reconstituted community. Thus, in both accounts, reading is a multifaceted practice consisting of explaining, interpreting, and applying the law in light of the new circumstances of the post-exilic community. This was for the sake of the understanding, joy, and covenantal obedience of the people, and for the exaltation of torah in their midst.

---

57. Ibid., 293; Venema, *Reading Scripture*, 180.
58. Throntveit, *Ezra-Nehemiah*, 99.
59. Ibid.

Following Trajectories: Haggai 2:11–13

As the returned exiles settled in Jerusalem and the temple still remained to be restored, YHWH spoke to Haggai the prophet, commanding that he go and ask the priests for a ruling (lit: תורה) (Hag 2:11). There are two cases the priests are asked to adjudicate. First, they are questioned: "If someone carries holy meat in the fold of his garment and touches with his fold bread or stew or wine or oil or any kind of food, does it become holy" (2:12a ESV)? This question makes specific reference to the law, particularly the regulations concerning offerings in Leviticus 1–7. The prophet describes a situation in which someone is carrying consecrated meat from a sacrificial meal, a circumstance quite relevant to religious life in Israel.[60] It is important to the question that the meat is carried in the fold of his garment, which formed a sort of bag and prevented direct contact with other foods.[61] If, in such a situation, the corner of the cloak touches any other kind of food, will that food then become sacred? The priests give the brief response: "No" (Hag 2:12b). Pertinent to their consideration would be such texts as Exod 29:37, 30:29, and Ezek 44:19, which all affirm that something or someone coming into contact with a holy object is made holy. For example, the last text states: "When they go out into the outer court to the people, they shall remove the vestments in which they have been ministering, and lay them in the holy chambers; and they shall put on other garments, so that they may not communicate holiness to the people with their vestments." Is there a contradiction? No, since the issue at hand is that of direct versus indirect contact with what is sacred. The latter does not make holy what is profane.[62] Furthermore, the contagious character of holiness is limited in the case of Exod 29:37 and 30:29, where only something that has the explicit potential of being holy may become holy.[63] Therefore, the priests' negative response to the prophet's question is in full accord with the teachings of the law, although no precedent is found in prior authoritative literature.

---

60. The offering may have been a fellowship or sin offering. See Petersen, *Haggai and Zechariah*, 76, and Verhoef, *Haggai and Malachi*, 117, for an outline of possible options.

61. Wolff, *Haggai*, 91.

62. For a similar interpretation, see Meyers and Meyers, *Haggai and Zechariah*, 56; Wolff, *Haggai*, 91.

63. Petersen, *Haggai and Zechariah*, 78.

The second case is presented as follows: "If one who is unclean by contact with a dead body touches any of these, does it become unclean" (Hag 2:13a)? The law, in multiple places, states that a person becomes unclean through contact with a corpse (Lev 21:11; 22:4; Num 5:2; 9:6–7, 10; 19:11–13). The question of the prophet, however, focuses on the result of contact between the defiled person and the aforementioned food items (cf. Hag 2:12). The priests reply in the affirmative to this query (12:13b), for the law provides a precedent, stating, "All who touch a corpse, the body of a human being who has died, and do not purify themselves, defile the tabernacle of the Lord" (Num 19:13) and, more generally, "Whatever the unclean person touches shall be unclean, and anyone who touches it shall be unclean until evening" (Num 19:22). Holiness and defilement operate differently. While holiness cannot be communicated indirectly, uncleanness can.[64] Only a few things may become holy, while almost everything is capable of becoming defiled by contact with anything unclean.[65] Therefore, the priests' response is in accord with torah and this is evidenced by Haggai's implicit approval and subsequent illustrative use of their judgment (Hag 2:14). In both cases, we see how the priests interpreted and applied torah in relatively new and specific situations. Priestly reading is thus principled and particular—it follows trajectories and precedents of prior texts, while also paying close attention to detail in order to be able to make the fine distinctions sometimes necessary for living faithfully before the Lord.

Conclusion: Priestly Reading as Pedagogy

As interpreters, civil and cultic judges, and instructors in the law, the various strata of the OT depict the priests as the paradigm for didactic, public-oriented Scripture reading. In some cases they were called simply to articulate what God had prescribed through Moses and the prophets. In other cases they were called to apply torah to different sets of circumstances, thus making it more transparently relevant to contemporary hearers. In still other cases, they were summoned to employ their torah-formed wisdom to adjudicate in difficult or complicated legal and cultic matters. They were also called to pronounce God's blessing upon Israel, bestowing upon the people the promise and guarantee of YHWH's con-

---

64. Meyers and Meyers, *Haggai and Zechariah*, 57.
65. Petersen, *Haggai and Zechariah*, 79.

tinual grace toward them. Like the king, priests were indeed expected to model torah-piety, but their central duty was to communicate God's revelation to God's people from generation to generation and, by doing so, preserve their identity as a holy people and a royal priesthood set apart by and for YHWH. The ideal priest was the exemplar of the centrifugal aspect of Israel's corporate calling vis-à-vis the Word of God, enacting practices that point towards the ideal reading practices of all God's people—reading performed for the sake of others, for the sake of the church.

PART TWO

Royal Priesthood and
"Reading" in Christ's Church

5

Royal Priestly Reading in Christological Perspective

Jesus Christ as the Ideal Reader

The Old Testament story ends with a sense of anticipation. Israel's kings, as the embodiment of torah-piety, and her priests, as faithful public-directed interpreters of the law, failed largely to provide actual models of devotion to torah. Thus, throughout the Scriptures of Israel there are sprinkled expressions of longing for leaders who would direct the people into covenant obedience through a proper relationship with torah. Then enters Jesus Christ. In him Israel's hopes and destiny are realized. He is the pious King, faithful High Priest, and the fulfillment of Israel's call as a royal priesthood. This chapter argues that Christ fulfills these callings in part by being the supreme "reader" of God's Word. In his person and work he demonstrates that to be king, priest, and Israel (that is, a royal priesthood), is to be oriented to the Word of God in a particular way that reflects OT expectations of torah fidelity and practices, but also transcends them. It is contended, first, that traditional construals of Christ's threefold office do not take adequate account of how central "reading" the Word of God is to each of the offices, especially the priestly. Second, with particular attention given to the royal and priestly offices, it will be demonstrated that these forms of the one office of mediator are united, in a sense, by their centering on the Word of God. In the end, to be "Christ" is to display a certain relationship to God's Word that is typified in the anointed offices and corporate calling of Israel in the OT. In that light, the chapter attempts to fill out the picture of Christ's kingship, priesthood, and Israel-as-royal priesthood by examining the Gospels' portrayals of his ministry and calling. While making mention of other ways to conceive Christ's offices, attention will be given to Word-related functions. Finally, the chapter concludes with three episodes of Jesus' "reading" of torah in Mark's Gospel, in order to provide concrete examples of Jesus as the ideal royal-priestly reader of Scripture. What emerges ultimately is that Christ is the model and standard of "reading" Scripture, as well as its chief subject matter. We begin with an examination of the doctrine(s) of Christ's threefold office.

The Munus Triplex Christi Traditionally Conceived

The received doctrine of Christ's offices no doubt derives from the scriptural witness to his mediatorial work. Christians of the first centuries drew categories for understanding Christ's saving work from the Old Testament and thus envisaged the mediatorial office of the Lord as having a threefold division, namely, Christ as *the* Priest, King, and Prophet.[1] The shape(s) of this *munus triplex* and its relationship to the Word of God in the history of dogma is the central concern of this section.[2]

Early and Medieval

The *Ecclesiastical History* of Eusebius of Caesarea (ca. 263–339 AD) furnishes us with the first clear use of the triadic formula. After discussing the various anointed offices—priests, kings, and prophets—of the Old Testament, he writes:

> All these [priests, kings, and prophets] have reference to the true Christ, the divine and heavenly Word, who really is the only High

---

1. Barth observes that the early and medieval church commonly spoke of a *munus duplex* of Christ. He observes that as early as the *Testaments of the Twelve Patriarchs* and into the time of Justin, Athanasius, Augustine, and Peter Lombard there was the tendency to speak of Christ as High Priest and King. The settlement on a twofold office is understandable, he acknowledges, since "the material content of the doctrine of reconciliation is in fact exhausted by what has to be thought and said from these two christologico-soteriological standpoints." However, the twofold structure needed to be deepened in light of other scriptural considerations, such as Rev 3:14, which describes Christ as the Amen, the faithful and true Witness (Barth, *CD* IV/3.1, 5–13).

2. There is no intention here to be exhaustive. Early examples are only representative, and the focus is primarily on broadly Reformed treatments.

Priest of all, the only King of all creation, and the Father's only Archprophet of the Prophets. And the proof of this is that no one of those symbolically anointed of old, either of priests or of kings or indeed of Prophets, possessed so great a power of divine virtue as was displayed by our Saviour and Lord Jesus, the only true Christ.[3]

Jesus Christ as the true Anointed One surpasses all previous officeholders because of the "divine virtue" which he uniquely displays. Peter Chrysologus, a fifth-century bishop, similarly writes: "He is called Christ by anointing, because the unction, which in former times had been given to kings, prophets, and priests as a type, was now poured out as the fullness of the divine Spirit into this one person, the King of kings, Priest of priests, Prophet of prophets."[4] Jesus is the Christ due to his preeminent Spirit anointing. All three OT offices point to and are fulfilled in the one person of Jesus Christ. Not much, however, is said in these accounts about the specific character or functions of each office.

In the thirteenth century, Thomas Aquinas forcefully articulated the dimensions of Christ's priestly office. He identifies the characteristic function of the priest as mediating between God and his people, which involves teaching people the law, interceding on their behalf, and making reparation for their sins. Since Christ performs these duties to "an eminent degree" he is a priest "in the fullest sense of the word."[5] Not only does he possess the "grace" of priesthood, as the "Head of all men" he also possesses "the fulness of all graces." Therefore Thomas writes: "In the case of other men one individual is lawgiver, another is priest, a third is king; but all of these prerogatives are united in Christ as in the source of all graces. *The Lord is our judge, the Lord is our lawgiver, the Lord is our king; he will come and save us* [Isa 33:22]."[6] Again, all three offices converge in the one Person Jesus Christ. The noteworthy feature of this account is that Thomas ties teaching to the priestly office, a move that is rare in later dogmatic expositions, as we will see.

---

3. Eusebius, *Ecclesiastical History* I.3, 48. Cf. Wainwright, *For Our Salvation*, 110.
4. Peter Chrysologus, *Sermon* 59, quoted in Wainwright, *For Our Salvation*, 111.
5. Aquinas, *ST* 3a.22.1, 137–39.
6. Ibid., 139–41.

John Calvin

The doctrine of Christ's threefold office takes its characteristic form in Calvin's *Institutes*.[7] The reformer views the knowledge of these offices as essential to understanding the purpose of Christ's coming and what was accomplished in his work. Thus the exposition of Christ's threefold office is the explication of his saving work.[8] The name "Christ" pertains to all three offices in that all of their OT manifestations received an anointing, even though it refers most properly to kingship.[9] As prophet, first, Christ is the herald and witness of Isa 61:1–2, whose special anointing (i.e., the Holy Spirit) and superior doctrine (i.e., the gospel) place him above all teachers. He fulfills his prophetic office by teaching his people God's ways and wisdom, and empowering them to do the same.[10] Thus, the prophetic office is the teaching office. Second, Christ's kingship is spiritual and characterized by its eternal nature and power.[11] The Father governs, protects, nourishes, and sustains the church through his Son and has given him "the whole power of God's dominion."[12] As eternal King, Christ is able to care everlastingly for his own by providing them with everything necessary for eternal happiness and protecting them from all their spiritual foes.[13] Judgment will be the last act of his reign.[14] Finally, the priestly office of Christ consists in his own holiness, which qualifies him to reconcile sacrificially the church to God. His atoning death purchased forgiveness and cleansing for God's people and grants access to all the benefits of his priesthood. Moreover, as priest he intercedes for us and makes our prayers acceptable to God because of his everlasting intercession on our behalf.[15] Thus, the priestly office is

---

7. In his first edition of the *Institutes*, he includes only two offices—king and priest (Calvin, *Institutes 1536*, 54). Interestingly enough, at this stage the teaching ministry of Christ is comprehended in the two offices. For a brief survey of the development of Calvin's account of the threefold office, see Jansen, *Calvin's Doctrine of the Work of Christ*, 39–51.

8. Calvin, *Institutes*, II.15.1, 494.

9. Ibid., II.15.2, 495–96.

10. Ibid., II.15.3, 496.

11. Ibid.

12. Ibid., II.15.5, 500. "Such is the nature of his rule, that he shares with us all that he has received from the Father" (II.15.4, 499).

13. Ibid., II.15.4, 498.

14. Ibid., II.15.5, 501.

15. Ibid., II.15.6, 501–2.

primarily sacrificial—atonement—and secondarily intercessory. In sum, Calvin's foundational exposition of Christ's threefold office identifies the prophetic office with teaching, the kingly office with rule, protection, and provision, and the priestly office with sacrifice and intercession.[16]

Francis Turretin and the Reformed Tradition

It is this basic structuring of the work of Christ that becomes most common in subsequent confessional and dogmatic accounts, especially in the Reformed tradition.[17] Various writers expanded on and further systematized Calvin and the confessions, such as Francis Turretin in his *Institutes of Elenctic Theology*.[18] He follows his predecessors in using the *munus triplex* to explicate the mediatorial ministry of Christ. According to Turretin, the tripartite structure of Christ's saving office is necessitated by Scripture. Old Testament passages, such as Isa 9:6, 61:1-2, and Psalm 110, speak of Christ in three offices. Such New Testament texts as John 14:6, moreover, join together the three offices: "The Way in his priesthood, when by his own blood he opened a way for us to heaven (Heb 10:20); the Truth in his prophetic office because he reveals to us the word of the gospel, the only saving truth; the Life in his kingly office by which he quickens and protects us through his efficacy; the Way in death, the Truth in word, Life in the spirit."[19] Both testaments make necessary a threefold saving ministry. The threefold misery of humanity, consisting of ignorance, guilt, and bondage to sin further necessitates a threefold office, as each of these impediments is overcome by the specific

---

16. The point is that this account, on its own, is a reductive summary of the threefold office of Christ. Taken alone it can be misleading. One finds a more nuanced account, however, by consulting Calvin's commentaries. I am indebted to Todd Billings for alerting me to this latter fact.

17. For example, question 31 of the Heidelberg Catechism reads: "Why is he called Christ, that is, Anointed? Because he is ordained of God the Father, and anointed with the Holy Ghost, to be our chief Prophet and Teacher, who fully reveals to us the secret counsel and will of God concerning our redemption; and our only High Priest, who by the one sacrifice of his body has redeemed us, and ever liveth to make intercession for us with the Father; and our eternal King, who governs us by his Word and Spirit, and defends and preserves us in the redemption obtained for us" (Schaff and Schaff, *Creeds of Christendom*, 3:317–18). See also questions 23–26 of the Westminster Shorter Catechism.

18. In what follows, I will primarily examine Turretin's account (*Institutes*) and supplement it with Heppe's compendium of Reformed doctrine (*Reformed Dogmatics*).

19. Turretin, *Institutes*, 2:393.

functions of each office: ignorance by the prophetic, guilt by the priestly, and the tyranny of sin by the kingly.[20] Finally, the nature of the salvation to be conferred (as annunciation, acquisition, and application), the acts common to a Mediator (speaking for God to us, satisfying and interceding, and procuring salvation), the fulfillment of types (anointed OT offices), and the three attributes of God (wisdom, mercy, and power) correspond to and call for Christ's triadic mediatorial office (prophet, priest, king, respectively).[21]

The Mediator's prophetic office denotes "that full and august revelation of the mysteries of salvation which Christ (as the highest teacher of the church) has exhibited to us."[22] Against those who desired to subsume the prophetic ministry under the priestly and kingly offices, Turretin argues that, though priests and kings were given the power to preach and legislate respectively, the prophetic office is distinct by its revelatory nature.[23] The matter of the prophets' revelatory preaching is the explication or exposition of the law, the proclamation of the gospel, and the prediction of future events.[24] Christ performs these prophetic functions immediately and mediately, externally and internally, efficaciously, authentically, perfectly, eminently, and with the confirmation of miracles and a holy life.[25] Other Reformed writers make a twofold distinction in Christ's prophetic ministry: *prophetia legalis* and *prophetia evangelica*. The first refers to Christ's teaching of the true intent of the law and corresponds to the earthly and external dimensions of his prophetic ministry. The second refers primarily to the illumination of the heart by the Holy Spirit, and corresponds to the heavenly/eternal and internal dimensions of his prophetic office.[26] What is noteworthy about Turretin's account is that he nearly defines the prophetic office by its fresh revelatory nature, on the one hand, and by its exposition of the law on the other. In doing

---

20. Ibid.
21. Ibid., 393–94.
22. Ibid., 397.
23. Ibid.
24. Ibid., 398–400. Heppe, citing Alsted, lists the prophetic functions as (1) teaching, (2) the confirmation of this teaching by miracles, which include healings, foretelling the future, and revelation, and (3) prayer (Heppe, *Reformed Dogmatics*, 456). Most accounts of the *munus triplex*, however, reserve prayer for the priestly office.
25. Turretin, *Institutes*, 2:400–402.
26. Heppe, *Reformed Dogmatics*, 455.

so, he blurs the distinction between prophets and priests, which he affirms beforehand in passing. Furthermore, not only is the exposition of the law tied to the prophetic office, but also the preaching of the gospel. Yet, as we saw in chapters 2 and especially 4, these functions find at least an equally fitting home within the priestly office.

The priesthood of Christ "is the function of the mediatorial office according to which he performs those things with God which must be performed for sinners; both by offering himself up once as a victim for them and by interceding for them always with the Father."[27] Thus, the priestly office of Christ is comprised of his *satisfaction* and his *intercession* for believers. Satisfaction, according to Reformed writers, consists of his voluntary self-offering and obedience to the Father's will as well as his bearing the punishment prescribed in the law on behalf of the elect.[28] In other words, satisfaction involves both his active and passive obedience. Regarding active obedience, there is a twofold distinction between natural and federal subjection to the law. The first pertains to the rule of the eternal law to which every creature is subject. Therefore, Christ as a true man was subject to the law in this way. The second refers to submission to the law as the condition of blessedness. In this case Christ is only subject to the law for the sake of the elect, not for his own benefit.[29] Thus, it follows that the active obedience of Christ was *pro nobis*, a subjection and obedience to the law for us and our salvation. Although both active and passive obedience are essential, most of the stress in Turretin's (and the Reformed) account of the priestly office is on the latter, that is, the death of Christ as the atoning sacrifice for sins. Intercession receives marginal treatment.[30] In addition, Turretin argues that Christ fulfills both the Levitical and Melchizedekian priesthoods, though his office corresponds more closely to the latter. With reference to the persons involved, the manner of their institution, their efficacy, perfection, and duration, the priesthood of the Mediator differs substantially from

---

27. Turretin, *Institutes*, 2:403.

28. Heppe, *Reformed Dogmatics*, 458–59.

29. Ibid., 459–63. Turretin adds a third distinction in active obedience, i.e., penal subjection, which describes the necessary punishments exacted upon violators of the law. Christ was obviously not subject to the law in this way (Turretin, *Institutes*, 2:449).

30. In this edition of Turretin, intercession is given four pages compared to the sixty-five pages devoted to satisfaction.

Aaron's.[31] Melchizedek's priesthood, on the other hand, comports with Christ's in terms of their common "name" (king of righteousness, king of peace), origin, immortality, office, dignity, and uniqueness.[32] Hence Turretin somewhat distances Christ's priesthood from the Levitical priesthood with regard to their relative eminence, yet interestingly ties them together by the common and defining functions of sacrifice and intercession. Thus, the Lord's priestly office is defined by both priestly orders. Christ is in the *taxis* of Melchizedek as to his dignity, but in the order of Aaron as to his priestly functions.

Finally, Christ is the King, whose mediatorial kingship is necessary on three grounds: (1) the decree of God who elected him in eternity, (2) the need not only for the annunciation and acquisition of redemption, but also for its application and conservation forever by the King, and (3) that the most powerful enemies of the church can only be vanquished by the King of kings and Lord of lords.[33] Correspondingly, Christ administers this office in calling and gathering the church, preserving and governing her, protecting the same against all her enemies, and glorifying her in the last day.[34] Turretin takes pains to emphasize the spirituality of Christ's kingship over against those who expect an earthly reign of the Messiah. One proof of the spiritual nature of the Lord's kingdom is the way he governs and preserves his church, namely, by the Word and Spirit of God.[35] Christ rules the church not by a scepter or sword, but by his royal promises and commands, which enable the faithful to attain

---

31. Turretin, *Institutes*, 2:406–8.

32. Ibid., 409–10.

33. Ibid., 486. Turretin distinguishes between Christ's *natural* and *economical* kingship. The first concerns the second Trinitarian Person's sovereignty over all creation as God. The second refers to the "economy of grace," where Christ as God-man is made King over the church by the institution of God. It is the economical kingship of Christ that concerns us here (ibid.).

34. Ibid., 487. Heppe distinguishes Christ's kingship as both a *vocatio* and a *judicium*. The first concerns the outward proclamation of the gospel and the inward illumination of the Holy Spirit. The second pertains to Christ's exercise of judgment on earth upon the elect and the godless, since he acquits and protects the former and inflicts temporal punishments on the latter. Other dogmaticians make further distinctions in the functions of Christ's kingship, such as (1) calling others to participate in his kingdom, (2) legislation, (3) bestowal of good things necessary for salvation, (4) doing away with the evil, and (5) judgment (Heppe, *Reformed Dogmatics*, 483).

35. Turretin, *Institutes*, 2:488.

the goal of their salvation. Thus, the kingly office of Christ is at once a ministry of the Word in which he strengthens and sustains the church.

What we find in Turretin is a classic expression of the post-Calvin Reformed doctrine of the *munus triplex* of the Mediator. Christ is the proclaiming Prophet, sacrificial and interceding Priest, and governing and protecting King.[36] Both in his humiliation and exaltation he exercises these three offices in order to accomplish everything necessary for the salvation of his people. What is important to observe for our purposes is that the Word of God is tied very closely to the prophetic office and somewhat to the kingly, while no significant link is established with the priestly dimension of Christ's saving work.

Karl Barth

Subsequent accounts of the threefold office diverge only slightly from this course.[37] Karl Barth, however, departs from traditional Reformed accounts by more closely uniting formally the person and work of Christ.[38] Materially, he covers much similar territory, but does not give

36. Turretin does make the important qualification that, since all offices are so united in Christ, the same act may proceed at the same time from all three offices. Thus, the gospel is "'the law of the prophet' (Is. 2:2, 3), 'the scepter of the king' (Ps. 110:2), and 'the sword of the priest,' by which he penetrates even to the dividing asunder of soul and spirit (Heb. 4:12) and an altar upon which the sacrifice of our faith ought to be placed" (ibid., 394).

37. Even Friedrich Schleiermacher follows the Reformed line, making only one significant alteration. He rejects the notion of Christ's state of humiliation, since the term presupposes a higher preexistent being to which we have no epistemic access. Rather, what we know is that the Person of Christ began when he became a man and we only know the unity of the Person. The divine in him, which existed from all eternity, cannot experience actual humiliation, compulsion, or division, but gives off the appearance of these because it is united to the Person of Christ. It is proper, then, to speak only of Christ's exaltation from a "state of lowliness" to the right hand of God, but not of a humiliation. These qualifications relate to Christ's offices in at least two ways. First, to hold to the traditional two natures doctrine inevitably results in the divine nature absorbing the human, which imperils the sympathetic mediatorship of Christ. Second, each of the three offices must be viewed as exercised from the state of lowliness and subsequently in the state of exaltation. There is no natural kingship or preexistent prophetic ministry. What Christ performs in his mediatorial office is as a man—both a lowly and exalted man (Schleiermacher, *Christian Faith*, 473-75). In most other ways, however, Schleiermacher does not depart from traditional categories.

38. Barth writes: "Jesus Christ is not what He is—very God, very man, very God-man—in order as such to mean and do and accomplish something else which is atonement. But His being as God and man and God-man consists in the completed act of

the *munus triplex* specific and independent treatment as that which sums up the mediatorial office of Christ. He entitles the sections corresponding to Christ's priestly, kingly, and prophetic offices, respectively, "Jesus Christ, the Lord as Servant," "Jesus Christ, the Servant as Lord," and "Jesus Christ, the True Witness." The three central aspects of the Mediator's work of atonement and reconciliation are justification as the Priest, sanctification as the King, and calling as the Prophet.[39] Finally, the three offices are correlated to Christ's state of humiliation, exaltation, and guaranteeing of the covenant.[40] Thus Barth combines many of the traditional aspects of the doctrines of the person and work of Christ to give a full-orbed picture of the reconciliation enacted by the Mediator.

In what corresponds to the priestly office, Barth describes the work of the Christ in forensic, non-cultic, categories, under the rubric of "The Judge Judged in Our Place."[41] For the most part, the priestly office for Barth involves Christ in the state of humiliation, and is a ministry of atonement that involves what earlier writers termed the Son's active and passive obedience. However, he goes further than prior dogmatic accounts by highlighting the soteriological significance of Christ taking our place as Judge. As both man and God, Jesus displaces every human and establishes God as supreme Judge, and in doing so liberates each person from the burdensome task of trying to justify himself or herself.[42] Although Barth does view the priestly office in terms of sacrifice and obedience, he also broadens it and creates space for other acts of libera-

---

the reconciliation of man with God." He acknowledges that the distinction between the person and the work of Christ is convenient and potentially helpful heuristically, but asks whether this division corresponds with the facts. Jesus Christ is who he is in the act of reconciliation he performs (Barth, *CD* IV/1, 126–27).

39. Barth, *CD* IV/1, 147.

40. Ibid., 132–37.

41. Although Barth selects his imagery from the legal sphere, he acknowledges Scripture's use of a variety of images to depict the saving work of Christ. He points to financial and military imagery as valid but insufficiently comprehensive. He admits that cultic imagery might have been able to capture the length and breadth of Christ's work, but opted for forensic categories because he reckoned them more understandable to modern readers. He explains that the cultic imagery could have been used somewhat interchangeably with the legal. Jesus Christ as Judge approximates to Jesus Christ as the High Priest who represents us. The Lord as judged and judgment corresponds to his being offered up as a sacrifice for sins. Finally, Christ as the just and obedient one is synonymous with Christ as the *perfect* sacrifice (ibid., 274–83).

42. Ibid., 231–34.

tion by the Savior. Yet there is no direct correlation between the priestly office and the ministry of the Word of God.

In Barth's treatment of the kingly office, he speaks of Jesus Christ as "The Royal Man," who by virtue of his exaltation as the Son of *Man* actualizes sanctification for all humanity.[43] While the accent on the priestly office was on the Son of God's humiliation, the emphasis for the royal office is on his exaltation as a man. Most relevant for our discussion is how Barth attempts to understand the person of Jesus, the Royal Man, in the act accomplished by him. The "life-act" of Christ takes two primary forms—his "concrete speaking" and his "concrete activity" which accompanies his speech.[44] The first, Barth observes, is the "primary and controlling aspect of His life-act: the most human form, basically, of all action; impartation, His self-impartation by the Word which he spoke to His disciples, the people, the publicans and sinners, the scribes and Pharisees as His opponents, the high-priests and Pilate as His judges."[45] Human speech is the basic form of his royal life-act, and may be further divided into three categories: preaching the gospel (εὐαγγελίζεσθαι), teaching (διδάσκειν), and preaching/heralding (κηρύσσειν). Jesus is *the* bearer of Good News—both publishing and uniquely enacting it in his person and work. He is also the *didaskalos*, the preeminent expositor and applier of the Law and Prophets. Lastly, he is the supreme herald of the kingdom of God, declaring the establishment of the eschatological reign of God.[46] Thus Christ exercises his royal office by imparting the realities of the kingdom of God in various modes of speech.

The second aspect of Jesus' life-act is the concrete works he accomplished, particularly his deeds of power that accompanied his speech. This activity is the "kindling light of his speech—the light of the truth of His speech kindling into actuality. . . . It is the demonstration of the coincidence, or identity, of His proclamation of the kingdom of God, the lordship of God, the divine *coup d'état*, with the event itself."[47] A miraculous act of Jesus adds confirmation to his verbal proclamation of the kingdom and at the same time is itself a Word spoken in power. "As an action," Barth writes, "it points to the fact that it is a Word which

43. Barth, *CD* IV/2, 155.
44. Ibid., 194, 209.
45. Ibid., 194.
46. Ibid., 195–209.
47. Ibid., 209.

is spoken in fulfilled time by the One who fulfils it, so that it is no longer a promise, but itself that which is promised; a definitive Word in the unequivocal form of a definitive action." The works of Jesus are the continuation of his preaching and teaching in another form, a "cosmic" form.[48] Therefore, Jesus largely fulfills his royal office by Word-acts—his heralding and teaching as a *speech*-act and his miraculous deeds as a speech-*act*, both working in tandem.

Finally, the prophetic office of Christ is a revelatory ministry. For Barth, it is the history of the humiliated and exalted God-man that is his prophecy, consisting mainly in the declaration of the reconciliation that he himself embodies and accomplishes. His prophetic ministry corresponds to his being the theanthropic Mediator, whose glory it is to reveal himself decisively and effectively as God, and as a man to ascribe prototypically the praise and honor due to God. The glory of Christ the Mediator is that of the covenant faithfully fulfilled by both God and humanity. As such, the life of Jesus Christ is the light, revelation, and truth that leads to life, and thus is his prophetic office.[49] Against all falsehood, the history of this God-man is true. Jesus Christ is the true prophetic Witness. Barth presents the prophecy that is the life of Christ as transcending all particular OT prophets, since he, unlike them, did not need an official call, speaks to *all* nations, declares the *presence* of the kingdom of God, and is a *mediator* between God and man. The only thing the prophets and Christ share is their common testimony to the real covenant of God with humanity.[50] Rather, it is the history of Israel as a whole that accurately typifies the prophetic ministry of Christ.[51] Finally, Barth describes Christ's resurrection, the impartation of the Spirit, and his final coming comprehensively as the *parousia*, the continuation and culmination of his history of liberation, and thus his prophetic activity.[52] In the end, the prophetic office of Christ is a revelatory ministry that takes the form of the concrete history of the God-man in the world.

---

48. Ibid., 210.

49. Barth, *CD* IV/3.1, 48.

50. Ibid., 49–52.

51. Ibid., 53–65. "The prophecy of the history of Israel in its unity is comparable to that of Jesus Christ in an unqualified sense which is not true of the testimonies of any individual prophets, even the greatest of them" (ibid., 65).

52. Ibid., 292–93.

This brief exposition of Barth's treatment of the *munus triplex* hardly does justice to his contribution. For our purposes, what is especially important about his account is the thoroughness with which he connects the ministry of the Word to *two* offices, not just one, and how he broadens what it means for Christ to be the bearer of the Word. He departs from the Reformed line by assigning all of Christ's *earthly* didactic functions—evangelizing, teaching, and preaching—to the kingly office as opposed to the prophetic. Like the Reformed tradition, however, he identifies the prophetic office as a revelatory ministry. Yet Barth again diverges from this line by viewing the *history* of Jesus as prophetic revelation, not just his earthly and heavenly teaching ministry. Significantly, by including Christ's miraculous works and his history as God-man as true Words, he was able to connect more fully the ministry of Word to the Word himself. Not only did Jesus have the ministry of the Word as the Prophet, but he and all his activities were that Word. Nevertheless, Barth ultimately does not ascribe any teaching ministry to the priestly office, and in this way largely remains true to the tradition.

Much of the tradition concerning the threefold office of Christ affirms similar things, namely, the Mediator is Prophet as teacher, Priest as sacrifice and intercessor, and King as governor and protector of the church. Yet few bring this schema into meaningful contact with the OT material regarding the relationship between kingship and priesthood and the Word of God. For example, the expected king of the OT, as was outlined, would embody torah-piety in a way unseen by all former kings. Indeed, a characteristic mark of his kingship would be his love for and obedience to torah. This aspect of kingship corresponds somewhat to the active obedience of the priestly office, but might also be a function of Christ's kingship. Moreover, the Old Testament is clear that the regular teaching function belongs to the priesthood. Yet apart from a few writers the task of expounding the law is regularly situated within the prophetic office. It appears, however, that the proper teaching of the law could, more properly in line with biblical theology, be located rightly within the priestly office, possibly as a form of Christ's active obedience. What Barth's proposal makes clear is that the lines cannot too neatly be drawn as far as which office performs which ministry of the Word. There is an aspect of proclamation to both prophetic and kingly offices as well. As Prophet, Christ did announce the fulfillment of past promises, while as King he proclaimed the onset, the presence of the kingdom of God in his person. But the fact that teaching is rarely ascribed to Christ's priestly office appears strange in light of the OT material. It is the task of subsequent sections to explore more fully the New Testament's depictions of Christ's offices of king and priest and draw meaningful connections with his approach to and ministry of the Word of God.

Christ's Royal Priesthood Reconsidered

The tradition's faithful upholding of the anointed offices of Christ as being explicative of his saving work is well rooted in the Scriptures. However, what one finds in these dogmatic accounts is a dependence on only a few texts or sections of Scripture for forming a picture of Christ's offices. This narrowness of focus is especially evident in portrayals of the priesthood of Christ, in which material is drawn significantly from the book of Hebrews. What inevitably follows is that the Mediator's office of priest is construed primarily in sacrificial terms, to the potential neglect of other dimensions of his priesthood.[53] To a far lesser degree similar things can be said about the royal office. The aim of this section, therefore, is to present a fuller picture of the kingship and especially the priesthood of Jesus in light of sometimes neglected portions of the New Testament witness. This brief survey of material is intended to set up a meaningful connection of these offices with the use and ministry of the Word of God by Jesus.

Jesus' Kingship in the New Testament

The theme of Christ's kingship is pervasive in the NT and is articulated in a number of forms. The following are some expressions of Jesus' kingdom observed most commonly by scholars.[54] First, the basic proclamation of the primitive church was "Jesus Christ is Lord" (κύριος Ἰησοῦς Χριστός) (e.g., Phil 2:11). That Christ is *Kyrios* means that he takes the name of the only God and represents him fully. The destinies of men and

---

53. We do not ignore that all four Gospels present Jesus as the self-sacrificing priest, nor that dogmatic accounts make use of the Gospels. The point, rather, is that dogmatic accounts of the priestly office tend to center on sacrifice, which may be the cause or result of focusing particularly on these biblical texts.

54. E.g., Beasley-Murray, "Romans 1:3f," 147–54; Evans, "Images of Christ," 34–72; Fee, *Pauline Christology*; Hengel, *Studies in Early Christology*, 119–225, 333–89; Hurtado, *Lord Jesus Christ*, 108–18; Visser't Hooft, "Jesus is Lord," 177–89.

women are entrusted to him (Acts 2:21; 4:12). He rules over all other lords (Eph 1:21; Rev 17:14). As "Lord," Jesus Christ is the unique ruler over the entire cosmos.[55] He is the royal referent, the "Lord," of Psalm 110, the OT text most often cited in relation to Jesus' kingship.[56] Second, he is the "Son of David" (Matt 1:1, 20) who reigns over the house of Jacob forever (Luke 1:30–33). He is appointed the "Son" as the anointed king of Psalm 2 (Luke 3:22). Third, the kingdom of God is present in his person. When Jesus proclaims the nearness of the kingdom, he is not merely announcing the future advent of God's reign but its very presence in himself. In his miraculous works Jesus manifests the presence of God's eschatological kingdom (Matt 12:28; Luke 11:20). When he exercises dominion over sickness, nature, people, and demonic forces, he brings the realities of the kingdom into the here-and-now. Finally, he is explicitly given a kingdom and called a "King." Jesus speaks of "my kingdom" (John 18:36); believers are said to be translated into the kingdom of the Son (Col 1:13); he will further hand the kingdom over to the Father after his reign (1 Cor 15:24–28); his kingdom is the same as God's (Eph 5:5; Rev 11:15; 12:10); and he rules over all other lords and kings as the "King of kings and Lord of lords" (Rev 17:14; 19:16). The NT presentation of Jesus' kingship is certainly more robust than this brief account suggests. However, what is important to note in all of these statements of Christ's kingship is that the emphasis rests on his power, dominion, and the subjugation of contrary forces—human and non-human, spiritual and natural—by his actions and words. Thus far most dogmatic expositions of Christ's kingship accord well with the content and proportions of the NT witness. But might there be other ways that the NT implicitly describes Jesus' fulfillment of OT royal expectations?

A few episodes in the Gospels suggest that Christ's kingly office, in the state of humiliation, may be construed as constituted by a certain relationship to the Word of God. First, Matt 21:1–5 presents Christ's kingly entry into Jerusalem and his accompanying actions as patterned after, indeed fulfilling, the prophetic word found in Zech 9:9. He marches toward his death with the express purpose of bringing to completion

---

55. Visser't Hooft, "Jesus is Lord," 178–80.
56. Bauckham lists the following references in Scripture: Matt 22:44; 26:64; Mark 12:36; 14:62; 16:19; Luke 20:42–43; 22:69; Acts 2:33–35; 5:31; 7:55–56; Rom 8:34; 1 Cor 15:25; Eph 1:20; 2:6; Col 3:1; Heb 1:3, 13; 8:1; 10:12–13; 12:2; 1 Pet 3:22; Rev 3:21 (Bauckham, "Throne of God," 61).

what was written of him in Scripture—in the way "prescribed." Second, during his arrest (Matt 26:53–56) Jesus claims implicitly that he is the royal commander of the army of heavenly angels. This king, instead of availing himself of his army, yields obediently to the words of the prophets—"so that the scriptures of the prophets may be fulfilled" (26:56). As king, Jesus is the obedient Son who follows the Word even to the point of death. Finally, during his examination by Pilate, Jesus declares that his kingship and mission consist in "testifying to the truth" (John 18:37). The "truth" here and throughout John refers to God's covenantal character—his faithfulness to his promises—as revealed in Christ; it is what God is now doing in the person and mission of Christ, in fulfillment of the Law and Prophets.[57] Jesus, *as king*, is the faithful messenger of God who has spoken "the truth which I heard from God" (8:40, 45). "His role as king," J. Ramsey Michaels writes, "cannot be separated from his role as the revealer of God, for his authority to 'testify to the truth' rests on his kingship, the royal authority the Father has given him over 'all flesh' (17:2) to make known 'the truth'—that is, 'the only true God,' and himself as God's messenger."[58] Moreover, in his life and speech, Jesus is "grace and truth" personified (1:14, 17). Craig Keener writes: "John accepts the witness of the law to the fullness of grace and truth in Christ, but Christ is the full embodiment of the law, *the actual model of lived-out commandments*, in flesh."[59] The history of Jesus Christ is the story of the law fulfilled and the manifestation of the glory of God. Thus, taken together with Matthew's depiction above, Christ is king *as* the obedient Son who testifies to the truth of God's self-revelation as its faithful follower, manifestation, and messenger.

Jesus the Priest in the Gospels

As mentioned earlier, the dogmatic tradition regarding Christ's priestly office focuses primarily on the book of Hebrews and the sacrificial work of the High Priest. However, when one looks outside this epistle, one finds a picture of Christ's work as a priest that enriches that painted by

---

57. Keener, *John*, 2:1113. Beasley-Murray speaks of "truth" here as "God's saving sovereignty," which Jesus reveals in word and deed (Beasley-Murray, *John*, 331–32). Carson speaks of "truth" as God's self-disclosure in his Son (Carson, *John*, 594–95).

58. Michaels, *John*, 925.

59. Keener, *John*, 1:421 (italics added).

the author of Hebrews. Moreover, according to Crispin Fletcher-Louis, one of the common mistakes in Jesus scholarship regarding his messiahship is its one-sided focus on royal motifs to the neglect of the place of priesthood in Jesus' Jewish world and his own messianic consciousness. Regardless of the specific features of the messianic hopes of the Jewish people, what is clear is that there was a priestly dimension to these expectations.[60] If this picture of Jewish messianism is correct, then one should expect to find more interaction with priestly categories in the Gospels. Hence, it is to Mark, Luke, and John that we turn for this fuller, complementary portrait.

A number of passages in the first seven chapters of Mark's Gospel provide a priestly portrait of Jesus: Mark 1:40–45 (along with 5:25–34 and 5:35–43), 2:1–13, 2:23–28, 3:1–7a, and 7:14–23. Mark 1–6 is a literary unit that is programmatic for the Gospel's picture of Jesus' ministry.[61] The priestly profile provided is meant to elucidate the various features of his life and work throughout the Gospel.[62] Mark 1:40–45 records Jesus' healing of a leper. In the OT, the healing ritual and pronouncement were clearly the prerogative of the priest (Lev 13–14). Here Jesus performs these functions and sends the leper to the official priests to bear witness to his power and ultimate compliance with the law and, simultaneously, their impotence and evident ignorance of God's ways.[63] Taken together with Mark 5:25–34, where he heals the woman with a discharge, and

---

60. Fletcher-Louis shows from the intertestamental material that there were basically three possible forms of government anticipated by the people of Jesus' day: (1) the nation ruled by one anointed high priest and him alone; (2) the nation ruled by an "anointed one" who is both a priest and king; and (3) the nation ruled jointly by an anointed priest and an anointed king, with the latter subordinate to the former. He concludes that royal messianism is not prominent in the Gospels and when present is coupled with a hope for a high priestly Messiah (Fletcher-Louis, "Jesus as the High Priestly Messiah: Part 1," 161–67).

61. Fletcher-Louis, "Jesus as the High Priestly Messiah: Part 2," 61–62, and Broadhead, "Christology as Polemic," 23–24. For a study of Mark 12, its use of Psalm 110, and its presentation of Jesus as a priest, see Gray, *Temple in the Gospel of Mark*, 86–89.

62. It must be said that Mark's priestly Christology is certainly neither the only Christology nor emphasis in this or any other part of the Gospel. The only point here is to highlight sometimes neglected priestly motifs in Mark.

63. Broadhead, "Christology as Polemic," 24–25; cf. Guelich, *Mark 1–8:26*, 77; Lane, *Mark*, 88. That the witness of the leper is *against* the priests and religious leaders is suggested by the fact that the typical function of μαρτύριον with the dative connotes incriminating evidence against a defendant (Strathmann, "μαρτύριον," *TDNT*, 4:502–3).

Mark 5:35–43, where Jairus' daughter is raised from the dead, Jesus touches people who fit the three conditions for impurity outlined in Num 5:1–4.[64] One point of these healing encounters is to show that it is Jesus' holiness, rather than the impurity of the sick, that is contagious. He reverses the order of impure to pure by transferring purity to impurity.[65] How this relates to the priestly presentation of Jesus is found in Ezek 42:14 and 44:19. Both passages speak of the priest's garments as having the ability to communicate holiness to the people they touch. In Jesus' day, the people understood that power emanated from his garments (see Mark 6:56).[66] Hence, it is probable that the Markan depiction of Jesus is here a priestly one, since the only precedents for such contagious holiness and power from a garment refer to the priest.

In Mark 2:1–13 Jesus offers and mediates the forgiveness of sins. In the OT, the process leading to and the pronouncement of forgiveness was reserved for the priesthood and confined to the cult (Lev 16:32–34). Here, in the face of opposition from the religious authorities, Jesus claims the priestly power of effecting the cleansing of sin apart from the cult. What his opponents were unable to do, he performs with authority. He goes beyond mere pronouncement and, requiring no animal sacrifice, brings God's forgiveness.[67] He is more than just the average priest.

In Mark 2:23–28, Jesus supposedly violates the law by giving his disciples the priestly bread to eat on the Sabbath. Three things must be observed here. First, only the priests were allowed to work on the Sabbath, but their work was temple work. Second, only priests were permitted to eat the special bread. Third, Jesus and his disciples were not in the temple but a cornfield. What these observations suggest is

---

64. Numbers 5:1–4 reads: "The Lord spoke to Moses, saying: Command the Israelites to put out of the camp everyone who is leprous, or has a discharge, and everyone who is unclean through contact with a corpse; you shall put out both male and female, putting them outside the camp; they must not defile their camp, where I dwell among them. The Israelites did so, putting them outside the camp; as the Lord had spoken to Moses, so the Israelites did."

65. Fletcher-Louis, "Jesus as the High Priestly Messiah: Part 2," 64–66; cf. Guelich, *Mark*, 74.

66. Ibid., 66–69.

67. Broadhead, "Christology as Polemic," 27–28. There is no need to downplay the Christological significance of Jesus' forgiving sin by arguing that he merely mediates God's forgiveness. Though that is true, he does more than mediate. Jesus claims to put away the man's sins decisively, thus assuming the role of God in this instance (see Edwards, *Mark*, 77).

that (1) Jesus as the royal High Priest was himself the location of the sacred space, (2) his disciples were given rights as priests to work on the Sabbath in that sacred space, and (3) as priests they were allowed to eat in that holy place, as David and his men did.[68] Jesus permits his followers to do on the Sabbath what was by law reserved for Israel's priest. Thus he implicitly declares himself a priest.

In a related Sabbath controversy (3:1–7a), Jesus again takes to himself the Levitical exemption from Sabbath work by healing the man with a shriveled hand. As any good priest should do, Jesus ministers on the Sabbath, working for the healing of the people.[69] More central to our purposes, by his interrogation and subsequent action, Jesus also teaches the people the proper interpretation of the law, again demonstrating ties to the priesthood.

Finally, Jesus plays the role of teaching priest again in 7:14–23 by reinterpreting the laws concerning clean and unclean foods (e.g., Deut 14:6, 9–10). He establishes a "new" standard by declaring that it is not what enters a man's mouth that makes him unclean, but what proceeds from it (Mark 7:15). In the OT, it was the responsibility of the priest to apply the standards of clean and unclean to the community. Here, Jesus takes that responsibility as the true teacher of Israel.[70]

This Markan portrait of a priestly Jesus is further sharpened when two additional features of these opening chapters are considered. First, Jesus' healings, pronouncements, and other priestly activities in this section are set against the backdrop of his continual conflict with the religious authorities of his day. The quality and nature of Jesus' priestly leadership stand out in the context of controversy with those who were the established priestly officers. Jesus is the ideal priest; his opponents are mere weak images of priestly leadership. Second, Jesus is declared the "holy one of God" (1:24), a title whose human precedent can only be found in Aaron (Num 16:7; Ps 106:16).[71]

---

68. See Fletcher-Louis, "Jesus as the High Priestly Messiah: Part 2," 75–77. Cf. Broadhead, "Christology as Polemic," 28.

69. Broadhead, "Christology as Polemic," 28.

70. Ibid., 28–29.

71. Fletcher-Louis, "Jesus as the High Priestly Messiah: Part 2," 63. Fletcher-Louis also argues that the title "Son of Man" from Dan 7:13 refers to Israel's eschatological high priest, whose coming to God on the clouds "evokes the Day of Atonement when the high priest enters God's presence surrounded by clouds of incense" (ibid., 57–58). He claims that this reading of "Son of Man" was common in the first century. Among

Therefore, although it is not the only image of Jesus in the opening chapters of Mark, the Jesus presented here is certainly a priestly one. For our purposes, we observe that his priestly office is not in these chapters exercised in the form of an atoning sacrifice, but in the various functions of healer, purifier, mediator of forgiveness, and true teacher and interpreter of the law. One could even say that all of his priestly actions were a commentary on the law—whether by explicit instruction, enacted reinterpretation, or by the execution of its commands. Thus, his priestly office is centered on God's Word.

Luke's portrait of a priestly Jesus is perhaps more subtle. Nevertheless, several features of the Gospel suggest such a priestly conception. First, the temple features prominently in the early chapters and proves significant in the final episodes of the book. When Jesus is twelve he is found in the temple, sitting among the teachers, reasoning about the law, and amazing his listeners by his wisdom and understanding (Luke 2:46–47). The image of the Holy Spirit overshadowing Mary (1:35) alludes to the descent of glory on the Mosaic tabernacle (Exod 40:34–35). In later chapters, Jesus comes to the temple, clears it, occupies it as teacher, and the people marvel at his authority (Luke 19:45–48). In addition, the "threshing floor" to be cleared by the one coming after John (3:17) may be the temple that Jesus later cleansed (19:45–46), since Solomon did build the temple on the site of a threshing floor (2 Sam 24:18–25; 2 Chr

---

his reasons include: (1) Rev 1:13–16 presents Jesus as the Son of Man dressed in the distinctive foot-length robe and golden girdle that the High Priest wore on the Day of Atonement (cf. Lev 16:4; Josephus, *Ant.* 3:153–55, 159); (2) the Son of Man of the Gospels comes in divine glory and power (Mark 8:38; 13:26), just as the high priest embodies God's glory (Exod 28:2, 40); (3) In Mark 14:62, the Son of Man title is closely related to the issue of blasphemy. Slandering the high priest was also blasphemous and a capital offense because he represented God (see Josephus, *Ant.* 13:294). Jesus' claim to be the Son of Man was a claim to the office of high priest, and therefore a blasphemous challenge to the current high priest; (4) the Son of Man is predicted to suffer at the hands of his generation (e.g., Mark 8:31; Luke 17:25). The clearest Jewish precedent for such suffering is that expected of the true high priest (see 4QTLevi[d] with Q 17.24–25); and (5) the closest parallel to the image of the Son of Man as a ransom (Mark 10:45) is that of the Levites, who were to act as ransom monies in place of the lives of the firstborn sons of Israel (Num 3:12, 41, 45) (ibid., 59–60). If this is the case, then Jesus' numerous references to himself as the Son of Man, especially in these early chapters of Mark, are also references to his priesthood. For a classic view of Son of Man language in the Gospels, its ambiguity, and lack of reference to an individual, see Dunn, *Christology in the Making*, 65–97.

3:1).⁷² Second, the priesthood is also a prominent feature of the early chapters of the Gospel. John the Baptist's priestly descent is clearly highlighted. Numerous parallels between John's and Jesus' life suggest that Luke presents the latter as John's younger twin.⁷³ Third, the transfiguration points towards a priestly Jesus: the inner circle of disciples is told to "hear" Christ the teaching Son (Luke 9:35); the event occurs on the "eighth day" after Peter's confession (9:28), as Aaron began his ministry on the eighth day (Lev 9:1); Jesus' garments are gloriously transformed to resemble those worn by the high priest (Luke 9:29); Peter suggests building "tabernacles" (9:33); and Moses and Elijah disappear after the cloud overshadows the mountain (9:34; cf. Exod 40:34–38). After this occasion Jesus sets his face toward Jerusalem, where he will cleanse the temple, teach the people, and offer the priestly sacrifice of his life. The transfiguration in a sense proclaims the truth of Jesus' high priesthood.⁷⁴ Finally, in Luke 20:1–2 Jesus is questioned by the chief priests and teachers of the law about his authority to cleanse the temple (cf. 19:45–46). This is a question of Jesus' authority in God's house, his priestly authority. Jesus responds by asking them to pass a (priestly?) judgment about the origin of John's baptism (20:3). Jesus clearly insinuates that his priestly authority is from God, who gave him the right to cleanse the temple and teach the people (20:1).⁷⁵ He is Israel's true teaching priest. Therefore, at the beginning and end of Luke's Gospel, he depicts Jesus as the priest who has divine authorization to govern the affairs of God's house. The primary emphasis seems to be on Jesus' priestly teaching ministry, particularly around the precincts of the temple. Unlike his opponents, he

---

72. Leithart, *Priesthood*, 112–13. The Spirit's overshadowing (ἐπισκιάσει) may also allude to God's creative power, his presence protecting his people (Ps 91:4), and the cloud that enveloped the disciples at the transfiguration (Luke 9:34). It is his glorious presence among his people (Bock, *Luke 1:1–9:50*, 121–22).

73. Similarities include announcement scenes to Zacharias and Mary (Luke 1:5–38), their "songs" (1:46–55, 67–79), their stories of circumcision and naming (1:59–63; 2:21), the use of "growth in wisdom and stature" to both boys (1:80; 2:40, 52), and the fact that they were both teachers of Israel (3:18; 19:47–48). There are also similarities with the early life of Samuel that intimate a parallel calling and ministry, that is, to raise up a faithful priest (1 Sam 2:35) (Leithart, *Priesthood*, 114–15).

74. Ibid., 119–20. Many scholars view this incident as pointing to Jesus as the eschatological Prophet. However, a priestly reading seems more likely in light of the Aaronic and tabernacle/temple imagery throughout this passage. For those holding the prophet view, see, e.g., Bock, *Luke 1:1–9:50*, 872–74; Marshall, *Luke*, 380.

75. Leithart, *Priesthood*, 120.

teaches the people in truth and with divine authority, and leads them to the Father.

The Johannine Jesus is also a unique High Priest, and this over against the official high priesthood, as demonstrated in at least two passages. First, in John 11:45–53 Jesus is contrasted with Caiaphas the high priest. The latter, in accord with his high priestly office, suggests that it is expedient that Jesus is sacrificed in order that the whole nation not perish (John 11:49–50). Yet Caiaphas' words were spoken without insight into the true depth of their meaning—they were not spoken "on his own" (11:51). Jesus, by contrast, would knowingly offer the high priestly sacrifice of himself to greater effect—not only for the preservation of Israel but also for the ingathering of many nations (11:51–52). One high priest envisions a relatively small political end, while the true high priest is destined to accomplish the salvation of all peoples.[76] Second, and more pertinent to the discussion, during Jesus' trial before the high priest he is questioned about his disciples and teaching (18:19). Jesus responds that he has taught the Jews openly in the temple and synagogues, not taking secret counsel like the high priest and his companions. That Jesus "spoke" (λελάληκα) refers to his public offering of the revelatory Word of God.[77] Therefore, in contrast to the high priest, Jesus was the true High Priest who openly spoke divine revelation to the Jewish people, and thus demonstrated the superiority of his priestly leadership over the established high priesthood.[78] The Johannine portrait of Jesus, therefore, includes a high priestly component. Jesus is the self-sacrificing priest, but also the priestly teacher and revealer of God's Word.[79]

The priestly presentation of Jesus in the Gospels, therefore, takes on a number of dimensions. He is, as emphasized in the tradition, the sacrificed priest who atones for the sins of the world. However, he is more. He is also priest as healer, purifier, mediator of forgiveness, and true Sabbath-keeper. He performs his sacral service by bringing *shalom* to the broken, unclean, and lost. More central to this study, the three

76. See Heil, "Jesus as the Unique High Priest," 731–35.

77. De la Potterie, *La Vérité*, 40–42.

78. Heil, "Jesus as the Unique High Priest," 739–40. Jesus' seamless tunic (John 19:23–24) corresponds to the high priestly robe worn under the ephod (Exod 28:31–32), and therefore may also suggest Jesus' high priestly status (ibid., 741–44).

79. The numerous references to Jesus as "rabbi" or "teacher" may also be seen as implicit references to his ministry as teacher (see O'Collins and Jones, *Jesus Our Priest*, 16–17).

Gospels just examined consistently present Jesus as the teaching priest, over against the priests and teachers of the law.[80] He correctly interprets the law, instructs in cleanness/uncleanness, and reveals God's Word to the people of Israel. This depiction of the didactic aspects of Jesus' priestly work complements what is commonly emphasized in discussions of his priesthood by suggesting that Jesus as the fulfillment of the priestly office performs the teaching as well as the more "cultic" functions. In at least this way he is the ideal public-directed, didactic "reader" of the Word of God.

Jesus as Israel, the Royal Priesthood

Israel was designated a royal priesthood—kings and priests to God. To be Israel was to be those chosen and set apart by YHWH, bound to covenantal obedience, and called to be a light to the nations. The Israel of the OT, however, largely failed in their vocation. At the canonical beginning of the NT (and elsewhere in the Gospels), the history and calling of Israel are revisited and recapitulated in the story of Jesus Christ, so that it may be said that Jesus is truest Israel and therefore the embodiment of its calling as a royal priesthood. In what follows, we will focus on Matthew's portrayal of Jesus in the first four chapters of his Gospel, with the hope of filling out our picture of Jesus Christ as *the* royal priestly reader.

The Gospel of Matthew commences with the genealogy of Jesus, tracing his ancestry through David and back to Abraham, the patriarch of Israel (Matt 1:1). By linking Jesus to Abraham, Matthew announces that God's promise to bless his people and the nations is being fulfilled through Jesus, the true descendant of Abraham. Jesus, then, is true Israel, everything that Israel, Abraham's offspring, was to be and performs much of what the nation was intended to do. Moreover, Jesus, as the son of David, is Israel's promised king and, therefore, *represents* true Israel.[81] While the genealogy does function to recapitulate the history of Old Testament Israel, it stresses that Jesus is the focus of Israel's history and that from this point on Israel cannot be defined apart from reference

---

80. O'Collins and Jones make the point that if the apostle Paul's preaching can be described as priestly (Rom 15:16), then Jesus' preaching ministry should be all the more (*Jesus Our Priest*, 16).

81. Holwerda, *Jesus and Israel*, 32–33.

to Jesus Christ.[82] He is the faithful Son, the embodiment of what Israel was intended to be, as the ensuing Matthean narrative confirms.

Joel Kennedy highlights a number of ways Jesus "passively" and "actively" relives Israel's history. The central events that Jesus passively recapitulates, particularly in Matt 2:1–23, are those surrounding Israel's exodus from Egypt. Jesus' reliving of Israel's story is suggested by such correspondences as the prophetic warnings associated with Moses' and Jesus' births, the latter's flight to and subsequent return from Egypt for safety, the parallels between Pharaoh's and Herod's treatment of "Israel," Jesus' fulfillment of the exodus motif of Hos 11:1, the employment of Jer 31:15 (Rachel's lament) for the events surrounding the slaughter of the innocents, and the similarities between Jesus' and Moses' return to Israel to accomplish the redemption of God's people.[83] The story of Israel in the OT is Jesus' story in Matthew. He is the new Israel.

The Gospel also presents Jesus' active recapitulation of Israel's history in the baptism and temptation narratives. The baptismal account begins with the crowds coming to John to be baptized, followed by the religious leaders. The first group receives no divine response, while the second receives a negative one. Jesus then comes to be baptized and receives a favorable divine response. Thus the story narrows its focus until it reaches Jesus, the true Israelite, who submits to baptism "in order to fulfill all righteousness" (Matt 3:15).[84] This enigmatic statement is best understood as Jesus presenting himself in solidarity with Israel, as the "representative embodiment" of Israel. As William Kynes writes, "John gives the prophetic call to Israel, and Jesus, the true representative of Israel, gives the righteous response."[85] Baptism is not the sum total of "all righteousness" but the beginning of Jesus' official fulfillment of Israel's righteousness through his obedience to the demands of God.[86]

The baptismal narrative is presented as an image of the exodus. Just as Israel passed through the waters of the *yam suph*, so Jesus passes

---

82. Ibid., 36. For a thorough study of the genealogy as a recapitulation of Israel's history, see especially Kennedy, *Recapitulation*, 25–102.

83. Ibid., 111–53. Parallels to Moses must be seen as parallels to Israel since he was the representative of Israel. Matthew is clearly not concerned with Moses per se since he makes no mention of him. Israel is his concern (see Holwerda, *Jesus and Israel*, 37).

84. Kennedy, *Recapitulation*, 171–72.

85. Kynes, *A Christology of Solidarity*, 26 n. 91.

86. Kennedy, *Recapitulation*, 173.

through the waters of the Jordan. This reading seems especially likely in light of the subsequent event in Jesus' and Israel's life—"entrance" into the wilderness to be tested (Matt 4:1–11). The quotation of Isa 40:3 in Matt 3:3, which refers to a "second exodus" of God's people, further draws attention to the exodus and its recapitulation. In addition, Rikki Watts ties the baptismal narrative to the remembrance of the exodus and the Spirit's involvement therein found in Isaiah 63. In Isa 63:14 LXX, we read κατέβη πνεῦμα referring to the Spirit's descent among the people of the exodus generation. In Matt 3:16 those words are applied to the Spirit's descent on Jesus. Both Isaiah and Matthew uniquely link the descent of the Spirit with the exodus and the coming out of water.[87] Moreover, the plea that God would rend the heavens (Isa 64:1 or 63:19 MT/LXX), which takes place in the context of the exodus remembrance, corresponds well with the opening of the heavens at Jesus' baptism (Matt 3:16).[88] If, therefore, the exodus is tied to God's Spirit descending and resting upon his people, then Jesus' baptism is likely a recapitulation of Israel's exodus experience. Jesus is the Son for whom the heavens are rent and upon whom the Spirit rests. He is Israel and the one who will deliver Israel.

After Jesus' baptism, two signs of divine approval are witnessed: the descent of the Spirit and the voice from heaven. In the latter, the Father declares Jesus "my Son, the Beloved, with whom I am well pleased" (3:17). Each of these appellations is significant for understanding how Jesus recapitulates Israel's history. The first, "Son," is used of national Israel in numerous OT texts (e.g., Exod 4:22–23; Hos 11:1; Isa 1:2; 63:16; Jer 31:20). Israel's king is also referred to as God's son (e.g., 2 Sam 7:14; Ps 2:7; 89:26–27; 110:3 LXX). It is likely, therefore, especially given our previous discussion, that two aspects of sonship are here combined—Israel as God's son and the king as God's son. When applied to Jesus, "Son" refers to his recapitulation and embodiment of Israel as model and king.[89] The two remaining appellations—"Beloved" and the one "with whom I am well pleased"—are likely references to Isa 42:1–4, which speaks of the servant who will bring salvation to the nations. The servant of Isaiah 42 is best understood as Israel *and* the one who by represent-

---

87. Watts, *Isaiah's New Exodus*, 103–4.
88. Ibid., 106.
89. Ibid., 181–82.

ing Israel brings renewal to Israel.[90] Thus Jesus is eschatological Israel, the Servant, the royal priesthood, through whom God's purposes for the world will be accomplished.

After his baptism, Jesus is driven into the wilderness to be tested as God's Son just as Israel was tested (Matt 4:1–11). As Israel languished in the desert for forty years, so Jesus fasts for a period of forty days and nights. He must be tested before bringing the kingdom, just as Israel needed to be tested before entering the Promised Land.[91] Crucial to understanding the temptation narrative is grasping the significance of the three quotations from Deuteronomy 6–8 employed by Jesus against Satan's promptings. Each quotation alludes to an episode of failure in Israel's wilderness wanderings, following the chronological order of Exodus: the trial of hunger (Exod 16; cf. Deut 8:3), their testing of God (Exod 17; cf. Deut 6:16), and the golden calf incident (Exod 23; cf. Deut 6:13; 10:20).[92]

The first temptation (Matt 4:2–4) recalls Israel's hunger in the wilderness (Exod 16:1–36). Deuteronomy 8:2 specifies that YHWH led his people into the wilderness for forty years in order to test and humble them, that he might see what was in their hearts. In this test, God intentionally subjects Israel to hunger in order to drive home the lesson of their absolute dependence on him for sustenance.[93] In a similar way, Jesus, the Son of God, is led into the wilderness for forty days to be tested and humbled. Israel did not pass the test of hunger, but yielded to doubt, discontentment, unbelief, and grumbling, desiring a different way of sustenance than that provided by God. Jesus, on the contrary, resists the tempter's prompts to secure bread miraculously to fend off his extreme hunger by responding with Moses' words that one is to live by faith in and obedience to God's commands, not by seeking to acquire bread by his or her own means (Deut 8:3b).[94] By quoting these words, he places himself in the place of wandering Israel, succeeding in the wilderness where they were tested and failed. He, the obedient Son of God, would

---

90. Holwerda, *Jesus and Israel*, 43.
91. Ibid., 45.
92. Kennedy, *Recapitulation*, 187.
93. Ibid., 199; cf. Sarna, *Exodus*, 86.
94. Ibid., 197–98.

submit to and believe the Word of God and trust YHWH for his ordained provision during this time of testing.[95]

The second temptation (Matt 4:5–7) corresponds to Israel's testing of God at the waters of Massah (Exod 17:1–7). Testing God in the OT is understood as a sign of unbelief and a violation of the covenant between YHWH and his people. It asks the question: "Is the covenant God really among us or not?" It calls into question the Lord's trustworthiness, reliability, and faithfulness to the covenant. Testing God, therefore, incurred the strictest of punishments.[96] When Israel cried out for water at Massah, they in fact doubted the Lord's presence, provision, and faithfulness. In the Gospel narrative, Satan recalls YHWH's covenantal promises of protection in the wilderness (e.g., Exod 23:22) and from the temple (e.g., 2 Chr 7:15–16), and uses Psalm 91 to urge Jesus to test God's faithfulness to him. If Jesus truly lives by every word of God, then he should believe the promise of protection in Ps 91:11.[97] Jesus responds as the obedient Son, again declaring his fidelity to the commands of Moses that no one should ever put YHWH to the test (Deut 6:16). He would not, like Israel, demand evidence that God is with him (Exod 17:7), but would simply trust YHWH's words.

The third temptation (Matt 4:8–10) is more straightforward. Satan offers Jesus what rightly belongs to the Son of God—universal dominion—if Jesus would but worship him. Instead Jesus responds with Deut 6:13 and 10:20, two passages which in their Deuteronomic context refer to the exclusive worship due YHWH and the people's failure to render that worship. The first passage borders the *Shema* and speaks in general terms about fearing, loving, and obeying YHWH alone. The second passage alludes to the golden calf incident (Deut 9:7–10:11; cf. Exod 32) and calls Israel to a renewed resolve to serve the Lord alone. Instead of bowing to another god, Jesus remains faithful to YHWH and thus reverses the outcome of Israel in the wilderness.[98] Hence, in all three trials Jesus recapitulates the history of Israel's wilderness testing by remaining obedient to the Word of God amid the many temptations of Satan. He proves himself to be the faithful Son of God, whose wilderness humbling manifested what was truly in his heart—love for and reliance

---

95. Gerhardsson, *Testing of God's Son*, 51–52.
96. Ibid., 28–29.
97. Kennedy, *Recapitulation*, 201.
98. Ibid., 210–12.

upon God's Word. As the personification of Israel's royal priestly calling, he both embodies torah piety and declares the Word of God (to Satan, at least), especially in the midst of trial and suffering.

Before concluding, it might be appropriate to make a brief comment about the election, sanctification, and covenant of Jesus Christ. As corporate Israel along with its kings and priests were chosen, sanctified, and graciously covenanted with by YHWH, so Jesus is the elect (Matt 12:18; Luke 9:35; Heb 5:5–6; 1 Pet 1:20; 2:4) and holy One (Mark 1:24; Luke 1:35; 4:34; Acts 2:27; Heb 7:26–28), and faithful covenant partner (Heb 7:20–22). The privileges enjoyed by Israel and its leaders are granted to Christ, the embodiment of faithful Israel, in full measure, and form the foundation of and proper context for understanding his ministry of the Word of God.

The recurrent theme of Jesus' recapitulation of Israel, whether in Matthew's genealogy, the exodus allusions, his baptism, or the wilderness temptation, is that he is the obedient Son who will accomplish the "mission" of Israel—a mission depicted in the royal and priestly offices—by being obedient to the Word and declaring it to all peoples.

Jesus Christ as the Royal Priestly Reader: Three Episodes

Whether one examines Jesus as king and priest, or as the personification of the royal priesthood, Israel, it becomes clear that much of his work *pro nobis* concerns his own relationship to the Word of God. As king, he is the royal Son who willingly submits to the demands of God's law. As priest, he is the teacher of torah—both by his words of instruction and deeds of compassion and healing. Indeed, it might be said that part of Christ's active obedience in his priestly office is his teaching and application of torah. He willingly and obediently follows YHWH's prescription for proper priestly service. Moreover, the emphasis of the presentation of Jesus as Israel is his obedience to the Word of God, his living on "every word that proceeds from YHWH's mouth." It is by his submission to God's Word that he mediates the presence of God to both Jews and Gentiles. Therefore, from whatever angle one chooses to view Jesus' offices and ministry, he is the ideal "reader" of God's Word according to the Gospels. In that light, episodes of Jesus' readings of Scripture become instructive examples of the fulfillment of his calling as mediator, king, priest, royal priesthood, and Word, and should point readers of the Gospels toward proper engagement with God's Word. What will hopefully be clear in Jesus' example are the "personal" and "public" dimensions of any adequate "reading" of God's Word. It is with three such accounts in Mark's Gospel that this chapter comes to a close.

The Way of Christ: Mark 2:23–28

Mark 2:23–28 is the first of two Sabbath controversies recorded in the Gospel between Jesus and the religious leaders. The account begins with Jesus' disciples plucking grain as they walked through a grain field (2:23). The Pharisees protest their actions and question Jesus as to why they are breaking the Sabbath (2:24). The accusation against the disciples is that they were harvesting or doing work, which is forbidden on the Sabbath (Exod 34:21).[99] It is not only the action of the disciples that is at issue, but Jesus' authority to permit such a violation of the law. Jesus responds to the Pharisees' query with his own question: "Have you never read what David did . . ." (Mark 2:25a)? He certainly knew that his opponents had read the Scripture to which he referred (1 Sam 21:1–6). The issue is their understanding of the significance of the particular actions of David.[100] The former king is described as breaking the law of the showbread (Lev 24:5–9), and this likely on the Sabbath, in order to satisfy his hunger and that of his companions (Mark 2:25b–26). Somehow David's actions form a precedent for those of Jesus and his disciples. First, Jesus emphasizes the hunger of David's men to show that it was for good reason that David behaved "unlawfully." Indeed, Scripture nowhere explicitly condemns his actions. Therefore, Jesus avers that in certain circumstances, particularly those benefiting others, the law may be "broken." This conclusion is confirmed in his closing saying: "The Sabbath was made for humankind, and not humankind for the Sabbath" (2:27).[101] Mary Healy summarizes well this "humanitarian" aspect of the Sabbath when she writes: "The whole purpose of the Sabbath was to raise human beings above the routine of earthly labors each week, to fulfill

---

99. Stein, *Mark*, 145. Cranfield notes that according to the Mishnah there are thirty-nine classes of work, of which one-third is reaping (*m. Sabb.* 7.2). In addition, the Mishnah states that stoning is the punishment for repeated violation of the Sabbath, particularly after one has been warned (*m. Sanh.* 7.4). Perhaps this account in Mark is one such warning (Cranfield, *Mark*, 115).

100. Legasse, *Marc*, 200.

101. Westerholm, *Jesus and Scribal Authority*, 98–99.

their unique privilege of living in covenant relationship with God. Any Sabbath observance that hinders rather than enhances the fulfillment of that purpose is a contradiction to the Sabbath itself."[102] Jesus is not abrogating the law but bringing out its true intent, something the Pharisees evidently missed. In addition, Jesus invokes the story of David to answer the question of his authority. Many commentators detect an *a fortiori* argument based on two correspondences: David's authority/Jesus' authority and David's era/Jesus' eschatological age. If David could break the law and permit his men to do the same, how much more does the Son of Man have authority to do so with his disciples?[103] Moreover, the days of David are superseded by Jesus' eschatological moment. With the dawning of the kingdom comes a new relationship with the law and the onset of the true Sabbath rest.[104] As an authority far greater than David, indeed as the eschatological Son of Man who is Lord of the Sabbath (2:28), Jesus may permit the rightful "breaking" of the Sabbath law. The Pharisees, thus, missed at least three things in their reading of Scripture. First, they did not understand the heart of God's law, but substituted the "letter" for the "spirit." They did not recognize the humanitarian core of God's commands—that they are for humankind and not vice versa. Second, they did not discern that the eschaton was upon them and that their relationship to the law would have to be reconfigured in light of this new age. Finally, and most importantly, they failed to recognize that one must (re-)interpret all of the law in light of the person of Jesus, for he is the primary subject matter of Scripture and the new standard for how it should be read. Prior interpretations may no longer be assumed valid.

The Way of Love: Mark 3:1–6

The Sabbath controversies continue in Mark 3:1–6, where Jesus' healing of a man is called into question by the religious authorities. Jesus enters the synagogue and the Pharisees watch to see if he has the gall to heal, and thus to work, on the Sabbath (3:2). According to their tradition, healing could only occur in a life or death scenario. The Mishnah, for example, states: "Whenever there is doubt whether life is in danger this overrides the Sabbath" (*m. Yoma* 8:6). Judging that this man with a

---

102. Healy, *Mark*, 65.
103. France, *Mark*, 145–46; Legasse, *Marc*, 202; Stein, *Mark*, 147–48.
104. Witherington, *Mark*, 130–31.

shriveled hand was not facing death, the Pharisees believed that healing him on the Sabbath would be a clear violation of the law.[105] In quiet defiance of their conclusions, Jesus summons the crippled man (Mark 3:3) and turns to question his interlocutors, asking: "Is it lawful to do good or to do harm on the Sabbath, to save life or to kill" (3:4a)? Here Jesus requests a judgment similar to those rendered by OT priests and contemporary rabbis. The answer is obvious. To refrain from helping someone in need is to do evil. There is no neutrality. To omit healing the handicapped man would be akin to killing him. The Pharisees respond with silence (3:4b), presumably because to say it is lawful to do good would be to permit a "violation" of the Sabbath and demonstrate the falsity of their piety. Yet to say the opposite would be to endorse the notion that God permits doing evil on the Sabbath. They do not provide their honest answer.[106] Jesus becomes enraged at his opponents because they failed to understand God's law due to their "stubborn" or "hard" hearts (3:5a). James Edwards notes that "stubborn" (πωρώσει) refers to an unwillingness to understand. Healy characterizes it as an obstinate refusal to be open to God. Cranfield views it as referring to a type of blindness.[107] All of these together capture the spiritual and moral aspects of the Pharisees' response to Jesus and to God's Word. They are spiritually blind and unable to perceive God's intention in the law. They are culpable moral agents who refuse to love people and be open to God's visitation. Jesus, however, reaffirms and sharpens the truth that the way of love, for God and for fellow people, is the way to a proper reading of torah.

The Way of Holiness: Mark 7:1–23

Further on in Mark's narrative, teachers of the law from Jerusalem travel to investigate and dispute with Jesus (7:1). Again it is the actions of Jesus' disciples that are called into question. The religious leaders inquire as to why Jesus' followers do not wash their hands before meals "according to the tradition of the elders" (7:2–5). The issue is not regarding transgression of the OT law, but customs developed and enforced in Pharasaic circles. Surely a prominent teacher like Jesus would require

---

105. Cranfield, *Mark*, 119; cf. Lane, *Mark*, 122.
106. Cranfield, *Mark*, 120.
107. Edwards, *Mark*, 100; Healy, *Mark*, 67; Cranfield, *Mark*, 121.

that his disciples be as scrupulous as those of the Pharisees.[108] Jesus responds by applying Isa 29:13 to his opponents: "This people honors me with their lips, but their hearts are far from me; in vain do they worship me, teaching human precepts as doctrines" (Mark 7:6b-7). The basic charge is phrased in two complementary ways: (1) their worship was lip service, not from the heart and (2) it was vain because it cherished human traditions as if they were the direct commands of God. Jesus summarizes his indictment, stating that the teachers of the law "abandoned" God's commands and have rather clung to human tradition (7:8). Worship is hypocritical when, under a pretense of piety, layers of human customs supersede the very Word of God. After repeating his charge (7:9), Jesus provides an example of his interlocutors' conduct. He cites Exod 20:12/Deut 5:16 ("Honor your father and your mother") and Exod 21:17 ("Whoever speaks evil of father or mother must surely die") and proceeds to demonstrate how they violate these basic commands (Mark 7:9-13). A scribal tradition developed wherein items could be dedicated to God by an unalterable oath, while still remaining at the disposal of the one offering it.[109] This is the background of Jesus' accusation. Scribal legislation allowed a man to withhold financial support (i.e., honor) from his parents by providing him with a pious "out" in the form of a Corban vow. Jesus summarizes his indictment by charging that the teachers of the law "make void" (ἀκυροῦντες) the Word of God in favor of their tradition (7:13). The term ἀκυρόω is a legal term, having the sense of "to annul" or "repeal." Thus, in this and many other areas the religious leaders ruled God's Word unlawful, effectively annulling it by their preference for human traditions.[110] Turning to the crowd, then to his disciples, Jesus provides his explicit response to his interlocutors (17:14, 17-18a). What defiles a person is not unclean food (Lev 17:15) or unwashed hands, but the things that come from within the person's heart (Mark 17:14-15, 18a-23). Everyone—scribes, crowd, disciples—who interprets the law as being primarily concerned with external actions is "dull" and "lacking in understanding" (17:18a). To comprehend the law is to grasp its overriding concern with the inner dimensions of the worshiper's life (though not at the expense of outward behaviors). To be a true follower of torah demands greater moral purity than simply

---

108. France, *Mark*, 280-81.
109. Ibid., 286-87.
110. Ibid., *Mark*, 288.

guarding what one eats and how one follows traditional prescriptions for outer purity.[111] Jesus underscores the importance of virtue in reading the Word of God.

Other reading episodes could have been included, but these prove striking because they pit Jesus the obedient and faithful king-priest against the sinful elements in the religious establishment, particularly many of the teachers of the law. Jesus' teaching shines brightly against the dark backdrop of official teaching and practice. He penetrates to the heart of God's law, practices it, and proclaims it. He simultaneously demonstrates what it means to live under the Word of God and how one is to understand and apply it properly to the present circumstances of God's people.

Conclusion: Jesus the Word Who Submits to and Declares the Word

> Jesus Christ comprised in Himself both God's saving action toward man, and man's perfect obedience toward God . . . Here we have the complete Word of God to man in grace and truth, and the complete witness of man to God's grace and truth, in one. Here we have One who steps into the midst of our religious estrangement from God which rests upon a perversion both of Scripture and priesthood, and calls scribe and priest alike to account. He is the Word who has power on earth to forgive sins and to cleanse the sick. He has authority over the Sabbath and over the Temple itself, which He insists on cleansing before the "hour" of sacrifice. He is the Messiah, the Anointed One, Prophet, Priest, and King in One, the Lord Himself suddenly come to His Temple. Throughout, it is primarily as Word of God that Christ presses toward reconciliation, and insists that in His Word God's own sovereign Kingdom breaks in.[112]

The tradition has largely relegated Christ's ministry and use of the Word of God to his prophetic office, with some reference to the kingly office. While there is slight mention of a priestly teaching office, the notion remains by and large undeveloped. Furthermore, the primary royal Word-function of Christ is rule and dominion by his Word. Other aspects of the relationship between God's Word and the kingly office, however,

111. Witherington, *Mark*, 230–31.
112. Torrance, *Royal Priesthood*, 7–8.

have also for the most part gone unexplored in the dogmatic literature. Therefore, what the second part of this chapter sought to investigate were the other dimensions, specifically the "reading" dimensions, of Jesus' royal and priestly ministry. What surfaced was that the Gospels present Jesus as the kingly obedient Son, who faithfully follows, manifests, and proclaims God's self-revelation. He is furthermore depicted as the teaching priest, the ideal didactic "reader" of the Word of God, who correctly interprets the law, instructs about true cleanness, and reveals God's ways to his people. He is thus the bearer of the Word who satisfies Israel's longing for leaders—kings and priests—who would lead the people into covenant obedience through a proper relationship with torah. Moreover, as royal priestly Israel—her embodiment and representative—he arises from his baptism and temptation as the obedient and reverent Son who declares the will of God and mediates between God and humanity. It deserves mentioning again that it is difficult to parse minutely which office performs what function in relation to the Word of God, especially in the Gospels. However, the conclusion intimated in Barth and made clearer in the Gospels is that the entirety of Christ's mediatorial office is in some sense a ministry of the Word of God. He exemplifies devotion to as well as deep knowledge of torah; he both internalizes God's Word and brings its true intent to bear on all those around him. He is the Word and the ideal reader of the Word. To be a right reader of Scripture is to read in light of Jesus Christ—the subject matter of and standard for "reading" the Word. This last point will be developed in the final chapters. Before then, however, we turn to Luther's articulation of the priesthood of believers, as he brings together many of the strands of this study, though in an undeveloped manner.

6

Martin Luther, the Priesthood of All Believers, and the Word of God

Toward a Theology of Readers

Thus far we have traversed much biblical territory seeking to establish the link between royal priesthood and a proper relationship to the Word of God. This chapter explores one important instantiation of this connection in the theology of Martin Luther. The reformer makes an important contribution to this study for a number of reasons: he brings together many of the central biblical-theological themes related to royal priesthood, offers the clearest and most explicit arguments available for universal priesthood up until and even immediately following the Reformation, and ties royal priesthood to the Word of God in a variety of explicit ways. Luther protests the loss of a biblical vision for royal priesthood, which, accompanied by an increased emphasis on the sacramental character of ordained priesthood, resulted in the tragic decline in the use, proper interpretation, and general attention to the Word of God—the very thing most central to any notion of priesthood. "Proclamation" of the Word—a Word that exists in many forms—is the primary occupation of the priesthood. The aim of this chapter is to (1) examine Luther's proposals in detail and (2) offer them as a helpful and concrete, though underdeveloped, attempt to integrate these two themes, while providing a bridge between the biblical theology material of earlier chapters and the dogmatic and ethical synthesis in the final chapters. Through his voice, it is suggested that regaining a vision for the royal priesthood of all believers might open up possibilities for the Word's broader activity in and transformation of the church's life.

Luther and the Priesthood of All Believers

Since clergy were at the heart of medieval church life, a reformation in the accepted understanding of priesthood was at the very root of Luther's reform.[1] The power that Rome arrogated to its priesthood was central in Luther's criticism and partially fueled his emphasis on the priesthood of every believer.

The Two Stände

In Luther's day, the official ecclesiastical stance was that the clergy had absolute power over spiritual things. Consequently, it was commonly held that within the church there were two "estates" (*Stände*), the worldly (or temporal, secular) and the spiritual.[2] Luther, however, railed against this notion of two *Stände* and its consequences in the church. He thus focused many of his attacks on the Roman sacrament of ordination because, according to him, (1) it is not found or promised in Scripture, and (2) elevates the ordained to unhealthy levels of power, which (3) creates a separation between clergy and laity, and (4) denies the priesthood of every Christian.[3]

---

1. Gounelle lists four criticisms of the Roman priesthood which underlie Luther's doctrine of universal priesthood: (1) a mediation between God and believers other than that of Jesus Christ; (2) the necessity of the ministry; (3) the idea of a sacrifice offered to God in the Eucharist; (4) the notion that the clergy have a "character" different than the laity. It is the last of these that is most relevant to this study (Gounelle, "Le sacerdoce universel," 429–32).

2. "Estate" is an older term meaning "walk of life" or "standing" (Wengert, *Priesthood, Pastors, Bishops*, 5).

3. Herman Preus helpfully points out that Luther's opponents and therefore the target of his polemics changed throughout his career. Prior to 1525, he focused on the elevation of clergy over laity (the Roman Church), while after 1525 he fought against the reverse (the radicals) (Preus, "Luther and the Universal Priesthood," 55). Luther also rejects the sacrament of orders because, in his opinion, it was behind many clerical abuses. I will not treat this concern of Luther's here. See, for example, *Against the Spiritual Estate of the Pope* (1522), LW 39:270–99; *Defense and Explanation of All the Articles* (1521), LW 32:50–51; *To the Christian Nobility of the German Nation Concerning the Reform of the Christian Estate* (1520), LW 44:142.

In *The Babylonian Captivity of the Church* (1520), Luther protests the apparent tyranny of the papacy, exercised through the misuse of the sacraments. Though focusing most of his attention on the Eucharist, he addresses the other Roman sacraments, particularly ordination. "Of this sacrament," he writes, "the church of Christ knows nothing; it is an invention of the church of the pope. Not only is there nowhere any promise of grace attached to it, but there is not a single word said about it in the whole New Testament."[4] Luther does not say that the ordination rite should altogether be condemned, but rather that it should not be presented as a divine institution. Accordingly, he argues that the church has no right to make new promises of grace attached to its own rites simply because it claims to be guided by the Holy Spirit. Rather, he says, "it is the promises of God that make the church, and not the church that makes the promise of God."[5] To say that the sacrament of orders confers a particular grace is to put the church in the place of God.

It is not only the idea of sacramental grace *per se* that was problematic for Luther, but the type of grace supposedly bestowed.[6] Rome, with much tradition on its side, argued that ordination conferred an indelible character on those ordained. Luther, however, rejects this tradition and what he deems to be the detrimental consequences of this teaching. He calls the doctrine of *character indelibilis* a "fiction" and a "laughingstock," writing: "I cannot understand at all why one who has been made a priest cannot again become a layman; for the sole difference between him and a layman is his ministry."[7] It is by this indelible character that two Christian *Stände* are created and perpetuated because it permanently allows clergy to have spiritual power over the laity, including temporal authorities. Therefore, already in the title of another of his tracts of 1520, *To the Christian Nobility of the German Nation Concerning the Reform of the Christian Estate* (Stand), Luther does the remarkable thing of reducing the Christian estate to a single one.[8] He goes on to argue that

---

4. *LW* 36:106–7.

5. Rome, however, argued on the basis of Heb 7:12 ("Where there is a new priesthood there is of necessity a change of laws . . .") that it had the right to make new laws. Luther refutes this claim in *The Misuse of the Mass* (1522), *LW* 36:137–38.

6. Eastwood makes the point that a difference in the concept of grace underlies much of Luther's protest against the prevailing priesthood as well as his arguments for the priesthood of all believers (Eastwood, *Priesthood*, 3).

7. *LW* 36:117.

8. Wengert, *Priesthood*, 5.

the Romanists use their power to build three "walls" around themselves that prevent any reform from occurring. First, when pressed by secular authorities, they claim that temporal powers have no jurisdiction over spiritual authorities, and the spiritual is always above the temporal. Second, when the attempt is made to reprove them from the Scriptures, they declare that only the Pope can interpret Scripture. Finally, if threatened by a council, they maintain that only the pope can call a council. By exercising this kind of power, Rome effectively takes away the three "rods" of the Christian by which he or she may punish sin and bring to light the work of the devil.[9] That is why Luther asserts that if this sacrament and the doctrine of indelible character were ever to fall to the ground, the papacy would scarcely survive.[10]

What seemed unavoidable to Luther was the dramatic cleavage between clergy and laity that was nurtured by this dogma. We are now nearer the heart of Luther's criticism of the Roman sacrament. He writes:

> They have sought by this means [ordination] to set up a seed bed of implacable discord, by which clergy and laymen should be separated from each other farther than heaven from earth, *to the incredible injury of the grace of baptism and to the confusion of our fellowship in the gospel*. Here, indeed, are the roots of the detestable tyranny of the clergy over the laity. Trusting in the external anointing by which their hands are consecrated, in the tonsure and in vestments, they not only exalt themselves above the rest of the lay Christians, who are only anointed with the Holy Spirit, *but regard them almost as dogs and unworthy to be included with themselves in the church*.[11]

If everything pertaining to the spiritual life was in the hands of the ordained few, where did that leave the laity? They were often passive recipients of whatever was handed down to them. In a real sense the church resided in the clergy. However, for Luther, there was only one

---

9. *LW* 44:126–27. Cf. *Concerning the Ministry* (1523) where Luther lodges a similar complaint: "For by a petty invention . . . the papal theory perpetuates its ministry through an *indelible character* and safeguards it against removal by any kind of wrongdoing" (*LW* 40:10). Moreover, these "walls" can be seen as a carryover from the time of the Gregorian reforms, in which clergy were protected from temporal punishment. Luther makes reference to this law in *Against the Spiritual Estate of the Pope* (1522) and argues that no leader is above reproof (*LW* 39:249–54).

10. *LW* 36:117.

11. Ibid. (emphasis added).

Christian estate, which is entered into through a common baptism. To say otherwise is to divide Christians into different classes and do injury to the fellowship believers have in the gospel.[12] Thus it might be argued that Luther opposed priestly ordination largely because it divided the church. In his *Treatise on the New Testament, that is, the Holy Mass* (1520) he laments that canon law has created so many sects, orders, and divisions that Christian unity is all but destroyed. As a result, the clergy cease to see laypersons as true Christians.[13] Furthermore, the laity begins to believe that service to God only occurs in the spiritual estate.[14] These problems flow from a misapprehension of priestly ordination.

Ordination should rather be seen as the conferring of the office of the ministry to a member of a Christian congregation. In his attempt to exonerate the ordination practices of the church fathers, Luther points out that the former anointed with oil and added other accoutrements for the purpose of making clear who was to exercise the office of preaching and baptizing on behalf of the community. They had no intention of creating a special class of people. However, though they meant well, their additions to the simple ordination ceremonies of the apostolic era led to the obfuscation of the true intent of the rite. Luther writes: "This good intention of the fathers and their consecration developed to the point where baptism and Christ were weakened and obscured by them, and there no longer remained a consecration to a calling or to the ministerial office, but it became a private consecration, ordaining private clerics for the private mass, and now at last it has resulted in a real division and distinction between true Christians and the devil's clerics."[15] As we will see in more detail later, Luther was acutely aware of the fact that ordination in his day was a far cry from that in the New Testament and the church fathers. What his opponents called a priestly or spiritual estate was no more than a ministry, office, or service, according to Scripture.[16]

---

12. Speaking of the pope, he writes: "[H]e divides the priestly people of Christ into clergy and laity. The clergy he calls his religious ones . . . He makes them religious simply by tonsuring them, anointing their fingers with oil, and having them wear long garments. He claims that he is imprinting on their souls an indelible character . . . This institution they call holy orders or ordination, one of the seven sacraments, [is made] much holier and better than baptism itself" (*LW* 36:201).

13. *LW* 35:80. Cf. *The Freedom of the Christian* (1520), *LW* 31:356.

14. See, e.g., *Against the Spiritual Estate of the Pope* (1522), *LW* 39:268.

15. *The Private Mass and the Consecration of Priests* (1533), *LW* 38:186–87.

16. Luther discusses at length the proper use of the term "priest" and its synonyms

Moreover, vows of celibacy, anointing, vestments, and tonsure—all additions to the ordination rite—further contributed to the separation between lay and clergy and were impediments to a proper understanding of priesthood.[17] It is this confusion regarding the nature of Christian priesthood that forms Luther's most important grounds for opposing Rome's clergy.

Throughout his works he protests that the elevation of the ordained priesthood eclipses the reality of the priesthood of every Christian.[18] He contends that all Christians are of the spiritual estate and, in fact, consecrated priests by virtue of their common baptism and faith.[19] It is, therefore, a gross act of usurpation for one to take upon himself what is common to all Christians (the priesthood) without the authority and consent of the community. "It follows from this argument," Luther writes, "that there is no true, basic difference between laymen and priests, princes and bishops, between religious and secular, except for the sake of office and work, but not for the sake of status. They are all of the spiritual estate, all are truly priests, bishops, and popes."[20] Priesthood is the calling of every Christian and it is only from among this priesthood that priests (correctly, ministers) are called to fulfill an office. Instead Rome ignored the common priesthood in favor of a special one. Luther goes so far as to say that to become a papal priest one had to reject his natural Christian priesthood: "For in carrying on their hateful office they make no one a priest until he denies that he was a priest before. Thus in the very act of making him a priest they in fact remove him from his priesthood, so that before God their ordination is a mockery, but also a veritable and serious degradation. For to say, 'I am ordained a priest,' is only to confess, 'I was not, and am not now a priest.'"[21] Thus Luther is

---

in *Answer to the Hyperchristian, Hyperspiritual, and Hyperlearned Book by Goat Emser in Leipzig—Including Some Thoughts Regarding His Companion, the Fool Murner* (1521), *LW* 39:154–55. Cf. *Concerning the Ministry* (1523), *LW* 40:35.

17. See, e.g., *LW* 36:114 and *LW* 45:46 on the issue of celibacy and priesthood.

18. "Thus [the pope] removes and eradicates our Christian priesthood with this damnable priesthood, for hardly anyone knows of any other priesthood except that of the pope. As soon as anyone hears a priest mentioned he imagines one who is tonsured, anointed and dressed in long garments" (*LW* 36:202).

19. *LW* 44:127. Cf. *Dr. Luther's Retraction of the Error Forced Upon Him by the Most Highly Learned Priest of God, Sir Jerome Emser, Vicar in Meissen* (1521), *LW* 39:237.

20. *LW* 44:129.

21. *LW* 40:20. For Luther, the priesthood of all believers is actually the foundation

persuaded that the NT avoids using *sacerdos* to refer to apostles or any other office in order to prevent this confusion. If Rome desires to do right it will simply call people from among this natural priesthood to the office of the ministry and not produce "new, holier, and better clerics" than baptized Christians.[22] Among other important things, what was at stake for Luther was each Christian's sense of his own election, consecration, dignity, and calling before God. All believers are loved, chosen, sanctified, and called to worship God and minister to others. Instead, he decries, "the pope has usurped the term 'priest' for his anointed and tonsured hordes. By this means they have separated themselves from the ordinary Christians and have called themselves uniquely the *'clergy of God,' God's heritage and chosen people*, who must help other Christians by their sacrifice and worship."[23] In the end, it is the very idea of what it means to be a Christian that was being called into question by Rome's doctrine. Therefore, his task was not only to bring to light their error but to correct it by a fresh examination of Scripture's teaching on Christian priesthood. It is to a fuller exposition of his biblical proposal that we now turn.

The Biblical Doctrine of Universal Priesthood

Luther builds his biblical and theological argument for the priesthood of all believers in three ways. First, he establishes Christ's preeminent priesthood and believers' priesthood by virtue of their connection to him. Second, he examines the explicit New Testament statements concerning universal priesthood. Finally, he contends that the functions normally attributed to OT priests are common to all believers according to Scripture. Ultimately, there is nothing sacred that is denied to every Christian because all are priests of God.

The reformer is always quick to point out the preeminence of Christ's priesthood over all other so-called priesthoods. In his exposition of Ps 110:4, for example, he highlights that Christ's priesthood is of the

---

of the office of ministry or priesthood. Cf. Lieberg, *Amt und Ordination*, 40–103.

22. *LW* 38:188. Thus, contrary to many misconceptions, Luther's doctrine of universal priesthood, as we will see, concerns both the office of ministry and the ministerial task of each believer. Cf. Gounelle, "Le sacerdoce universel," 432–34, for three common misinterpretations of the reformer's doctrine.

23. *Commentary on Psalm 110:4* (1535), *LW* 13:329 (emphasis added).

Melchizedekian order and therefore superior to the Jewish priesthood.[24] According to Luther, the NT has no outward and visible priest. Rather, he retorts, "we have only one single priest, Christ, who has sacrificed himself for us and all of us with him." It is he alone who died for our sins (1 Pet 3:18) and by his offering has perfected believers for all time (Heb 10:14).[25] Moreover, since it is also the priest's task to teach God's Word and intercede for his people, Christ is the supreme priest because he performs these functions supremely.[26] Christians, then, derive their priesthood from Christ's because they are "children" of the High Priest.[27] They become priests by a kind of birth. Luther writes: "No one can be called a priest unless he has been born to this heritage of and through Christ, just as a child has its name and rights by heredity from its father. It is clear, therefore, that those who will be priests must be born as children of this Priest, and that those who are born of Him are, and are called, priests—all of them."[28] Psalm 110:4 speaks of the Messiah-Priest as having children and heirs. These offspring, according to Luther, are not born in a natural and human way, but in a spiritual and heavenly manner, that is, by God's activity working through baptism.[29] Therefore, just as all Christians share a common baptism, Gospel, heavenly inheritance, Spirit, Lord, and God (Eph 4:4–6; cf. John 17:22; Gal 3:28), so they ought to share the name "priest."[30] What this means, moreover, is that the sacrifices and service we offer are "through Christ" (Heb 13:15) and are acceptable only on that account. Christ receives our prayers and sacrifices, and through his intercession and mediation makes them pleasing to God (Rom 8:34; Heb 9:24).[31] Thus, the central aspects of our

---

24. *LW* 13:312. Cf. *Lectures on Genesis Chapters 6–14* (1536), *LW* 2:393–94.

25. *LW* 36:138.

26. See, e.g., *LW* 13:315–24; *LW* 35:99; *LW* 36:138–39.

27. *LW* 36:138.

28. *LW* 13:329. Luther however does not exclude the idea that a special "priesthood" is also derived from Christ's priesthood and must undertake the same tasks (cf. Schwarz, "Geistliche Vollmacht," 80).

29. "Consequently every baptized Christian is a priest already, not by appointment or ordination from the pope or any other man, but because Christ Himself has begotten him as a priest and has given birth to him in Baptism" (*LW* 13:329).

30. Ibid., 330–31.

31. "We lay ourselves on Christ by a firm faith in his testament and do not otherwise appear before God with our prayer, praise, and sacrifice except through Christ and his mediation" (*LW* 35:99).

priesthood derive their legitimacy from our connection to the one High Priest.[32]

The passage of Scripture that Luther treats most often when speaking of the priesthood of all Christians is, not surprisingly, 1 Pet 2:1–9. Some of his clearest expositions of it are found in his correspondences with the Leipzig theologian Emser.[33] With regard to his teaching on universal priesthood, Luther is accused by Emser of interpreting Scripture "by the letter" and not "by the Spirit" and, in doing so, bringing death (2 Cor 3:6). The reformer responds that he is only teaching 1 Pet 2:9, so that if he is teaching death by the letter so is the apostle.[34] Emser charges Luther with teaching that all Christians are consecrated priests, when in fact the text speaks only of a common internal, spiritual priesthood. Luther concurs that Peter speaks of a spiritual priesthood and, in fact, nowhere deals with a consecrated priesthood.[35] At the same time, Emser understands the text to be addressing two priesthoods, but Luther apparently cannot see this because of his "letter" way of interpreting the text.[36] However, for Luther, Peter's words have only one meaning that encompasses both letter and Spirit. That is, when 1 Peter 2 is interpreted literally it yields a spiritual, living priesthood. However, if whatever is not of the Spirit is dead, and Emser's "spiritual" interpretation yields only natural, dead priests, his argument self-destructs. How is it, Luther asks, that a dead interpretation produces living priests and a living interpretation produces dead priests?[37] What his opponent calls a "priest" is in the NT called a servant, minister, or elder, and refers to an office not a status.[38] Thus one should not impose the then-current meaning of the term "priest" on the Scriptures. With that he dismisses

---

32. Luther illustrates this point elsewhere by use of a husband-wife analogy. As in marriage where all that belongs to the husband belongs to the bride, so in the Christian life all that belongs to Christ belongs to his people. In this way he gives believers his priesthood and its accompanying tasks (*LW* 31:354).

33. *Answer to the Hyperchristian*, *LW* 39:140–224 and *Dr. Luther's Retractions*, *LW* 39:229–38.

34. Ibid., 151–52.

35. Ibid.

36. Ibid., 152–53.

37. Ibid., 153.

38. Luther cites Acts 20:17–18, 28; 1 Cor 4:1; 2 Cor 11:23; 2 Tim 2:24; Titus 1:5, 7; and 1 Pet 5:1–2, 5 as examples of the interchangeable use of minister, priest, presbyter, elder, bishop, etc. (ibid., 154–55).

the notion of two priesthoods in Peter's epistle.[39] The apostle instead addresses all Christians, bidding them all to grow in grace and long for pure spiritual milk (1 Pet 2:2). It is the whole church that is to be built up into a holy priesthood (2:5).[40] Peter clearly speaks of the whole congregation when he calls them a royal priesthood and commands them to proclaim the deeds of God. "[Emser] may interpret 'priests' as he pleases," Luther objects, "but all Christians are nevertheless such priests through this passage. If all of us should preach, then the tonsure-bearers must keep silent, since they have a different, special priesthood above all Christians."[41] The outward trappings of clerical priests do not make priests or give power. "Rather," says Luther, "priesthood and power have to be there first, brought from baptism and common to all Christians through the faith which builds them upon Christ the true high priest, as St. Peter says here."[42] Thus 1 Peter 2 supports only a spiritual priesthood common to all believers.

Luther identifies Rev 5:9–10 and 20:6 as the only other passages in the NT that speak about a priesthood.[43] Both passages affirm that all Christian people are kings and priests, not visibly but spiritually. In *The Freedom of the Christian* he claims that believers' kingship and priesthood are defined by their faith. By this faith they rule over all things as kings and have every circumstance work for their good. Moreover, by the same faith Christians have priestly access to God and may pray for and teach divine things to others.[44] This royal and sacral dignity and calling belong to every believer. For Luther, these three explicit and soli-

---

39. Luther, however, later concedes that 1 Peter could speak of two priesthoods. It does so by including the consecrated priesthood as comprehended in the general priesthood. If the passage speaks of both priesthoods in one breath, then everything that is ascribed to the physical priesthood is given to all Christians, since Peter is addressing all Christians as priests. He is convinced, however, that Emser would not accept this interpretation, for it would allow even women and children to preach and administer the sacraments (ibid., 233; cf. *LW* 36:141).

40. *LW* 36:141.

41. *LW* 39:236.

42. Ibid., 236–37.

43. He was, however, reluctant to build a case from these Revelation texts. He writes, "Although the Book of Revelation is hardly of such significance as to be useful for citing in controversy, yet I wanted to confront our opponents with some evidence from it..." (*LW* 36:140).

44. *LW* 31:606–7.

tary references to priesthood in the NT are self-evident and unassailable foundations for the doctrine of the priesthood of every Christian.[45]

He further argues that the functions of OT priests are assigned to NT believers, thus making the latter priests. It is abundantly clear from Scripture that the task of Levitical priests was to offer sacrifices, pray, and teach the law on behalf of the people.[46] Moreover, already in the OT, the common believer is spoken of as offering sacrifices: a broken spirit (Ps 51:17), thanksgiving (Pss 50:14, 23; 116:16–7), and righteousness (Ps 4:5). In the NT, Christians are called to present themselves as a sacrifice to God (Rom 12:1), offer spiritual sacrifices (1 Pet 2:5), sacrificially put to death the misdeeds of the body (Rom 8:13), and offer sacrifices of praise (Heb 13:15). Sacrifice is a priestly work intended to be carried out by all of God's people. Therefore, every Christian is a priest.[47] All Christians, furthermore, have access to God and may intercede for others. Luther writes, "We may boldly come into the presence of God in the spirit of faith [Heb 10:19, 22] and cry 'Abba, Father!' pray for another, and do all things which we see done and foreshadowed in the outer and visible works of priests."[48] Thus, the numerous calls in Scripture to pray for one another only testify to the common priesthood of God's people. Finally, Luther very often cites Mal 2:7 to demonstrate that the chief task of OT priests was to teach the people the law of God.[49] In fact preaching the Word of God was what defined a priest, so that Luther could say: "Whoever does not preach the Word . . . is no priest at all."[50] Yet this

---

45. It should be noted that Luther does make brief mention of the believers' priesthood in his sermons, lectures, and commentaries on other relevant biblical texts. See, e.g., *Lectures on Deuteronomy* (1523–1524), *LW* 9:124; *Commentary on Joel* (1524), *LW* 18:106, 109; *Commentary on Zechariah* (1527), *LW* 20:346; *Lectures on Isaiah 40–66* (1527–1530), *LW* 17:97–98, 337, 414–15; *Sermons on the Gospel of John 14–16* (1537), *LW* 24:242–44; and *Commentary on Psalm 51* (1538), *LW* 12:402–3.

46. *LW* 13:315.

47. These arguments constitute part of Luther's second "assault" on the papal priesthood in *The Misuse of the Mass* (*LW* 36:145–46).

48. *LW* 31:355.

49. Mal 2:7 says: "The lips of a priest should guard knowledge, and men should seek instruction from his mouth, for he is the messenger of the Lord of hosts" (Cf. *LW* 13:315; *LW* 36:113; *LW* 36:148). Luther, however, rarely made explicit reference to Scriptures pertaining to the other two functions of Levitical priests. This was likely because it was obvious that these were priestly tasks in the Bible and few disputed this in his day.

50. *LW* 36:113.

priestly prerogative is not solely the property of the ordained, either in the Old or New Testaments. Luther argues that Paul refers to all Christians as "able ministers of the new testament" (2 Cor 3:6). All who have been called out of darkness into God's light are to declare his praises (1 Pet 2:9). He further contends that the command to keep order (1 Cor 14:40) only becomes necessary if everyone has the right and power to preach.[51] Thus another priestly task is democratized by Scripture. He concludes: "Through these testimonies of the Scriptures the outward priesthood in the New Testament is overthrown; for it makes prayer, access to God and teaching (all of which are fitting and proper to a priest) common to all men."[52] Therefore, the priesthood of believers is a biblical doctrine that flows from an understanding of Christ's priesthood and the benefits of our relationship to him, explicit NT passages concerning believers' royal and priestly status, and biblical statements regarding the priestly prerogatives distributed to all Christians. It is in fact the last of the priestly duties highlighted above—the proclamation of the Word—that points us toward the central concern of this chapter, namely, how Luther relates the priesthood of believers to the proper "reading" of the Word of God.

The Priesthood of Believers and the Word of God

To understand best how Luther relates the Word of God to the priesthood of believers, it is essential to grasp what he means by the "Word of God." It will be evident in the following that this term has many dimensions, which make its connection to Christian priesthood all the more rich.

The Manifold Word

It is understandable to assume that when Luther speaks of the Word of God he has Scripture in mind, as the primacy of Scripture was a central commitment of his reform. However, this would be a false assumption. In Luther, the Word of God consists in three broad forms: oral, sacramental, and written. He writes in the *Smalcald Articles* (1537) that the gospel is given, first, "through the spoken word, by which the forgiveness of

---

51. Ibid., 148–49.
52. Here he puts access to God in place of sacrifice as part of this triad of priestly duties (ibid., 139).

sins is preached to the whole world (which is the proper function of the Gospel); second, through baptism; third, through the holy Sacrament of the Altar; fourth, through the power of keys and also through the mutual conversation and consolation of brothers and sisters."[53] Through these various forms of his Word, God graciously presents himself to human beings. More than just pointing to God and his disposition toward sinners, these forms of his Word actually convey and perform his saving will. Writing on Luther's view, Robert Kolb observes: "God designed his Word in these forms as instruments of his re-creating power which accomplish what they announce. More than performative speech, they are creative speech, parallel to God's speaking in Genesis 1."[54] Luther presents God as "a *person* who engaged his people in conversation through his Word in its several forms," and through it "exercises *his* power to claim and restore sinners."[55] Let us examine each of these forms in order.

God encounters his people primarily in his Word. For Luther this Word is predominantly a spoken word uttered in the proclamation of the gospel and in the absolution of sins. The oral proclamation of the Word, first, places emphasis on the living confrontation and conversation between the Creator and humanity. Luther writes:

> The word "Gospel" signifies nothing else than a sermon or report concerning the grace and mercy of God merited and acquired through the Lord Jesus Christ with His death. Actually, the Gospel is not what one finds in books and what is written in letters of the alphabet; it is rather an oral sermon and a living Word, a voice that resounds throughout the world and is proclaimed publicly, so that one hears it everywhere.[56]

---

53. *SA* 3, 5 in *BC*, 319. We will return to these specific forms of the Word and expand this list in what follows.

54. Kolb, *Martin Luther*, 132. Lohse argues that Luther's view is rooted in Augustine's distinction between the sign and reality. For Augustine, words were only a reference to a reality behind them which could not be communicated or expressed. Words were merely signs. Luther retained those distinctions but went beyond Augustine by tying word and reality, or outer and inner word, more closely together. For him the human word becomes the "bearer of the divine Spirit" and actually conveys the reality in some real way. Lohse points out the parallels with Luther's view on the Lord's Supper (Lohse, *Martin Luther's Theology*, 191).

55. Ibid., 131 (emphasis added).

56. *Sermons on the First Epistle of St. Peter* (1522), *LW* 30:3.

Since God is a God who speaks, one most powerfully encounters him through the medium of the human voice. This truth is summed up well in the eighth of the *Marburg Articles* (1529) which states that "the Holy Spirit, ordinarily, gives such faith or his gift to no one without preaching or the oral word or the gospel of Christ preceding, but that through and by means of such oral word he effects and creates faith where and in whom it pleases him."[57] The Word of God as the proclamation of the gospel brings Christ to us and us to Christ through a human voice.

Second, the pronouncement of forgiveness in the sacrament of penance is a word of God's comfort to troubled sinners. In his treatise *The Sacrament of Penance* (1519) Luther argues that the Word of God and not the priest accomplishes what is important in the sacrament of penance, namely, absolution from the guilt of sin.[58] He does not deny the role of the priest in extending God's forgiveness, but he emphasizes that God's Word itself conveyed forgiveness to those who trusted in it. The words of the priest "show, tell, and proclaim to you that you are free and that your sins are forgiven by God according to and by virtue of the above-quoted words of Christ to St. Peter [Matt 16:19]."[59] That is, the word of Christ's promise that whatever is loosed on earth will be loosed in heaven is articulated and rearticulated through the word of the priest's absolution. To disbelieve it is to make God out to be a liar. However, if with "unshakeable faith" we "give place to the word of God spoken through the priest" we may receive the forgiveness of our sins and have

---

57. *The Marburg Colloquy and The Marburg Articles* (1529), *LW* 38:87. In *The Sacrament of the Body and Blood of Christ—Against the Fanatics* (1526), he moreover writes: "I preach the gospel of Christ, and with my bodily voice I bring Christ into your heart, so that you may form him within yourself. If now you truly believe, so that your heart lays hold of the word and holds fast within it that voice, tell me, what have you in your heart? You must answer that you have the true Christ . . . [T]he one Christ enters so many hearts through the voice, and that each person who hears the sermon and accepts it takes the whole Christ into his heart" (*LW* 36:340). See also *The Adoration of the Sacrament* (1523), *LW* 36:278 and *A Brief Instruction on What to Look For and Expect in the Gospels* (1521), *LW* 35:121.

58. "It follows further that the forgiveness of guilt is not within the province of any human office or authority, be it pope, bishop, priest, or any other. Rather it depends exclusively upon the word of Christ and your own faith" (*LW* 35:12). Cf. Kolb, *Martin Luther*, 134.

59. *LW* 35:11.

a joyful conscience.[60] It is this oral Word that, in the hearing of the one who has faith, conveys what it promises.

The sacraments—baptism and the Lord's Supper—are also forms of God's Word to his people. Concerning the first, Luther typically presents speech as an image of the mode of God's activity in baptism. He asserts that "baptism is nothing other than God's Word in the water, commanded by God's institution."[61] Baptism proclaims and actualizes the promises of God for forgiveness, cleansing, and new life: "In Baptism . . . it is said to us: 'I am the Lord your God, do not be troubled! I will care for you! Cast your care on Me! You have a God who has promised that He will care for you."[62] It is precisely its attachment to God's Word of promise that renders baptism itself a word, and particularly a word of any value.[63] The emphasis in baptism is on divine action and initiative, not on the response of the recipient.[64] The God who graciously makes the promise provides a visible word through which he effects what he has pledged. Similar things may be said of the Eucharist. Following Paul's account (1 Cor 11:24-26), Luther holds that the sacred meal proclaims Christ. As the signs of bread and water are combined with the words of institution, they preach and praise Christ, glorify his sufferings, and speak of his grace, "to the end that our faith, provided with and confirmed by divine words and signs, may thereby become strong against all sin, suffering, death, and hell, and everything that is against us."[65] Contrary to Rome's view, the sacrament was not a sacrifice but a

60. Ibid., 14–16. It is noteworthy that when Luther later excluded penance from the list of sacraments, he still urged Christians to partake of the absolution pronounced by pastors both publicly and privately (Kolb, *Martin Luther*, 134).

61. SA 3, 5:1 in *BC*, 319.

62. *Lectures on Genesis 37* (1544), *LW* 6:364. Cf. *Lectures on Genesis 17* (1539), *LW* 3:124.

63. Trigg helpfully draws attention to the multivalence of "word" in relation to the sacrament. The term may refer to the ministry of the word that accompanies baptism or the divine word of promise which is joined to the sacrament. The former is merely a human word intended to remind those who are weak in faith, while the latter is already given in Scripture and therefore continues to be given (Trigg, *Baptism*, 35).

64. In his earlier work on baptism, Luther emphasized the necessity of faith for the efficacy of baptism (see, e.g., *The Holy and Blessed Sacrament of Baptism* [1519], *LW* 35:33–36). However, in his later works he stressed the objectivity of baptism, sometimes over against the claims of the Anabaptists (see, e.g., *Concerning Rebaptism* [1528], *LW* 40:249).

65. *LW* 35:105–6.

testament of the forgiveness of sins and God's gracious disposition toward his own, and like baptism, bestows what it proclaims, particularly as faith receives the promises that are intertwined with the signs.[66] Yet the importance of faith is somewhat mitigated by the reality of Christ's presence in the Supper, which is made certain by Christ's creative words of institution, and this apart from faith. Thus there is a kind of objectivity to the work done in the sacramental word of the Lord's Supper. In fact, in at least this way, the sacrament is meant to arouse or strengthen faith.[67] For Luther, as Kolb points out, "all talk of Christ's presence in the sacrament must serve to assure the faithful that God works through the sacrament to give them eternal life, for 'the forgiveness of sins, consolation of souls, and strengthening of faith.'"[68] Luther's vehement opposition to the views of Zwingli and other Swiss theologians was intended to secure this assurance for God's people. Bread and wine are visible words that guarantee Christ's presence and promises, especially to those who believe.

That Luther holds Scripture to be the Word of God is beyond dispute.[69] What emerges from the above discussion, however, is the question of the interplay between Scripture and the oral and sacramental forms of the Word of God. Luther sometimes speaks of Scripture as merely the preservation of the prior proclaimed Word, leading some like Lohse to conclude too strongly that "Luther emphasized the priority of the oral proclamation *over* the written deposit."[70] Rather, by highlighting the

---

66. *LW* 35:84–87. On Luther's stress on the necessity of faith to receive the benefits of the sacrament, see *LW* 35:88–89 and *LW* 36:349–50.

67. The *Marburg Articles* state: "That the use of the sacrament, like the word, has been given and ordained by God Almighty in order that weak consciences may thereby be excited to faith by the Holy Spirit" (*LW* 38:88).

68. Kolb, *Martin Luther*, 147.

69. See, e.g., *LW* 34:284; *The Gospel for the Festival of the Epiphany, Matthew 2* (1522), *LW* 52:211; *The Small Catechism* (1529), SC Baptism 1–8, in *BC*, 359. Lohse rightfully points out that Luther's view of the relationship between God and Scripture is complex. He outlines three ways that Luther speaks of Scripture: as God's Word, containing God's Word, and as a mere creature. At the very least, what this alerts us to is the flexibility of Luther's statements about Scripture. However, this flexibility does not mute Luther's constant refrain that the Scriptures are the final authority in all matters (Lohse, *Martin Luther's Theology*, 188).

70. Lohse, *Martin Luther's Theology*, 189 (emphasis added). Also see *LW* 52:205–7, where Luther makes the point that the apostles first preached before they wrote and that their writings were for the preservation of what they had preached.

oral proclamation of the gospel Luther was making a basic distinction between the Old and New Testament eras and their respective scriptural writings. He averred that, although both testaments were written down, the NT should properly be "contained in the living voice which resounds and is heard everywhere." It is therefore not necessary that it be written. While the OT is available only in writing and merely points to the Christ who was to come, the gospel or NT "is a living sermon on the Christ who *has* come."[71] The gospel is an announcement of good news, and that news is the reality of Jesus Christ who has come to save humankind. Althaus more accurately captures Luther's heart. While affirming that for Luther the Word is "first and last the spoken word," he also notes that this living, oral Word is limited because its content is the apostolic Word. The apostles alone are the infallible teachers of the Christian message, whose writings are the authoritative accounts of their own preaching.[72] Therefore, all true Christian proclamation can only transmit and explain this apostolic Word.[73] Written Scripture provides the sure message, oral proclamation brings it into conversation with human persons, and each reinforces the other. Absolution functions in a more straightforward manner. The pronouncement of forgiveness is merely a repetition or re-verbalization of Christ's promise of clemency. Because the Lord pledges that what is forgiven on earth is truly forgiven, the priest who absolves simply gives breath and voice to the written Word and makes it a living word of comfort to the hearer amidst his circumstances.

Luther makes explicit the connection between Scripture and baptism in his *Small Catechism*, where he defines the latter as "water used according to God's command and connected with God's Word." What is God's Word? It is Matt 28:19, which commands Christ's followers to baptize in the triune Name.[74] The second question in this section of the catechism asks what gifts or benefits are bestowed by baptism. The answer: "It effects forgiveness of sins, delivers from death and the devil, and grants eternal salvation to all who believe, as the Word and promise of God declare." What is this Word and promise? Again it is Scripture, specifically Mark 16:16, which declares that all who believe and are bap-

---

71. *LW* 30:19 (emphasis added).
72. *LW* 52:206.
73. Althaus, *Theology of Martin Luther*, 72.
74. *SC* Baptism 1–8, in *BC*, 359.

tized will be saved.⁷⁵ Thus, baptism is commanded and defined by the written Word, and furthermore confers what it promises on the basis of God's promise in this same Word. The Lord's Supper also derives its power from the scriptural Word alone. Against anti-sacramentalists like Karlstadt, Luther avers that even if the bread and wine were only symbolic, the sacrament would still grant the forgiveness of sins on account of Christ's words of institution. "Everything," he says, "depends on the Word."⁷⁶ The sacraments as visible, tangible words are rooted in the prior Word that established them and continues to undergird their work in the lives of believers.⁷⁷

We may therefore sum up the interplay between Scripture and the other forms of the Word of God, and therefore Luther's view, as follows: Oral and sacramental proclamation are forms of the Word of God when they correspond to the written Word that instituted and makes promises through them. Now that we have some grasp of Luther's use of "the Word of God" we are better able to understand how he connects this to the Christian's priesthood.

The Mutual Ministry of the Word

One important way Luther establishes the priesthood of every Christian is to take what his opponents, and medieval Christianity generally, believed are the functions of a priest and demonstrate that all Christians are permitted to perform those same functions. In *Concerning the Ministry* he identifies seven priestly functions: (1) to teach and preach the Word of God, (2) to baptize, (3) to administer the Eucharist, (4) to bind and loose sins, (5) to pray for others, (6) to sacrifice, and (7) to judge all doctrine and spirits.⁷⁸ It should be no surprise that he views the first duty as the highest and the one upon which the others depend, for "we teach with the Word, we consecrate with the Word, we bind and absolve sins by the Word, we baptize with the Word, we sacrifice with

---

75. Ibid., 484–85. This is also Luther's argument against the Anabaptists. He argues that, if they believed God's word (Mark 16:16) about the efficacy of baptism, they would not rebaptize anyone (see *LW* 40:249).

76. *LW* 40:214.

77. See Trigg's entire discussion on the relation of water and word in Luther's baptismal theology (Trigg, *Baptism*, 61–109 [esp. 70]).

78. *LW* 40:21.

the Word, we judge all things by the Word."⁷⁹ These seven priestly duties are nothing other than expressions of the various forms of the Word of God outlined above. Everything a priest does is in essence a ministry of the Word, and this ministry defines priesthood.⁸⁰ The remarkable move Luther makes is to extend this manifold priestly ministry of the Word to all Christians—men and women alike. He argues that if all Christians are given access to the same Word of God, and if all as priests are given a ministry, namely, to proclaim the excellencies of God (1 Pet 2:9), then no priestly duty should be denied any believer since they are all derivative of the ministry of teaching and preaching the Word. Every "splendid" and "royal" duty is to be exercised by every Christian.⁸¹ In *Concerning the Ministry* and elsewhere he expands on what it means, and what it does not mean, for every believer to perform these priestly functions.

First, preaching, teaching, and proclaiming the Word is within the province of every believer. "Even though not everybody has the public office," Luther writes, "every Christian has the right and the duty to teach, instruct, admonish, comfort, and rebuke his neighbor with the Word of God at every opportunity and whenever necessary."⁸² Two things should be observed: (1) he distinguishes between the *office* and *function* of preaching, and therefore (2) grants every believer a non-official ministry of the Word. He is clear throughout his writings that the public ministry of the Word is for those called by a congregation to exercise this office on the congregation's behalf. No one may take it upon himself, but must be elected by the church.⁸³ Another way to understand Luther's view is

---

79. Ibid.

80. "The duty of a priest is to preach, and if he does not preach he is as much a priest as a picture of a man is a man" (*LW* 36:115). "The priesthood is properly nothing but the ministry of the Word . . . Whoever, therefore, does not know or preach the gospel is not only no priest or bishop, but he is a kind of pest to the church, who under the false title of priest or bishop, or dressed in sheep's clothing, actually does violence to the gospel and plays the wolf in the church" (ibid., 116). "To declare the praises of Christ is the priesthood and kingdom of the Christians" (*LW* 17:98).

81. *LW* 40:21.

82. *LW* 13:333. Cf. *LW* 20:346.

83. "Although we are all equally priests, we cannot all publicly minister and teach" (*LW* 31:356). Writing against radical reformers who used the doctrine of the priesthood of all believers to justify their usurpation of the office of pastor, he urges: "It is true that all Christians are priests, but not all are pastors. For to be a pastor one must be not only a Christian and a priest but must have an office and a field of work committed to him. This call and command make pastors and preachers" (*Sermons on Ps 82* [1530], *LW*

to note the way he distinguishes between "public" and "private" spheres. For him, these terms do not designate corporate versus personal spheres, but rather official versus non-official. Thus the priesthood of all believers obliges every Christian to declare God's Word in the private sphere, that is, to mediate the Word of God to a fellow believer in personal conversation.[84] A parent who acquaints her child with the gospel, a brother who teaches another the Lord's Prayer, or a peasant who admonishes an ignorant friend concerning the Ten Commandments—these are truly priests.[85] When any Christian speaks to another a word of correction, instruction, or consolation, the priesthood of all believers vis-à-vis the ministry of the Word of God is properly exercised.

Second, the administration of baptism is permitted to all the baptized. According to church law only priests were permitted to baptize. However, Luther's opponents allowed even ordinary women to baptize in emergency situations. According to their logic, he argues, every Christian is then made a priest since every Christian is allowed to baptize. And baptism, being the proclamation of the life-giving Word of God, is the greatest official ministry in the church. Therefore, every believer is given the great honor of visibly and verbally preaching Christ in the church.[86]

The third function of the universal priesthood is the consecration and administration of the Lord's Supper. Luther argues that the words of institution (Luke 22:19; 1 Cor 11:24) were originally spoken to all those present at the Last Supper and to those who in the future would come to the table. It follows, therefore, that what was given there was given to all. Furthermore, in 1 Cor 11:23 ("For I received from the Lord what I also delivered to you . . .") Paul addresses all the Corinthians, making

---

13:65). Cf. *LW* 39:157; *That a Christian Assembly or Congregation Has the Right and Power to Judge All Teaching and to Call, Appoint, and Dismiss Teachers, Established and Proven by Scripture* (1523), *LW* 39:310–11. Some even took the priesthood of believers so far as to exclude the need for training for the ministry. Luther rejects this notion (see *To the Councilmen of All Cities in Germany That They Establish and Maintain Christian Schools* [1524], *LW* 45:343). Luther did make necessity an exception to this hard and fast rule. If there were no official ministers, then anyone, including a woman, might preach to the congregation. The most important thing was the proclamation of the Word (*LW* 39:310; cf. *LW* 36:152).

84. Gerrish, "Priesthood and Ministry," 416–17. Cf. *LW* 40:34.

85. See *The Estate of Marriage* (1522), *LW* 45:46; *LW* 13:333.

86. *LW* 40:23.

each of them consecrators.[87] Finally, Luther concludes that if the two greatest ministries—preaching the Word and baptism—are given to all Christians, it is no great thing that all should be able to administer the Eucharist.[88] If God gives the greater, how much more would he grant the lesser?

Fourth, Luther holds that the power of the keys belongs to all Christians on the basis of Matt 18:15–20, which is spoken not only to the apostles but all believers.[89] Binding and loosing are nothing else than the proclamation and application of the gospel. "For what is it to loose," he asks, "if not to announce the forgiveness of sins before God? What is it to bind, except to withdraw the gospel and to declare the retention of sins?"[90] The word Christ spoke to Peter ("Whatever you loose... shall be loosed") is the power behind every absolution; "indeed every absolution depends upon it."[91] Thus, since the ministry of this and every form of the Word belongs to all, the power to forgive and withhold forgiveness is the prerogative of all.

Fifth, prayer is the common right of all believers. Luther does not make equally clear connections between prayer, the Word of God, and universal priesthood. He simply argues that since the Lord's Prayer is given to all Christians, all may take part in the priestly duty of making intercession for others.[92] Prayer is simply every believer's response to the command, promise, and provision of God.

The sixth function, sacrifice, is a spiritual activity carried out by all believers. The only sacrifice in the NT is a spiritual sacrifice, that is, our bodies, which includes our praise and thanksgiving (Rom 12:1; 1 Pet 2:5). Luther relates the Word of God to this sacrifice in two ways. First, the sacrifice is perfected by the Word, which means that it must be

---

87. Ibid., 24.

88. Ibid., 25.

89. Here Luther embarks on an argument against the false distinction between power and use. His opponents held that it might be true that all believers have the power of the keys, but they asserted that the use was not common to all. Luther objects that Scripture does not make such a distinction and, if it were to be upheld, it would have to apply to Peter as well (Matt 16:19) (ibid., 26–27).

90. The papist priests, on the other hand, bound and loosed on the basis of their own laws. In this way they undermined the gospel and closed the door of heaven to the church (ibid., 28).

91. *LW* 35:13.

92. *LW* 40:30.

offered according to Scripture and as a result of the gospel.[93] Second, he interprets the OT priestly sacrifice as the offering of Christians through the ministry of the Word. That is, the "office of slaughter and sacrifice signifies nothing else than the preaching of the gospel, by which the old man is slain and offered to God, burned and consumed by the fire of love in the Holy Spirit."[94] Sacrifice is putting to death the sinful nature by constant use of the Word of God, and this is something all Christians are permitted, indeed commanded, to do.

Finally, the right to judge doctrine belongs to the whole church, as is firmly established in Scripture by passages that deal with testing false teachers (John 10:5, 27; Matt 7:15; 16:6; 24:4–5; 1 Thess 5:21) and those which affirm that each believer has the Spirit of truth (John 14:26; 1 Cor 2:15; 2 Cor 4:13; 1 John 2:27).[95] The judging of doctrine is a corollary of the teaching ministry.[96] Both activities require knowledge of God's Word and are concerned with its proclamation. In this vein, both seek to edify—the latter by the positive presentation of the gospel, the former by the refutation of destructive teaching. If every Christian as a priest can preach the Word, the same may judge doctrine.[97] "It is the duty of the Christian," Luther exclaims, "to espouse the cause of the faith, to understand and defend it, and to denounce every error."[98] This is part of what it means for believers to live out their priesthood.

The relationship of the priesthood of all believers to the Word of God is a rich and multifaceted one. Far from being an affirmation of an individual's right to read the Bible and form private judgments, it combines the many different expressions of God's Word with an emphasis on ministry to others. Althaus captures the reformer's view well:

> Luther never understands the priesthood of all believers merely in the "Protestant" sense of the Christian's freedom to stand in a direct relationship to God without a human mediator. Rather he constantly emphasizes the Christian's evangelical authority to come before God on behalf of the brethren and also of the world. The universal priesthood expresses not religious individu-

---

93. Ibid., 29.
94. *Preface to the Old Testament* (1545), *LW* 35:248.
95. *LW* 40:32–33; *LW* 39:306–8; *LW* 44:135.
96. *LW* 40:32–33.
97. *LW* 44:135.
98. Ibid., 136.

alism but its exact opposite, the reality of the congregation as a community.[99]

All Christians have access to God's Word in order that they might minister it in its many forms to one another. Luther's linking of the priesthood of believers with the Word of God brings out the NT emphasis on the community—the "one another" aspects of the Christian's calling. As a priest, the baptized person lives for her Christian brother and sister. But the primary way she helps the other is by holding to and proclaiming the manifold Word of God.

Luther, Royal Priesthood, and Readers: Ways Forward

At this final stage, at least two questions should be posed to Luther's proposals. First, does his understanding of the dangers of the Roman priesthood, the priesthood of all believers, and the relationship of universal priesthood to the Word of God accord with the testimony of Scripture? Second, in what ways does he enrich our understanding of the priesthood of all believers, the Word of God, and their interconnectedness? The answers to these questions bring to the fore the contribution Luther makes to reflection on the theological nature of "reading" the Word and thus the central concerns of this study.

Chapter 2 of this project drew attention to a number of theological themes that accompany and help to define royal priesthood in the biblical material, particularly the election, sanctification, and calling of all of God's people. Luther's criticism of the medieval church generally and the priesthood specifically reflected his concern that Rome arrogated to the ordained those very privileges that in Scripture belong to whole church. By positing a *character indelibilis* for the clergy, two *Stände* are created, and the special election, holiness, and dignity of the laity are inevitably diminished. As a result, the laity's sense of calling and vocation as ministers of the gospel is replaced by a sometimes blind dependence on the ordained clergy. Luther saw clearly the connection between the diminution of the priesthood of all believers and the malaise of the church. First, if the ordinary Christian is worldly and has no power over the spiritual estate, the Christian's ability to initiate reform is removed from the outset. Second, although Rome recognized the dignity and calling of the laity on one level, the Word of God in all its forms was taken

---

99. Althaus, *Theology of Martin Luther*, 314.

from their hands and thus the power to bring change rested firmly in the hands of papal priests. Therefore, on the level of status (two estates) as well as calling (the use and proclamation of the Word) Luther rightly argued that the biblical view of priesthood was undermined by that of canon law, leaving the church in a weaker state.

In addition, it bears repeating that Scripture constantly connects priesthood in all its forms with the proclamation and teaching of the Word of God. Thus when Luther brings the two themes together he does it on the basis of a thorough and accurate reading of the Old and New Testaments. He begins with the priesthood of Christ as central, goes on to the main texts dealing with universal priesthood (1 Pet 2:5, 9; Rev 5:10; 20:6), stresses baptism as the entry point into priesthood, and further develops an understanding of the priestly vocation by examining the functions of priests in both testaments. On this last point, he regularly appeals to prophetic texts that condemn Levitical priests for not faithfully teaching torah as evidence that the priesthood is defined by the communication of God's Word. It should be registered, however, that Luther does not make much of the *royal* component of royal priesthood in relation to the Word of God. Nowhere in his discussions of the relation of the priesthood of believers to the Word does he point out that to be a "king" is to be an exemplar of virtuous "reading" practices. This undoubtedly would have strengthened his case against Rome, for he might have argued that to be a Christian is to be both royal and priestly, and thus to have royal access and responsibility to the Word of God—something somewhat denied to the laity. Nevertheless, in the end, Luther demonstrates a keen attentiveness to the biblical material on royal priesthood and more importantly the consequences of following or straying from this scriptural trajectory.

If we grant Luther's fidelity to the biblical testimony regarding priesthood, it is now necessary to ask how his perspectives might enrich our understanding of these issues. I would suggest at least four contributions Luther makes, which will be developed further in the final chapters. First, he is uniquely aware that when the priesthood of all believers is denied the proper use of the Word of God is diminished. Though the manifold Word of God might still be proclaimed by the ordained priesthood, its full effects, including its power to reform the church, are weakened because the laity is not encouraged to handle the Word as priests to one another. What Luther posits is that when the priesthood of believers is rightly understood and appreciated it results in freeing the Word of God to function more fully in the life of the church. Thus, in one sense Luther democratizes access to and ministry of the Word, but not to the exclusion of ordained ministers or to encourage individualism in Scripture reading practices. Rather, he delivers the Word of God to every believer so that each is made responsible for the encouragement, comfort, and discipline of others, and all this for the benefit of the whole church.[100] Luther's appeal to the priesthood of all believers may thus be seen as an affirmation of the centrality of the Word of God in the church's life. When one emphasis declines, the other is soon to follow suit.

Second, Luther's emphasis on the relative importance of oral forms of the Word draws attention to the living character of this Word. He gives prominence to preaching and proclamation because he sees the Word of God as a summons, a call to faith from almighty God. The gospel is presented most appropriately with a living voice; its proper form is oral; it is to be vocalized and heard. The practice of confession and absolution surfaces similar concerns. When forgiveness is pronounced verbally, the hearer is assured of God's promise of mercy as if God spoke the Word himself. What this points to is that believers are to be mouthpieces for the Word of God; they are mediators of an address the living God seeks to make to his people. Their words, when congruent with the written Word, become God's Word of invitation, promise, and discipline. Thus, what Luther unwittingly underlines is the need for sustained reflection on the place of orality in the theological reading of Scripture.

Third, by opening up God's Word to include sacramental forms such as the baptism and the Lord's Supper, he puts these rites in their proper light. Both sacraments are visible and effectual proclamations of the promises of God. Baptism heralds the promise of new life in Christ, while the Eucharist announces the reality of the Lord's death and the promise of forgiven sin. Rooted in the commands and assurances of Jesus, these sacramental events, furthermore, have the power to confer what they promise to those who believe. They are pictorial and tangible words designed to comfort and strengthen the hearts of God's people. Therefore, the sacraments are correctly understood only when seen as

---

100. Eastwood remarks that Luther rightfully places the task of ministry *in* the church and not *above* it. He adds that the Ministry of the Gospel, which is the primary ministry of the church, does not occur "outside the congregation but within it, and in this way the Gospel is mediated through the congregation" (Eastwood, *Priesthood*, 3–4).

ministries and forms of the Word of God. The all-too-Protestant denunciation of ritual may need some revision if Luther's contribution is to be taken seriously. What may become apparent is that fidelity to the Word of God is increased, not diminished, by the employment of visible, symbolic words—at the very least those in their sacramental forms.

Finally, Luther's emphasis on universal priesthood in relation to these oral and sacramental forms of God's Word underscores the ministerial and missionary components of the church's reading practices.[101] Preaching, absolution, baptism, and the Eucharist function to vocalize and symbolize God's words of promise and hope to those outside the church as well. In the case of preaching it is obvious that gospel proclamation is the publication of good news to sinners alienated from God. If one desires to "read" the New Testament most adequately, one must voice its message to those in need of it. Moreover, the enactment of the Lord's Supper is a declaration of the Lord's death for sin and a reminder that he will come again to reign. This visible Word should serve to point unbelievers to the mercy of God demonstrated in Jesus Christ. Similar things may be said of the other forms of the Word. Thus, for Luther, the proper use of the Word of God will always have others in mind. It involves more than just silently reading the Bible. In a real way, it seeks to bring the written Word to life in order that others might truly *hear* God and respond to him as the living Judge and Savior of their souls.

In Luther's vision of priesthood, to be a Christian is to be a priest, and this carries with it various rights and responsibilities. As God's priests in God's house, all believers are called to declare the Word of God in its many forms for the edification of one another and the salvation of the world. Only in this way will the royal priesthood of all believers come into its own and the Word of God be given full and free rein in the church. What Luther provides to this study is a concrete application of the biblical motif of royal priesthood to the reading of Scripture, one that accounts for both the dignity and calling of the epithet. The being and action of readers, or attention to divine initiative and human responsibility in depicting them, are a unity when viewed through the lens of royal priesthood. It is the task of the final chapters to expand on this last point while pulling together the various strands of this study.

---

101. Gounelle in fact concludes that the doctrine of the priesthood of all believers is an affirmation of the mission of the community to the world (Gounelle, "Le sacerdoce universel," 434).

PART THREE

Royal Priesthood and
"Reading" in Covenant Life

7

Divine Dramatics

Royal Priesthood as a Theological Account of the Readers of Scripture

The goal of this study has been to present a construal of the readers of Scripture that is explicitly and thickly rooted in the exegesis of biblical texts and takes seriously two poles within contemporary conversations regarding readers of Scripture—those which privilege divine agency and those that primarily emphasize readerly ethics. I have maintained throughout that the biblical-theological motif of royal priesthood, informed by the related offices of king and priest, brings with it themes that help to frame what it is to be a reader of Scripture before God. These themes serve to correct, corroborate, and complement current proposals in the theological interpretation of Scripture. As a first step towards seeing how this is the case, I will attempt to pull together the many strands of this study and summarize the argument thus far. Once that picture is clear, a synthesized proposal for the depiction of readers of Scripture will be offered in conversation with the proposals of other theorizers.

Chapter 2 sought to offer a brief outline of the theme of royal priesthood, to draw connections between royal priesthood and God's Word, to identify the surrounding theological themes that shape an understanding of royal priesthood and provide a context for construing how one should relate to God's Word. Thus, it provides a preliminary and skeletal portrait of what it means for royal priesthood to function as an important theological and ethical depiction of the readers of Scripture.

Exodus 19, to an extent the programmatic passage in this study, makes explicit the relationship between God's commands and royal priesthood. The pattern of God's relation to Israel as kings and priests formed the pattern of Israel's self-understanding vis-à-vis God's Word. Specifically, the election and sanctification of the people, along with the formation of a covenant, precede any form of ongoing interaction with the words of God. That is, apart from God taking to himself Israel and graciously designating them a royal priesthood, there would be no covenant stipulations for Israel to follow—there would be no "reading" of God's Word. The keeping of God's covenant stipulations is predicated on the existence of a gracious covenant relationship with YHWH. Nevertheless, the people are indeed called to specific forms of interaction with the Word of God. They are to be a holy and obedient people, who by their faithfulness are to mediate the blessing of God to the nations. This understanding of royal priesthood and the Word of God is carried on in Isaiah 59–62, which emphasizes the "reading" function of proclamation, that is, declaring to the nations the ways of the Lord. God's promise of eschatological restoration is at once the pledge of a renewed relationship to his laws and promises, again highlighting the dynamic of God's action and the resultant human response vis-à-vis the Word.

First Peter in many ways reiterates the themes of Exodus 19: the election (1 Pet 1:1; 2:9) and sanctification (1:2) of God's people; requisite holiness (1:15; 2:1, 11) and obedience (1:14); mission to outsiders (2:10, 12); and all of this within the covenant mediated by Jesus Christ (1:2, 19; 2:4, 6–8). For our purposes, the declaration of royal and spiritual priesthood in 2:5 and 2:9 is a statement of both the privilege and responsibility of being God's people. The church is chosen and sanctified by God, but then called to embody and proclaim the words of the One who delivered them. The Book of Revelation stresses that securing present and eschatological kingship and priesthood requires holding to, proclaiming, and obeying the Word of God, even to the detriment of one's life. Hebrews and the other NT passages also draw some connections between universal/royal priesthood and the ministry of the Word of God.

Therefore, "reading" God's Word in light of being a royal priesthood means relating to it as those privileged before God by virtue of gracious divine election and consecration. As a response, these kings and priests are called to demonstrate holiness by obeying God's law and to proclaim this Word to all peoples. This is a cursory sketch of how royal priesthood frames the reader (and reading) of Scripture in theological and ethical terms.

Chapters 3 and 4 sought to provide an expanded account of what "kingly" and "priestly" reading might entail, focusing on the ethical, communal, and ministerial dimensions of the reading of Scripture. The basic premise was that the offices of king and priest in Israel helped to shape the nation's self-understanding of what it means to be a royal priesthood. To be a king and/or priest was to have a particular set of relationships to the Word of God. By examining the kingship law, select OT narratives, and the Psalter, the third chapter described the (ideal) king as the exemplar of the pious torah reader. He was to (and sometimes did) embody the proper attitudes, aims, and responses that made his relationship to torah a model for all Israel to follow. The fourth chapter described priestly work as Word-work and demonstrated this by an exploration of a number of OT passages that legislate, describe, and condemn priestly reading practices. The priests were to be the ideal didactic readers of torah by teaching it, applying it to changing circumstances, wisely judging through its lens, blessing with it, and simply reading it aloud. The chapter aimed to provide a concrete picture of priestly reading activities and to demonstrate that these practices have primarily the interests of the community at heart. The failure to perform them faithfully is to the detriment of God's people. Israel, and eventually the church, as a priesthood, are in many ways to emulate the faithful priestly reading activities as part and parcel of who they are as a people.

In the fifth chapter we encountered Jesus Christ, the fulfillment of the offices of king and priest, as well as of the corporate calling of Israel as a royal priesthood. Though this fulfillment involves many facets, Jesus fulfills these roles largely by the way he relates to the Word of God. As king and Israel-as-royal priesthood, he is the faithful and obedient Son, who even in temptation chooses to keep God's Word. He is thus the ideal *exemplarist* reader of the Word, the embodiment of fidelity to torah. Moreover, the Gospels of Mark, Luke, and John consistently present Jesus as the teaching priest who correctly interprets the law, instructs in cleanness/uncleanness, and reveals God's Word to the people of Israel. This portrait demonstrates that Jesus' priestly work is both "cultic" and "pedagogic." He is thus, also, the ideal *didactic* reader of the Word of God. What this chapter demonstrates is that at the center of God's cosmic work in Jesus lies the all-important relationship between royal priesthood and the reading of Scripture, since even the life and ministry of the Lord as Mediator are oriented around the Word of God.

Finally, as a preliminary step toward synthesizing the biblical material, chapter 6 presented Martin Luther as one who in a concrete historical situation saw many important connections between the priesthood of God's people and the way of the Word of God in the church. Generally speaking, Luther argues that priesthood is the privilege of all believers and that when this is ignored the ability of the Word to reform the church is diminished. The whole church, instead, is responsible for the encouragement, comfort, and discipline of others. Furthermore, by stressing oral and sacramental forms of the Word, Luther underscores that this Word is God's speech and is, therefore, living. Finally, by foregrounding proclamation, he also highlights the "missionary," outward, or others-centered aspects of reading Scripture. Proper reading issues in believers summoning others to come under the reign of God. Hence, Luther's synthesis draws together the two themes of the dignity of the whole people of God and the communal/ecclesial aspects of reading, and thus provides a helpful though underdeveloped account of how "royal priesthood" helps to situate the readers of Scripture theologically.

Divine Drama and Dramatic Action: Readers as a Storied People

Far from providing what Ricoeur called a "de-regionalized" hermeneutics, this study has sought to present a radically "re-regionalized" theological hermeneutics. Webster describes this type of approach:

> The chief task of such a "re-regionalized" theological hermeneutics is not the construction of better theory to *ground* Christian reading of the Bible but the construction of theory which makes sense of that reading by depiction. Its main business, in other words, is making a map of the particular historical, social and spiritual space within which this interpretation occurs . . . Such a depiction of the "space" of Christian reading of the Bible is a matter of making a Christian theological construal of the field of reality within which such reading occurs.[1]

Indeed, the Scriptures do not present a hermeneutical model or theory that automatically renders successful readings of the Bible. Rather, Scripture *depicts* the reading situation, sometimes explicitly and some-

---

1. Webster, "Hermeneutics in Modern Theology," 57–58.

times *en passant*, by poetry, prose, prescriptions, and prohibitions. This project presents a scriptural map of the particular space—the story of Israel, Jesus Christ, and the church—within which reading occurs. More specifically, this map has been constructed by appeal to the motif of royal priesthood and is further furnished by the adjoining theological themes that define it. The "field of reality" within which reading occurs, therefore, is that of the ongoing history of the redemption of God's people. This narrative is determined primarily by divine action in the forms of election and sanctification, at the center of which is Jesus Christ the mediator of the covenant, who as the saving God initiates the new covenant and as the obedient human enacts it faithfully on our behalf. As Webster aptly notes, it is not a story that we write or fill in with whatever activities seem fitting to us. Rather, this history is a "situation within which the Christian reader of the Bible already finds herself."[2] And it is primarily within this field or locality that readers and their acts, as Webster writes, have real depth and meaning.

Reading acts in this scenario are surely then responses to the "entrances and exoduses" of God.[3] However, we do not want to overstate the case for the priority of divine action—something to which Webster sometimes falls prey. For example, he writes: "As Word, God is not absent or mute but present and communicative, not as it were waiting to be made sense of by our cognitive or interpretative activities, but accomplishing in us the knowledge of himself."[4] Indeed, envisaging God as Word points us to his sovereignty, self-communication, and purposefulness, as well as to our dependence on him for knowledge of himself. However, if the Word of God is God's speech to human persons in any meaningful way, then this grace should be conceived as the granting of freedom for appropriate human response. It is not clear that Webster takes seriously enough the reality that this Word is "heard" but not heeded, "read" but not understood. There is too much of a successful "event" character to Webster's depiction of reading and this does not sit well with a reading of the narrative examples provided in this study. For example, the "if you obey me fully and keep my covenant" of Exod 19:5 underscores the reality that God can be truly heard, yet still rejected. Adam disobeyed. Israel disobeyed. Kings and priests disobeyed. Knowledge of

2. Ibid., 63.
3. This phrase is taken from Vanhoozer, *Drama of Doctrine*, 38–41.
4. Webster, "Hermeneutics in Modern Theology," 64.

God is often not accomplished, though the Word was clearly heard. On a related note, elsewhere Webster too strongly states: "Theology should disabuse itself of the assumption that clarity about the nature of biblical interpretation demands nothing more than exquisite discussion of such matters as exegetical technique or readerly virtue."[5] Of course Webster is correct at one level, but, as Briggs rightly notes, the matter need not be presented as either-or: *either* thick description of the divinely initiated space within which interpretation happens, *or* anthropocentric accounts of "readerly virtue."[6] Webster's arguments overstress the passivity of human response in the reading situation: God the Word accomplishes the hearing of the Word; God determines the hermeneutical environment.[7] The shape of that determination must, however, be carefully drawn and not too dramatically presented. To be sure, the primary context of any creaturely act is the grace of God, as is seen in the creation, exodus, Sinai covenant, promise of restoration, the life, death, and resurrection of Jesus Christ, and the redemption of the church. Yet one must take special care when saying that Scripture as an instrument of divine action "determines" the shape of our reading.[8] In response to such claims, Briggs retorts, "It is difficult, to say the least, to reconcile such claims of 'determining' with much of the actual history of the shape of the church's reading of Scripture."[9] Not only the church's reading but also the mass of God's people throughout the Old and New Testaments are witness to this less than absolute determination. Therefore, the message to the reader of Scripture cannot be heard as, "All your active reading is futile," but rather "Strive to hear the Word in a different way." Thus enters the need for the cultivation of habits, practices, and virtues that, in, with, and from God's action, make for faithful reading.

---

5. Webster, "Resurrection and Scripture," 143.

6. See Briggs, *Virtuous Reader*, 167–71, for a critique of heavy-handed hermeneutical proposals about the primacy of divine action in biblical interpretation.

7. As might be evidenced by the use of terms like "consent." He writes: "That history, and within it the mystery of God's self-manifestation, is a history which is essentially twofold: a history of God's acts, acts which in turn evoke, sustain and bring to their final telos human acts; these human acts are truly human precisely in glad consent to the shapely givenness of reality, including their own human reality" (Webster, "Hermeneutics in Modern Theology," 64).

8. See ibid., 76.

9. Briggs, *Virtuous Reader*, 169.

A number of writers in both camps of the conversation about readers agree that the story, history, or drama of redemption is that which unifies dogma and ethics, theology and practice. Lest *I* overstate the case, it must be said that Webster himself is not unaware of this ethical pole. He writes:

> As a participant in this historical process, the reader is *spoken to* in the text. This speaking, and the hearing which it promotes, occurs as part of the drama which encloses human life in its totality, including human acts of reading and understanding: the drama of sin and its overcoming. Reading the Bible is an event in this history. It is, therefore, moral and spiritual and not merely cognitive or representational activity. Readers *read,* of course: figure things out as best they can, construe the text and its genre, try to discern its intentions, whether professed or implied, place it historically and culturally—all this also happens when the Bible is read. But as this happens, there happens the history of salvation; each reading-act is also bound up within the dynamic of idolatry, repentance and resolute turning from sin which takes place when God's Word addresses humanity. And it is this dynamic which is definitive of the Christian reader of the Bible. ... Reading Scripture is therefore a microcosm of the history of judgment and salvation, a point at which that history is realized in the process of God's communication.[10]

God's speaking through the text of Scripture is an episode in the history of redemption. Therefore, the reader of Scripture is caught up in that very history. Not only so, but if, as Vanhoozer and others argue, Scripture is itself one act of God in the drama of redemption, reading cannot but be an act in that history.[11] But this history is not just any history; it is the story of the presence and conquering of sin. Thus reading takes on an ethical and spiritual character. Yet, because reading occurs within the history of sin and its overcoming, the type of ethics and spirituality involved is made more particular. Webster indeed points us in the direction this project has desired to follow regarding the ethics of reading. By going to significant lengths to follow Scripture's prescriptions for and descriptions of faithful reading, as well as to provide examples of

---

10. Webster, "Hermeneutics in Modern Theology," 77–79. "Faithful reading of Holy Scripture in the economy of grace is an episode in the history of sin and its overcoming" (idem, *Holy Scripture,* 87).

11. On Scripture being a part of the history of salvation, see Vanhoozer, *Drama of Doctrine,* 48, 70, and Work, *Living and Active.*

the reading practices of particular kings (chapter 3), priests (chapter 4), and Jesus Christ (chapter 5), this study describes with some particularity those attributes of the reader that are *actually* commended or condemned within this history of salvation. Reading Scripture faithfully is part of what it means to participate fittingly in the drama of redemption. When we speak of ethics, virtues, practices, etc., we are trying to define more clearly what it means to be "fitting."

Moberly, in his attempt to integrate concerns for divine initiative and human response, moves us further along in our inquiry by speaking thus of reading:

> Consequent widespread assumptions about the "irrelevance" of the Bible (as "mere" history or ideology), with corresponding (and sometimes misplaced) attempts on the part of believers to demonstrate its "relevance," may be in some senses beside the point, which is rather what it means, and what is necessary, to "learn the language" or "inhabit the story" or "discern the mystery." It may be less a matter of doing different things or trying to acquire different kinds of experiences than it is to re-envision, re-interpret, re-contextualize, and re-live that life which is already under way; though the changes that this involves ("repentance") will never be straightforward, and it is only by attending to the content of scripture, and living accordingly ("faith"), that we may begin to find out what is involved.[12]

What is common and commendable in proposals from both poles is the call to "inhabit the story" in which we find ourselves. Hart speaks of it as an overlapping of stories, of Scripture's story becoming part of our own; Jones, as the development of a scriptural imagination.[13] Readers are depicted both theologically and ethically when their acts are seen as a re-living and re-contextualization of "that life which is already under way" (to follow Moberly) or as responsible performances in the divine drama (to follow Vanhoozer). Fitting performance in this drama requires specific practices and dispositions, such as faith and repentance. In that light, the kingship law, for example, must not be seen merely as political legislation, but as that which prescribes the future king's fitting participation in the unfolding drama of the salvation of Israel. As a responsible agent in this particular history, the king is to demonstrate reverence

---

12. Moberly, *Bible, Theology, and Faith*, 242.
13. Hart, "Tradition," 203; Jones, "Formed and Transformed," 21.

for God, submission to the divine will, and trust in divine provision. These are the "virtues" that precede and result from his reading of torah. Further along the historical timeline we encounter Josiah and Jehoiakim as examples or counter-examples of the ideal kingly reader of torah. The narrator implicitly and explicitly commends the virtues they do or do not display. But again, the nature of their virtues is circumscribed by the particular meta-narrative and smaller narratives within which they are embedded. Not only does the divinely initiated drama call for certain types of virtues, but these are in fact part of the story itself; indeed in one sense they move the story along. Put differently, readerly virtue is not just shaped or determined by the story, it *is a major part of the plot*—that of the victory of or over sin. Even the primal couple's lack of obedience to the divine command, for example, is the beginning of this multi-millennial dark history of humanity. By doubting the Word of God, they launched their descendants into the drama of creation, *fall*, and therefore redemption. Jehoiakim's blatant irreverence for the Word of YHWH only expedited the judgment coming on Judah. Jesus Christ's obedience as the Son and faithful performance of the Scriptures undo the work of our first parents. The divine drama calls for certain "reading" responses that drive the drama along.

On one level, this study may seem to be simply a presentation of the history of Israel as a royal priesthood of readers. It highlights what it means for God's people to interact faithfully with his Word in light of the dignity and responsibility bestowed upon them by YHWH. On another level, though, this study is concerned to depict readers of Scripture and their situation as governed by specific forms of both divine initiative and human response, and to do so by the use of biblical categories. The prior acts of the drama—Israel's designation as a royal priesthood, its unfolding throughout her history, and its fulfillment in Christ—give rise to and shape these categories, which themselves inform our present, and hopefully consistent, performance of Scripture as those involved in the last act of redemption's drama.[14] These final chapters, therefore, will highlight five themes that emerge from the foregoing biblical and historical survey of royal priesthood: election, sanctification, covenant, virtues and holiness, and ministry and mission. These themes underscore both the divine and human dimensions of the designation "royal priesthood"

14. This dramatic imagery is taken from Wright, "How Can the Bible Be Authoritative?," 7–32.

respectively, spelled out with the kind of specificity called for by the biblical narrative. Each of the following sections will draw out the themes as they appeared in the previous chapters, develop them, and suggest how they might aid in shaping an account of the readers of Scripture.

Readers by Grace Alone: Royal Priesthood as Divine Action

Few within this hermeneutical conversation would argue against the centrality of the prevenience of God's grace in the unfolding of history of salvation, and thus in giving an account of the readers of Scripture. Disagreements concern how one construes the interplay between divine and human agency in Bible reading: are they in a competitive, complementary, concurrent, and/or consequential relationship? Depending on the specific form of divine action, one could conceive the relationship in one or another of these ways. For example, if one is speaking of the generation of the Scriptures with which the reader interacts, the notions of consequence and concursus both come into play: God's speaking and acting in revelatory history are the beginning of the Scriptures, whose production then becomes a divine and human work. However, if one seeks to depict who are the proper readers of Scripture, it becomes necessary to speak of the reader as a consequence of prior divine acts, such as creation or election. Thus it seems preferable to follow generally a schema similar to Bowald's "divine rhetorical hermeneutics," in which divine agency is the ubiquitous *ethos* within which all readerly acts occur.[15] That being said, it must be asked what *specific* modes of divine agency should be highlighted—something not often developed in current proposals, including Bowald's. However, when he asserts, "Therefore the determinative *ethos* of the theological interpretation of the Bible is the divine *ethos*. It encompasses and precedes all human agencies that were elected and caught up in its salvific and sanctifying wake," he points us to two of the clearest prevenient acts of God in our account: election and sanctification.[16] Where these themes surfaced in our survey of royal priesthood and how they might shape an account of the reader are the focus of what follows.

---

15. See Bowald, *Rendering the Word*, esp. 174–79.
16. Ibid., 178.

Chosen Unto...? Election and the Reading Community

The LORD your God has chosen you out of all the peoples on earth to be his people, his treasured possession. It was not because you were more numerous than any other people that the LORD set his heart on you and chose you—for you were the fewest of all peoples... (Deut 7:6b–7).

God's action of selecting a community for himself from among created peoples—election—is the first theme framing the readers of Scripture. At least three aspects are central in a consideration of election in the biblical material: the primacy of divine initiative, the privilege bestowed by this divine act, and the consequent responsibilities enjoined upon the recipient(s). The election of Israel, as presented in Exod 19:3–6, strongly emphasizes God's initiative in rescuing Israel from Egypt and bringing them to himself to be his "treasured possession" and "royal priesthood." In verse 4, the eagle imagery points to the privilege of election, while the three "I" statements underscore divine priority in the salvation of Israel. The *telos* of their election is to worship, have fellowship with, and mediate for YHWH. If the conditional clause in 19:5a–6a is construed the way outlined in chapter 2, then the apodosis is a proclamation of the LORD's favor and Israel's election, and the protasis—obedience and faithfulness to the covenant stipulations—would be understood as a consequence of the election of the people. Thus, divine action in the form of election precedes the "reading" of the law in this most foundational episode in the history of Israel.

Election also proves to be critical to our understanding of kingship and priesthood in Israel. The *sine qua non* of both kings and priests, as alluded to earlier, was to be chosen by God. These particular elections, furthermore, help to elucidate the dignity, privilege, and responsibility entailed in Israel's election. The kingship law, for example, makes it explicit that the choice of YHWH precedes the torah-piety of the king. Yet by obeying, meditating on, writing, and reading torah the king fulfills the purpose of his election. By loving the Word of the Lord, Israel does likewise.

The New Testament focuses the theme of election on Jesus Christ and consequently the church. Implicit in the Gospels' depictions of Jesus as King, Priest, and Israel-as-royal priesthood is the presentation of Christ as the elect One *par excellence*. First Peter 2 then states the matter plainly, referring to Jesus as the elect Stone who is precious to God (2:4b,

6a). This elect One fulfills his offices largely through his proper orientation to and use of the Word of God. Included in the election of Christ, moreover, is the election of a community that bears his name (2:5a). This community, formed entirely by the gracious initiative of God, is given the dignity of being kings and priests to God presently (2:9a) and in the eschaton (Rev 5:10; 20:6), but is also given the vocation formerly ascribed solely to Israel: to offer spiritual sacrifices (1 Pet 2:5c) and declare the mighty acts of God (2:9b). Indeed, all the epithets of 1 Pet 2:9 draw attention to the elect status of God's people, and this prior to the mention of, and thus grounding, their vocation vis-à-vis the Word of God.[17]

The story of God's people as a royal priesthood is the story of their election, especially when conceived as God's intention and action to take to himself a particular people from among other peoples to accomplish his universal purposes. It is these that God calls into a specific relationship with his Word. In what follows, we will explore some ways in which the doctrine of election might be made serviceable to a discussion of one's proper orientation to God's Word. Along the way we will place our account in conversation with aspects of Barth's dogmatic treatment, in the hope that the latter will help elucidate what has emerged from the biblical material.

Election to Dignity

The election of God's people to royal priesthood is an act of free divine favor, which carries with it privilege and honor, but also deep responsibility. A treatment of election vis-à-vis readers of Scripture, if it is to remain within scriptural contours, must account for this dual aspect. There are at least five ways in which our theology of election helps to fill out a depiction of the readers of Scripture.

First, election points to the freedom of grace and thus should foster a deep sense of humility before God and his Word. A notable feature of many ethical accounts of the reader, particularly those that accent humility as a prime interpretive virtue, is that fuller accounts are not given

---

17. One could argue that Luther's crusade was to restore the dignity and privilege of election to all Christians. Although he does not employ the word "election" in his discussions of the priesthood of all believers, his rejection of the notion of two *Stände* is rooted in his view that the Roman priesthood went awry by presuming to be *the* chosen heritage of God. However, the closely related theme of sanctification probably lies closer to Luther's concerns.

as to *why* humility should characterize readers or from whence cometh humility—or at best the accounts given are only one-sided. Jones, for example, simply lists it among other interpretive virtues.[18] Fowl indirectly provides a fuller account when he describes the recognition that one is a sinner as essential to non-distorted, faithful readings of Scripture.[19] Surely the recognition of one's fallenness is an important source of humility, but it represents only one side of the coin. The inward turn—the move toward honest self-examination—must be a response to a look outward—to the electing God. Vanhoozer gestures in this direction, appealing to the Creator-creature distinction, humanity's dependence on God, and eschatology to ground humility in the reader's finitude and fallibility. He accordingly defines hermeneutical humility as "the virtue that constantly reminds interpreters that we can get it *wrong*."[20] As important as human fallenness, finitude, and fallibility are for fostering humility, our reading of Exod 19:4–6, for example, suggests the significance of election to an account of hermeneutical humility. Readers bring nothing to God rendering them worthy of handling the Word. Speaking of election's ability to humble, Barth writes:

> In His grace God is the One who unconditionally precedes the creature. Man with his decision can only follow. He cannot forestall God with any claim, or condition, or ground of action. But this fact carries within itself the final and severest humiliation of the creature. If it is really the case, then over against God the creature cannot produce or proclaim any inherent dignity, anything that is good within itself.[21]

In this light, readers are made worthy by a free act of grace and are, therefore, "passively" drawn into the society of readers within the economy of salvation.

Yet, second, election also points to the privilege of being those especially loved by God. "Although the whole earth is mine," says the Lord, "you will be for me a kingdom of priests . . ." (Exod 19:5b–6a). Election indeed places human limitations in stark contrast to the reality of the grace of God. At the same time, however, this humbling of humanity is not to be mistaken for its negation. Rather, as Barth observes, "The

---

18. Jones, "Formed and Transformed," 32.
19. Fowl, *Engaging Scripture*, 78–83.
20. Vanhoozer, *Is There a Meaning*, 464.
21. Barth, *CD* II/2, 27–28.

sovereignty of God is thus confirmed by the freedom of the election of grace, and that means for the creature not simply humiliation, but the humiliation which is really and in the same moment exaltation."[22] God in his freedom chooses to love. Human humbling is for the purpose of exaltation, salvation, and life. Election is the simultaneous humiliation and elevation, the lowering and raising, of humankind. It reveals the prior unfeasibility of the relationship humans share with God, while granting the greatest privilege imaginable. And if one allows that election is at heart the primal decision of God to be for us in Jesus Christ, then, since it is located in the doctrine of God, the force of the emphasis on election as gospel is great—even stronger than in traditional accounts. What this means for readers of Scripture is that the environment in which they find themselves is an overwhelmingly positive one, rooted in the eternal love of God. In this ethos the reading of Scripture is seen as a gift. Moses reminded Israel of this when they stood poised to enter the Promised Land: "What other nation is so great as to have their gods near them the way the Lord our God is near us whenever we pray to him? And what other nation is so great as to have such righteous decrees and laws as this body of laws I am setting before you today?" (Deut 4:7–8 NIV). There is potential here to temper concepts such as the Word "slaying and making alive" (Webster) and reading the Scriptures "over-against" oneself (Fowl and Jones) among divergent hermeneutical proposals.[23] As necessary as are these calls to note the seemingly adversarial character of Scripture, an equal emphasis needs to be placed on the opportunity of its reading as a gift. Election reminds us that not only does the entire economy of salvation proceed from grace, but specific acts within this economy are of grace as well. More to the point, when by God's grace Israel and the church are summoned to be a royal priesthood, they are called to be so *as readers*, which is part and parcel of the privilege bestowed.

Third, as we have seen, the primary referent of God's election and bestowal of royal priesthood is the community—Israel and the church.

---

22. Ibid., 29.

23. Webster writes: "Reading Holy Scripture is 'faithful' reading: exegetical reason caught up in faith's abandonment of itself to the power of the divine Word to slay and to make alive. 'Faithful reading' takes place in the economy of grace" (Webster, *Holy Scripture*, 86). Fowl and Jones adopt this term from Bonhoeffer, who used it to speak of reading Scripture in such a way that it challenges our presuppositions and practices. This way of reading the Bible is contrasted to reading it *for* us, that is, in a way that merely confirms our lifestyles (see Fowl and Jones, *Reading in Communion*, 135–64).

What is also distinctive about Barth's account is this focus on the election of the community as the living presentation of God's acts of judgment and mercy in Jesus Christ.[24] Although the next chapter addresses the ecclesial aspects of reading more fully, it should at least be mentioned here that such a prioritization of the election of the community is a dogmatic ground for the communal emphasis in many proposals in the theological interpretation of Scripture. For example, Fowl writes: "The vast majority of purposes for which Christians engage scripture both presuppose and work to establish and maintain particular sorts of communities."[25] The sinful and redeemed community that is presupposed, established, and maintained, exists on the basis of God's election. Reading in communion calls for an explicit acknowledgement of the primal source of that communion.

Election to Calling

The emphasis on the community leads to a fourth contribution emerging from the biblical material and expressed ably by Barth: election and calling are inseparable. To be elect in Jesus Christ is to be elect *to* something; the election of the community has a *telos*. Barth's account of election has a remarkably historical character, focusing on the community's (and individual's) response to their election—will they be obedient to their election by proclaiming the judgment and salvation of God or not? Election is not meant merely to foster a preoccupation with individual destinies (as important as they are), but to form the obedient human response of ministry within the community and mission without. The task of the church, as the perfect form of the community, for instance, is to proclaim the meaning of the death of Jesus Christ—to declare the mercy and good will of God, which are directed toward the establishment of fellowship with human beings. The church is "the bearer of God's positive message to the world in which the negative is—necessarily, but still only subordinately—included."[26] This assertion is essentially an affirmation of 1 Pet 2:9: "But you are a chosen race, a royal priesthood . . . that you may proclaim the excellencies of him who called you out of darkness into his marvelous light." To be a reading community in this arrange-

24. Barth, *CD* II/2, 205–6.
25. Fowl, *Engaging Scripture*, 6 (italics added).
26. Barth, *CD* II/2, 210–11.

ment involves viewing election as an imperative to bring the Word of God to bear on the community and the world, that is, to remind them of the judgment and mercy of God, the necessity to receive the Word by faith, and the glory that awaits them in the resurrection. More will be said about these particular "reading" practices in subsequent sections.

Finally, when Barth speaks of the election of the individual, he highlights that the individual is called to the same tasks as the community. However, he underlines one aspect not developed in the section regarding the community: that the individual is elected to be conformed to Christ.[27] Put differently, election is the context for holiness, which (as will be developed later) is often seen as obedience to the Word of God. The very people whom 1 Peter declares a chosen people and royal priesthood are subsequently commanded to embody the Word by abstaining from evil desires and living holy lives (cf. 1 Pet 2:9–17). Calvin also affirms this connection, arguing on the basis of Eph 1:4–5 that since election occurs before the creation of the earth it cannot be based on any merits. Rather, election precedes and empowers holiness, not vice versa.[28] Instead of short-circuiting obedience and holiness, election, having the "pursuit of good" as its "appointed goal," fuels well-doing.[29] Therefore, in light of election, the individual Bible reader understands his proper end: obedience, holiness, conformity to Jesus Christ.

In the end, the doctrine of election, as Colin Gunton explains, "should serve the cause of a due ecclesial self-confidence, one based not in individual assurance of future salvation, though that may be an integral part of it, but in a call to ecclesial faithfulness."[30] While election, as we have seen, should foster a due sense of privilege and honor before God, it is also a call to faithfulness. Gunton adds: "The proper interest served by the doctrine of election concerns not the numbers, but the *purpose* of the election of such quantities as there are."[31] Thus the community is faithful inasmuch as it tends toward the ultimate end of its election—the supremacy of Christ in the church and world (Eph 1:10; Col 1:17–18). Hence there is what Hendrikus Berkhof calls the

---

27. Ibid., 410–11.
28. Calvin, *Institutes* III.22.2, 934.
29. Ibid., III.23.12, 960–61.
30. Gunton, "Election and Ecclesiology," 139–55 (140).
31. Ibid., 146 (italics added).

"exceptional advantage" and "exceptional burden" intrinsic to election.[32] Reading Scripture in this situation takes on grander dimensions than simple devotional aims. To be a reader in light of election is to accept the favor bestowed as well as the mandate, which, according to Berkhof, is "to live from the love of this sovereign God in all areas of life," including reading Scripture.[33] It is to practice, perform, and proclaim the Word for the sake of the cosmos. In so doing, readers find themselves situated within and participating in the drama of the triune God's reconciliation of all things to himself.

A Holy Priesthood: Sanctification and the Readers of Scripture

For you are a people holy to the LORD your God . . . (Deut 7:6a).

When it comes to describing divine action in the cause of redemption, the notion of election logically comes to mind as the prototypical work of divine initiative, at least to many. That salvation is accomplished, at its very roots, by the will and action of God is essentially what election declares. However, corresponding to election, indeed having much conceptual and teleological overlap, is the biblical concept of sanctification. First Peter 1:1–2 places the two concepts together: "To God's elect, strangers in the world . . . who have been chosen according to the foreknowledge of God the Father, through the sanctifying work of the Spirit, for obedience to Jesus Christ and sprinkling by his blood." The emphasis here is on the initiatory action of God on behalf of his people. Logically, it is election that precedes and grounds this work of sanctification done by the Spirit, as Webster writes tersely: "Only God is properly holy; only God may elect the Church; only an elect Church is sanctified. The Church's holiness is thus grounded in the election of God the Father."[34] Logical order aside, God is the subject of both works; they are operations of divine grace, yet particular operations. In the last section we explored how the concept of election might function to situate rightly readers of Scripture. The question we face in this section is how sanctification, as another distinct aspect of divine initiative, helps to shape an account of readers. To get at an answer, this section will, first, isolate the relation-

---

32. Berkhof, *Christian Faith*, 249.
33. Ibid.
34. Webster, *Holiness*, 60.

ship between sanctification and the reader as articulated in various portions of previous chapters. In the process, sanctification will be defined more precisely, before expanding on its place in depicting readers.

Set Apart by the Triune God

The programmatic pattern for the sanctification of God's people is found in Exod 19:1–6, wherein the action of God to take for himself a people is emphasized. David Peterson writes: "For Israel, holiness was to be found in a relationship with the Holy One. The Lord himself sanctified Israel, *by* rescuing his people from Egypt, bringing them to himself at Mount Sinai, and giving them his law."[35] In fact, all three terms used to designate Israel ("treasured possession," "royal priesthood," and "holy nation"; Exod 19:5–6) refer to her holiness or separation from the nations.[36] Sanctification, then, is primarily by God's initiative. However, after God sanctifies the people by taking them to himself, he commands Moses to consecrate the people (19:14), and the priests (as representatives of the people) to consecrate themselves (19:22), so that there would be physical and ceremonial reminders of their holy status. Finally, the people are told that if they keep his covenant stipulations—ritual, legal, and moral—they would remain his royal priesthood and holy nation (19:5–6). By obeying God's law, the people would remain holy by not profaning the holy name of YHWH before the nations, but rather demonstrating the greatness of God. Peterson sums up this OT pattern of sanctification well: "The common element [in the OT] is an awareness of God's initiative in making himself known as the Holy One, taking possession of Israel as his own, and requiring his people to live in the light of his self-revelation in their midst."[37] Thus the rest of Exodus, along with Leviticus, Numbers, and Deuteronomy, might be seen as the legislation of the holiness that Israel already possessed objectively. More than election, sanctification, as a work of divine initiative, has a particularly intrinsic connection to active holiness. It is as those who have already been made holy that Israel is to maintain and foster holiness through obedience to the law of YHWH.

---

35. Peterson, *Possessed by God*, 19 (emphasis added).
36. Ibid., 19–20.
37. Ibid., 22.

This perspective on sanctification is carried into the NT but given a Christocentric cast. Here the ground of believers' sanctification is the blood of Christ.[38] A number of NT passages draw the connection between the work of Christ and the sanctification of the church. John 17:19, for example, speaks of Jesus' self-sanctification for the sake of his disciples' sanctification. The self-sanctification of which Jesus speaks is his death for sin. The means by which the disciples will be set apart is the "truth" or Word of God (17:17, 19), which at its root is a declaration of the good news concerning Jesus. The purpose for which the disciples are sanctified is summarized well by Peterson: "The goal of separation from the world, and from Satan as its ruler, is that disciples might actually be *sent into the world*, just as the Son was sanctified and sent by the Father (10:36), to bring the blessing of eternal life to the world (17:18). . . . Mission is clearly the goal of sanctification in John 17."[39] By this last point, the Gospel of John essentially echoes 1 Peter. As we saw earlier, it is those who are "sanctified by the Spirit" (1 Pet 1:2) who are later declared a royal priesthood, whose purpose is to declare the mighty acts of God (2:9). Another purpose for which the church is sanctified is that it would become spotless at the eschaton (Eph 5:25–27). In that light, the church is called to live in particular God-honoring ways, such as speaking the truth in love (4:15) and obeying the commandments of God (6:2). Here, as in the OT, sanctification is tied to holy living, but also public "reading" of the Word. Thus, in the NT, believers are given the "reading" tasks of obedience and proclamation by virtue of the sanctification wrought by Christ.

The sanctification of the entire people of God also lies at the heart of Luther's revolt against the Roman papacy. As a result of post-Cyprianic innovations regarding priesthood, what was common to all believers (according to the OT and NT) was relegated to the official clergy. However, it was not ordination and its *character indelibilis* that consecrated believers as a holy priesthood, but a common faith and baptism.[40] The ultimate consequence of this de-democratizing of sanctification was that the ministry of the Word of God became the calling of only a few, thus lessening the potential for this Word to reform the church and present it spotless before Christ.

38. Also see Heb 10:10 and 1 Cor 1:2.
39. Ibid., 30.
40. See, e.g., *LW* 44:127.

Sanctification, according to K. Bockmuehl, "is, in the first place, a work of God, more specifically of the Holy Spirit, both as a one-time act, valid for all time, imputing and imparting holiness, and as an ongoing progressive work."[41] God is the primary subject of sanctification, both by initially taking his people to himself and by empowering holiness on an ongoing basis. Thus, we might agree with Webster: "The Church is holy because God is holy. And therefore the *sanctitas ecclesiae* is at heart *sanctitas passiva*, a matter of faith's trustful reliance upon and reference to the work of the triune God."[42] With this divine act the church acquires a decisively new orientation within the economy of salvation. Those sanctified are called to live holy lives, thus demonstrating the holiness of God.

Set Apart for the Word

A noteworthy feature among theologians who desire to emphasize divine action in depicting the reader is that they rarely specify what type(s) of divine agency are important or what these forms of divine action do to/in/for the reader of Scripture. For example, Webster relates "sanctification" to reading generally when he writes: "Sanctification can more readily be applied to the full range of processes in which the text is caught up from pre-textual tradition to interpretation."[43] Sanctification, according to Webster, is the work of the Spirit through which creaturely realities are taken up by God for use in the economy of salvation.[44] In this light, the readers of Scripture, as part of the "post-history" of the text, are among those realities sanctified by God.[45] What sanctification means for the reader of Scripture is not, however, specified. While Bowald rightly calls into question proposals that either ignore divine agency altogether or give minimalist accounts of the role of divine action in relating the reader to the text, he does not provide much by way of specifics in his positive proposal.[46] He develops a notion of God's speech or "divine

---

41. Bockmuehl, "Sanctification," 615.
42. Webster, *Holiness*, 58.
43. Webster, *Holy Scripture*, 26.
44. Ibid.
45. Ibid., 30.
46. For his critique of functionalist proposals like Kelsey, Frei, and Fowl, see Bowald, *Rendering the Word*, 93–94.

rhetoric" and makes brief mention of election and sanctification, but does not present an account of how these latter forms of divine agency shape reading or the reader.[47] Our examination of the biblical material directs us to specify the forms of divine action that help describe the reader and to provide an account of how this might be so.

Moreover, sanctification puts theological meat on the bones of accounts that center on reading's ecclesial location and the virtues of readers. For example, Fowl and Jones advocate a form of active separation from the world in order to foster Christian communities, identifying baptism as the ritual act that signifies the move from "friendship" with the world to "friendship" with God through participation in his end-time community.[48] They write: "In and through our participation in Christian communities—called into being and sustained by the Triune God and marked as the Body of Christ—we are enabled to engage in the process of unlearning the ways of the 'world' and learning how to pattern our lives in Jesus Christ."[49] Something akin to what we have said thus far can be discerned in this quotation, as being "marked as the Body" and sustained might be what we have called sanctification. God's action of sanctifying and marking out of a people for himself sets them on a trajectory toward patterning their lives after Jesus Christ. The basic point is this: an appeal to objective sanctification can directly and intrinsically ground virtue- and ethics-oriented proposals in hermeneutics by following Scripture in linking character growth, more precisely progressive holiness, to being set apart by and for God.

There are at least two further ways in which sanctification, as I have deployed the term thus far, may be useful in depicting readers.[50] First, since God has made us holy by bringing us into a special relationship with himself we are destined to serve him and please him eternally. However, our failures to live up to our sanctification do not undo the definitive sanctifying work Christ has accomplished on our behalf. Those broken by temptation and sin can rest in the fact that they are incorporated into the holy people of God and will continue to receive God's enabling help as they press toward their eschatological end. Herman Bavinck writes:

47. See ibid., 174–83.
48. Fowl and Jones, *Reading in Communion*, 70–71.
49. Ibid., 71.
50. In the following, I am adapting some of Peterson's practical implications (see Peterson, *Possessed by God*, 47–49).

"For [sanctification] consists in the reality that in Christ God grants us, along with righteousness, also complete holiness, and does not just impute it but also inwardly imparts it by the regenerating and renewing working of the Holy Spirit until we have been fully conformed to the image of his Son."[51] Our renewal rests in the hands of the sanctifying Spirit through the work of Christ. A regular look to our sanctification can be a necessary stage in the development of people and communities of character who will embody the Scriptures, as Fowl suggests.[52] Indeed, the recognition that one is a sinner is a first step toward remaining/becoming single-mindedly focused on Christ. However, the process toward repentance, reconciliation, and virtue formation can often become derailed by despair and frustration because of our sins. Remembering that God has sanctified and will continue to sanctify us, and that we are not permanent residents in the realm of the profane, therefore, may provide the hope and impetus to overcome sinful tendencies: "How can we who died to sin go on living in it" (Rom 6:2)?

Second, and related, an emphasis on definitive sanctification has payoff in the communal sphere. Fowl describes the church as ideally the place where forgiveness and reconciliation are practiced. However, the church is often the place where those who recognize themselves as sinners are least welcome. New converts, for example, are sometimes rejected because they have not fully overcome their past sins or simply do not fit into local church culture. As a result, conditions are imposed upon them that serve as proof that they are truly converted. But as Peterson warns, this behavior is a distortion of the gospel of Jesus.[53] We confess one *holy* and *catholic* church: we are church founded on difference—we are catholic—whose members, in their difference, experience equally the sanctifying grace of the Spirit—we are holy. As much as Gentiles are now recipients of this gift along with Jews, so those formerly and presently perceived as unacceptable and profane now take rightful residence in the realm of the holy through Christ. When we recognize all Christians as those sanctified in Jesus Christ and trust that the final form of their sanctification is in the Spirit's hands, we will better embody those practices (forgiveness, friendship, etc.) that enable the church to perform the Scriptures faithfully. Charity practiced concretely and continually in the

---

51. Bavinck, *Reformed Dogmatics*, 4:248.
52. See Fowl, *Engaging Scripture*, esp. 75–91.
53. Peterson, *Possessed by God*, 49.

form of patient (though not entirely uncritical or unconditional) acceptance forms charitable readers. When we practice friendship with the newly converted "profane," we embody the ways of Scripture's Author who befriended Abraham, Moses, the disciples, and many others in order to bless them with ultimate goods. In the end, communal-ethical proposals are weakened when they fail to emphasize specific forms of prevenient divine action, such as sanctification. Though this consideration of the character-forming potential of objective sanctification by no means counters a proposal like Fowl's, it certainly supplements it.

Sanctification, understood as a mode of divine action, contributes to a theological depiction of the readers of Scripture. Like election, it helps to put human responsibility in proper perspective, namely, as a response to divine initiative. For example, sanctification intrinsically grounds and energizes any progress in holiness. For readers, this means that the character that precedes and proceeds from faithful Bible reading is rooted in God's work of setting them apart for his purposes. Coupled together, election and sanctification, therefore, root readers and their situation in the prior and ongoing action of God. However, talk of these modes of divine action, as we have seen, must in the same breath speak of an important end towards which they are directed, namely, the establishment of a covenant. But to speak of the covenant is at once to speak of the mediator of God's covenant with humanity—Jesus Christ. In the next section we will explore how Jesus as *the* covenant mediator informs our depiction of the ideal readers of Scripture.

Royal Priesthood and Covenantal Reading: Jesus Christ as Hermeneutical Mediator

Know therefore that the LORD your God is God, the faithful God who maintains covenant loyalty with those who love him and keep his commandments, to a thousand generations, and who repays in their own person those who reject him. He does not delay but repays in their own person those who reject him (Deut 7:9–10).

The notion of covenant is unavoidable in a discussion of Bible reading and readers, since Scripture as a form of divine speech is directed toward human subjects who are called to respond to it appropriately. Indeed, we saw in chapter 2 that the covenant is the very meeting point of divine initiative and human response, particularly as these intersect with "reading" the words of God: "I bore you on eagles' wings and brought you to myself. Now . . . obey my voice and keep my covenant . . ." (Exod 19:4–5). Reading rightly requires an acknowledgement of covenantal grace—divine grace that enables and calls forth an appropriate response. This notion of divinely initiated reciprocity that is intrinsic to covenants has consequently been deployed occasionally to depict the hermeneutical situation. However, surprisingly few authors have developed this connection significantly. This section, therefore, explores how "covenant," and more importantly, the Christocentric character of God's new covenant with humanity might inform descriptions of the readers of Scripture. First, the general hermeneutical use of covenant in Vanhoozer's work will be examined, as it represents the only extensive use of the concept in recent hermeneutical proposals (of which I am aware) and complements what will be said in the latter part of this section.[54] Second, since Christ is both the embodiment of the covenant—as initiating God and responsive humanity—and the fulfillment and mediator of the covenant—as obedient King, faithful Israel, and teaching Priest—it is argued that reading in light of God's covenant is to read in light of Christ.[55] Extending the conclusions of chapter 5, Jesus fulfills and mediates the covenant *by* his relationship to the Word of God. He is, moreover, both the primary subject matter of Scripture and the standard for proper reading practices. We are, therefore, formed into covenantally faithful readers of Scripture as we participate in and imitate Jesus Christ, the Mediator of the covenant.

---

54. Some, like Billings, also speak of reading as a covenantal act: "We read as those who are united to God in covenant through the person and work of Christ. Our covenantal union with God means that we read Scripture in fellowship with God, but also with covenant obligations toward God . . . Reading Scripture as those who are in Christ, we see how Scripture sets forth a playbook for how to be a covenant people." However, he borrows from Vanhoozer on this matter (Billings, *Word of God for the People of God*, 205–6).

55. It might be worth noting that Webster prefers to locate the church's "reading" acts within Christ's prophetic office (see, e.g., Webster, "Dogmatic Location of the Canon," 9–46 [35–36]). In doing so, he follows a traditional Reformed line: the exalted Christ proclaims himself—the *prophetica evangelica*—through the church in the power of the Holy Spirit. As we have seen, however, the priestly and kingly offices are Word-oriented ministries of the Son in his state of humiliation that should also, in part, shape the church's understanding of its reading of Scripture.

Discourse as Divine: The Hermeneutical Use of "Covenant"

The biblical concept of covenant is full of potential for projects that seek to rehabilitate the readers of Scripture. Accordingly, Vanhoozer deploys it impressively and extensively to address issues related to language and interpretation. In one essay, he uses "covenant" to develop (1) a theory of communication in general and (2) a theology of Scripture interpretation, making it his goal to "let the 'discourse of the covenant' (Scripture) inform and transform our understanding of the 'covenant of discourse' (ordinary language and literature)."[56] Thus, he seeks to let the biblical picture of covenant describe what occurs in all forms of communication.

He first develops a theory of communication, in which he identifies the concept of covenant as central, writing, "Here too the leading theme of covenant proves helpful, insofar as interpretation is largely a matter of fulfilling one's covenantal obligation toward the communicative agents, canonical or not, who address us."[57] All discourse is covenantal action, bringing with it certain privileges and responsibilities that all communicants—speakers, hearers, authors, and readers—must bear.[58] Reading, then, is a circumscribed activity, delimited by the requirements of the covenant of discourse.

Vanhoozer then applies this covenant-centered theory of communication to biblical interpretation. He does this by proffering "covenanting" as one illocutionary act that emerges at the canonical level and unifies all other illocutionary actions in Scripture.[59] "What God does with Scripture," he writes, "is covenant with humanity by testifying to Jesus Christ (illocution) and by bringing about the reader's mutual indwelling with Christ (perlocution) through the Spirit's rendering Scripture efficacious."[60] Scripture, as an instance of divine covenantal discourse, has illocutionary force that must be respected and understood before its perlocutionary effects may be properly felt. Responsible

---

56. Vanhoozer, *First Theology*, 161.

57. Ibid. Speaking of common points among speech act theory advocates, he writes: "We agree that *action*, rather than representation, should be the operative concept, and that this entails certain *rights* and *responsibilities* on the part of author and readers. In particular, we see the promise as the paradigm for what is involved in speech action (though in the present work I put forward covenant as an alternate)" (ibid., 164).

58. Ibid., 175.

59. Ibid., 193–95.

60. Ibid., 200.

reading in this covenantal scenario means not bypassing illocutions, but allowing the Spirit to use them to bring about the desired effects. Thus, Christians are to engage the discourse of the covenant (Holy Scripture) with appropriate reverence as participants in both the covenant in Jesus Christ and the covenant of discourse. Vanhoozer concludes: "The church is first of all a community oriented to the discourse of the covenant, the Christian Scriptures. Yet the church should also be a community that cares about the covenant of discourse in general. For . . . language is a divinely ordained institution with its own divine design plan."[61] What this means is that members of the church must become (1) "covenant keepers," that is, those who cultivate interpretive virtues, particularly honesty; (2) "witnesses," bearing truthful witness to authors' texts by not ascribing to them things they did not intend, trying to hear the text well, and listening to tradition; and (3) "disciples" who seek to understand the text, who follow and perform the Word, even to the point of death.[62] Whatever one makes of this general hermeneutical move, Vanhoozer's proposal is certainly apt in the realm of biblical hermeneutics: to be a right reader of Scripture is to be a faithful covenant partner, one who follows thoughtfully where the Bible leads. Building on this account, as well as receiving help from Vanhoozer's other works, we may further specify and further expand the notion of covenant and, by doing so, extend the theological-hermeneutical reach of the concept.

Covenant Mediation as Theological Hermeneutic

At one moment in Vanhoozer's essay, he points in the direction pursued in this section. Speaking of the rhythm of sentence and promise in the history of Israel's covenant, he writes: "The cross of Christ fulfills the sentence, the resurrection the promise. In this sense we could say that Jesus Christ is God's illocutionary act."[63] Jesus Christ and his work of mediating the covenant are what God meant to say to us as well as that which he desires us to follow. It is for the comprehensive fulfillment of earlier covenants and the mediation of the new covenant that Christ enters the fray. We could also speak of Christ fulfilling two sides of God's covenantal relations with humanity: he is the sign and bearer of

---

61. Ibid., 201.
62. Ibid., 201–2.
63. Ibid., 189.

the covenantal grace of God *and* the one who supremely demonstrates faithfulness to the covenant stipulations. In fact, it is here at the covenant in Christ, the very nexus of divine and human relations, that the two "poles" of our hermeneutical conversation find their unity. God's action and humanity's faithful response find perfect harmony in Christ. In this way, he both embodies and mediates the covenant of God with his people. Indeed, Jesus Christ *is* the covenant of God's grace: "I have given you as a covenant to the people" (Isa 42:6). Therefore, as we seek to discover the relationship between the concept of covenant and the depiction of readers of Scripture, we must inevitably look to Jesus Christ. The various episodes presented in chapter 5 suggest, and it is here contended, that Christ is subject matter—the *Sache*—of Scripture as well as the standard for proper reading practices in his role as king, priest, and Israel-as-royal priesthood. To read Scripture in light of the covenant is to see Christ as the culmination of God's acts in history, to participate in his life—new covenant life, life in Christ—and to imitate his practices. To read in light of the covenant is to read of and like Jesus. Covenantal reading is Christological reading. We begin our exploration of covenantal reading by exploring how union with Christ informs our account of readers, before examining Christ's account of faithful reading.

Reading in Light of the Covenant: Union with Christ

Reading Scripture in light of the covenant, at its root, demands participation in Jesus Christ, the embodiment, fulfillment, and mediator of the covenant. Indeed, it is union with Christ that grounds and empowers all Christian acts of covenant fidelity—including Scripture reading. Therefore, it is important to begin a constructive account of covenantal reading by addressing briefly this central Pauline and Reformational theme.

When believers are united with Christ by the Spirit, they receive all the benefits the Father bestowed upon the Son in order that he would distribute them to his children. Calvin, speaking of this union, writes:

> To share with us what he has received from the Father, he had to become ours and to dwell within us. For this reason, he is called "our Head" (Eph 4:15), and "the first-born among many brethren" (Rom 8:29). We also, in turn, are said to be "engrafted into him" (Rom 11:17), and to "put on Christ" (Gal 3:27); for ... all

> that he possesses is nothing to us until we grow into one body with him.[64]

By means of a Spirit-wrought faith, Christians are engrafted into Christ and experience all the gifts of the covenant. Two of the chief benefits are what Calvin terms the *duplex gratia*: justification and sanctification. He writes:

> Christ was given to us by God's generosity, to be grasped and possessed by us in faith. By partaking of him, we principally receive a double grace: namely, that being reconciled to God through Christ's blamelessness, we may have in heaven instead of a Judge a gracious Father; and secondly, that sanctified by Christ's spirit we may cultivate blamelessness and purity of life.[65]

This double grace that comes to us through union with Christ addresses well the relationship between God's agency and human response in the practices of believers. God graciously justifies us *in Christ*, regenerates us *in Christ*, and then empowers and calls us to live *like Christ*. The living out of love for God and neighbor—sanctification—is founded upon our union with the preeminent Lover of God and others. In addition, and more central to the concerns of this study, when Christians are united with Christ and anointed with his Spirit, they not only partake of his benefits, but also participate in his work. Echoing what we have discovered throughout this study, Calvin speaks thus of our participation in Christ's priesthood: "Now, Christ plays the priestly role, not only to render the Father favorable and propitious toward us by an eternal law of reconciliation, but also to receive us as his companions in this great office (Rev 1:6). For we who are defiled in ourselves, yet are priests in him..."[66] Similarly, after affirming Christ's anointing to the threefold office of prophet, priest, and king (Question 31), the Heidelberg Catechism makes explicit the connection between union with Christ and participation in his work (Question 32):

> Q. But why are you called a Christian?
>
> A. Because by faith I am a member of Christ and so I share in his anointing.

---

64. Calvin, *Institutes* III.1.1, 537. See Billings, *Calvin, Participation, and the Gift*, for his excellent exposition of Calvin's doctrine of participation.

65. Calvin, *Institutes* III.11.1, 725.

66. Ibid., II.15.6, 502.

> I am anointed
> to confess his name,
> to present myself to him as a living sacrifice of thanks,
> to strive with a free conscience against sin and the devil in this life,
> and afterward to reign with Christ over all creation
> for eternity.[67]

The very functions performed by Christ in his offices—proclamation as prophet, sacrifice as priest, and rule as king—are shared with us, though in a manner that preserves the singularity of his mediatorial work. For our purposes, it is as priests that we offer ourselves, pray, and *read* in a way that corresponds fittingly to him. In Christ, we experience the initiative and empowerment of God, so that we can respond to the imperative to imitate him faithfully. Those who enter into the new covenant and are united with Christ are enabled and called to participate in his covenantal faithfulness—his piety as well as his practices. Therefore, in Christ—indeed by union with him—proposals that privilege divine action and those that favor ecclesial response in depicting readers are not at odds, nor competitive, but rather find their unity. Participation in Christ becomes the bedrock for reading practices that are faithful to the demands of the covenant initiated by the Triune God. We are now ready to examine the content and, more pertinently, the character of Christ's reading of Scripture, in order that we as readers might learn what it is to follow God's ultimate illocutionary act—Jesus Christ the arch-reader.[68]

Reading in Light of the Covenant: Christ the *Sache*

That Christ is the center of Scripture in some way is hardly debated among those Christians who see Scripture as having some sort of unity. We saw at the end of chapter 5 that Jesus indicted the religious authorities for failing to reinterpret the Sabbath in light of his advent (Mark 2:23–28). They missed Jesus as the key to the Scriptures. Elsewhere Jesus condemns the Jewish leaders for failing to recognize Moses' testimony about him (John 5:31–47). The point here and elsewhere in the Gospels

---

67. *The Heidelberg Catechism*, 12. Cf. Billings, *Union with Christ*, chap. 5, for a helpful account of the relation between union with Christ and the ministry of believers.

68. Vanhoozer moves in a similar direction when he speaks of Jesus' "canonical practices." He writes, "Canonical practices are thus 'of Christ' both in the sense that they are *about* him and in the sense that they are *Christ's own practices*" (Vanhoozer, *Drama of Doctrine*, 220–21). We will return to Vanhoozer's exposition of these practices in what follows.

is that neglecting to read the Scriptures Christologically is often a moral as well as a methodological failure. To experience Jesus and yet fail to reconceive the Scriptures in light of that encounter is an indicator of something amiss in the reader. To Jesus, reading Christologically was a serious matter, for failure to do so resulted in missing God's work altogether.

Vanhoozer identifies this kind of rereading of Scripture as one of the most important "canonical" reading practices of Jesus.[69] He defines figural reading (or typology) as "that practice of interpreting Scripture, and history itself, as indicating and finding its unity in Jesus Christ." Appealing to the *locus classicus* for Christological interpretation, Luke 24, he shows that the pattern of using Scripture to interpret Christ and Christ to interpret Scripture originated with Jesus himself.[70] He points out that figural reading represents the "inner logic" of the canon by viewing the history of Israel and the story of Jesus Christ as one story. Figural reading, moreover, calls contemporary Christians to read their own stories in light of these histories, just as Jesus himself did.[71] This type of reading unites OT and NT, as well as the history of Israel and that of the church, thus fostering what Vanhoozer calls "typological realism," which insists that all history finds its coherence in Jesus Christ. The history of Jesus is thus the hermeneutical key not only to the biblical canon, but to all of life, since he is the Logos through which all things were created.[72] If we allow that God's relation to all creaturely reality is covenantal in character, then "typological realism" unites all God's covenantal works, that is, history itself, so that creation, the story of Israel, and our own stories are viewed as one story centered on Jesus Christ. On a preliminary level, therefore, to read in light of God's covenant(s) is to read in light of Christ.

---

69. A "canonical practice" is a "communicative practice in a canonical context with a covenantal aim" (ibid., 216). Or, more to the point, canonical practices are "rule-governed forms of covenantal behavior in Israel and the church that in turn direct the covenantal practices of the believing community today" (ibid., 220).

70. Ibid., 221.

71. Ibid., 222.

72. Ibid., 223.

Reading in Light of the Covenant: Christ the Standard

There is a second aspect to covenantal-Christological reading that we must reckon with, namely, Jesus' own faithful reading of the Word of God. Francis Watson writes, "The actions of Jesus are to be understood as oriented towards the restoration of authentic human community in situations where it is distorted or absent." He adds that these actions "shed light on the humanity of the Son—both his becoming human and the divine *philanthropia* that he incarnates. *They also offer anticipatory images of the perfected community of the eschatological future.*"[73] Thus Jesus' reading of Scripture, like all his other actions, helps bring about the restoration of the covenant community, while revealing what that community is to be eschatologically. What the community is to become is the model of what they are to strive for today in all practices, including Scripture reading. Hence, to be a right reader of Scripture is to be a reader like the eschatological man, Jesus Christ. Two broad aspects of Christ's royal priestly/mediatorial reading practices will here be considered: (1) his obedience to the Word of God, even to the point of martyrdom, and (2) his others-centeredness. Let us take these up in order.[74]

As the Son of God—both as Davidic King and as the embodiment of faithful Israel—Jesus exemplified covenantal faithfulness. Jesus responds to Satan's testing ("If you are the Son, then . . .") by demonstrating that to be the Son is to be submissive to the Word of God (Matt 4:4).[75] What Vanhoozer calls "interpretive martyrdom" is best applied to Jesus as the hermeneutical martyr *par excellence*.[76] Jesus is a martyr not merely on behalf of meaning generally, but rather on behalf of the intent of the entirety of God's words. He suffers and dies so that Scripture might be fulfilled. Jesus was the faithful covenant partner, triumphing where Israel and its office-holders stumbled. The suffering of the royal priestly Christ on behalf of the Word is the model for the suffering required of his royal priestly saints, as poignantly sketched in the book of Revelation (see chapter 2). Faithfulness to the Word requires ultimate devotion.

---

73. Watson, *Text, Church and World*, 247 (emphasis added).

74. Much of the last chapter expands on these practices. Thus I will only briefly outline Jesus' demonstration of them in anticipation of that treatment.

75. Bockmuehl likewise presents Jesus' reading of Scripture during the temptation as an ideal model of scriptural interpretation (see Bockmuehl, *Seeing the Word*, 94–96).

76. See Vanhoozer's discussion in *Is There a Meaning*, 438–41. Cf. Vanhoozer, *First Theology*, 201–2.

What the community of Christ is to be is also demonstrated by Jesus' others-centered reading practices. We saw that the Gospels of Mark, Luke, and John present Jesus as the teaching priest. He taught the people the proper intent of the law, instructed in cleanness and uncleanness, revealed the Word of God, enacted torah through healings and pronouncements, and re-interpreted the law according to his advent. For Jesus, reading the Scriptures of Israel was for the benefit of all Israel. The Word of God was to be spoken to those who had ears to hear, so that they might attain life. Again, hermeneutical martyrdom was the result of Jesus' reading practices. He was accused of deceiving the people and leading them astray, and suffered accordingly. This time Jesus suffers not merely for following the content of the Word, but for bringing the reading act to completion, namely, by proclaiming the Word. To read in light of the covenant is to recognize oneself as a member of a covenantal community whose Head saw it fit to die for the sake of others. In that light, proper reading acts cannot be selfish, self-centered, or shallowly pietistic. We read for the sake of Christ's flock, bringing the reading act to fulfillment by declaring the Word of God, which, by its very nature, is to be proclaimed, not just heard.

The notion of covenant presents a powerful way of conceiving the type of relationship readers are to have with God via the biblical text. God initiates a covenant with humanity and gives the Scriptures as a covenant document, specifying how one should rightly respond to him and his words—as a covenant keeper and follower of the Word of God. Furthermore, Jesus Christ is the embodiment and fulfillment of God's covenant(s) with humanity: he is both parties of the covenant, as God's loving action and humanity's faithful response. He fulfills the covenant between God and humanity. To be a reader in light of the covenant, therefore, is to participate in Christ and follow him faithfully, and this begins with viewing him as the center of Scripture and its ideal reader. We read all of Scripture in light of Jesus Christ and, more important to our present purposes, we follow his reading practices. In the course of this *imitatio Christi* we find ourselves most faithfully reading Scripture as the document of God's gracious covenant with his people.

8

Response and Responsibility

*Royal Priesthood as an Ethical Account
of the Readers of Scripture*

Therefore, observe diligently the commandment—the statutes, and the ordinances—that I am commanding you today (Deut 7:11).

The last chapter attempted to demonstrate that what primarily determines our reading of Scripture and who we are as readers is God's action—specifically election and sanctification—which has a view to establishing a covenant with humanity. David Scott summarizes this point well: "God's praxis, God's performance of allowing and enabling creatures to share in, show forth and be shaped by his life, is the real action. This divine praxis is the ultimate horizon or standpoint, therefore, for understanding—or or trying to understand—all aspects of Christian life," including Scripture reading.[1] However, as mentioned throughout, the covenant also requires a proper human response: "Now, therefore, if you obey my voice and keep my covenant, you shall be for me . . ." (Exod 19:5). Most in the hermeneutical conversation acknowledge that we cannot simply stop at divine action in our depiction of readers. As briefly outlined and highlighted by the example of Jesus in the last section, readers are called to be and do something. In one way or another, theologians and ethicists posit that there are certain dispositions, aims,

---

1. Scott, "Speaking to Form," 142. "This final purpose of God's grace—humans actually participating in God's performances—constitutes the ultimate horizon for understanding the church's life and the individual Christian's life" (ibid.).

and responses that are necessary for reading Scripture well. To depict readers accurately one must attend to what Scott calls the "dual reference" of every biblical text. Not only are we to direct our attention to the divine character and praxis revealed in the Scriptures, but as he observes, "every biblical text directly or indirectly has implications for those practices—or the goods, the rules, the virtues which sustain and guide those practices—by which human beings correspond in their relations to God and with one another to God's praxis in relation to us."[2] Plainly put, every Scripture directly or indirectly prescribes the right being and doing, attitudes and behaviors, or dispositions and practices of its readers. The *telos* of Scripture and its reading is to make our praxis correspond to God's holiness. Thus it might be fitting to say that Bible reading or interpretation is itself, at heart, a form of doing:

> Interpretation is meaning, and meaning can be said. But more basically, biblical meaning is done: meaning as relationships God intends between us and himself and between ourselves in relation to God. Because those relationships are forms of human life sharing in, showing forth and being shaped by God's own "performance" as triune life, the most authentic Christian biblical interpretation is human enactments of God-informed life.[3]

Reading, as interpretation, is not merely about achieving understanding in the cognitive sense, but also about the performance of the appropriate acts called for by Scripture itself. In fact, intrinsic to true understanding is the performance of that which the text demands.[4] Scott sums up the matter well: "Interpretation, then, in its final form, is God-formed human practice. What we do as the people of God *is* our interpretation of the Bible. . . . [I]nterpretation does not guide practice; practice, properly understood, is the interpretation. Everything else is commentary."[5] To read Scripture well is to follow its direction and creatively live out the ways of God—to have the right attitudes, the proper aims and interests,

---

2. Ibid., 145.

3. Ibid., 144.

4. This discussion is a variation on Christopher Spinks' notion of meaning as triadic, that is, involving roughly locutions, illocutions, *and* perlocutions. Meaning involves a doing, a carrying out of the perlocutionary effects of the text. See Spinks, *Bible and the Crisis of Meaning*, chap. 4.

5. Scott, "Speaking to Form," 145–46 (italics added).

the appropriate responses, and the corresponding practices that flow from and complete such fitting acts of reading.

Accordingly, this chapter seeks to provide a biblically- and theologically-informed ethical depiction of the readers of Scripture, accounting for human response and responsibility. The first section explores human response in the forms of virtue and character formation. The assumption throughout, following Briggs, is that it is crucial to commandeer biblical language and categories to describe the virtues more Christianly. Thus, this section revisits earlier chapters and draws out some interpretive virtues that follow from "low-key, ad hoc exegetical forays" into the biblical material.[6] In the end, it is argued that the overarching "virtue" which we must embody and for which we must strive in reading Scripture is holiness—holiness through obedience. The second and final section examines human response in its outgoing forms, namely, as ministry and mission. "Ministry" (or service, διακονία) refers to those others-oriented practices of reading Scripture, which are concerned with fostering Christ-honoring ways of living within the Christian community. "Mission" speaks of those reading acts that are directed toward those to whom we are sent outside the ecclesial community.[7] This final part of the chapter builds upon the suggestion that these outward forms of reading, these declarative deeds, bring to completion the broader act of reading the Scriptures.[8] Moreover, these proclamatory modes of reading bring to light issues related to the appropriation of oral and sacramental forms of the Word of God, which function as particular readings themselves. Thus the reader will be presented as one formed within an ecclesial community that prizes and fosters holiness and obedience to the Word through the mutual ministry of the manifold Word of God.

---

6. I borrow this language from Briggs, whose project in some ways resembles portions of this study (see Briggs, *Virtuous Reader*, 31). Our projects differ in that he (1) selects particular passages/characters of Scripture to describe virtues, while I use the offices of king and priest generally to describe the virtues, and (2) he is concerned only with depicting interpretive virtues, while I am concerned with the entire depiction of readers with respect to both divine and human agency.

7. This distinction is, of course, heuristic, since "ministry" is done to persons outside the church as well (e.g., 2 Cor 5:18).

8. This suggestion is broadly similar to Augustine, who writes at the beginning of *On Christian Teaching*: "There are two things on which all interpretation of scripture depends: the process of discovering what we need to learn, and the process of presenting what we have learnt" (I.1). He spends Book Four on the issue of communication.

Interpretive Virtues in Royal Priestly Perspective

Talk of character ethics among Christians, whether in general or directly related to biblical interpretation, divides roughly into two camps. On the one hand, there are those who are generally in the Catholic tradition and seek to rehabilitate a Thomistic notion of virtues as those internal and habitual dispositions of the heart that define moral identity and goodness more fundamentally than external acts.[9] On the other hand, there are those who seek to situate character ethics within the Christian community of formation. In this view, most common among Protestants, the main function of character is to embody the community's narrative and thus sustain the integrity of the community's identity and practices. As expressed in the thought of Hauerwas, objectivity with regard to moral action is not universal, but rather a function of the particular narrative that Christians inhabit. Right moral action is creative conformity to the story that defines the community over against the general culture.[10] The choice of terminology in both camps is significant. On the one hand, Lisa Cahill observes, "Virtue connotes *aspiration to* or *cultivation of* certain goods, values, or ideals, to which the moral agent is positively and habitually disposed." Character, on the other hand, implies resistance to and perseverance against the forces that threaten Christian identity, particularly sin.[11] These differing visions of character ethics reflect at some level well-worn dichotomies between Catholic and Protestant or even nature and grace versus creation-fall-redemption ground motifs.[12] These differences are somewhat reflected in recent hermeneutical proposals. There are those who emphasize the virtue of the interpreter (e.g., Rogers), others who stress character formation within a rightly functioning Christian community as essential to faithful interpretation (e.g., Fowl and Jones), and still others who try to mediate between the two (e.g., Vanhoozer). This section aims to bring together these ethical approaches by proposing a story-formed ethic that takes account of

---

9. Cahill, "Christian Character," 4–5.

10. Ibid., 5–6 (emphasis original).

11. Ibid., 6.

12. Cahill gets to the heart of the differences between these approaches: "In the background of these connotations, we may perceive the age-old theological debates about the primacy of a created nature that is able to discern basic goods and to strive after them in the present moral order versus the primacy of sin in human experience and the need for conversion away from the order of the world" (ibid.).

the non-narrative genres of biblical literature—legislative, hymnic, proverbial, and prophetic—as also constitutive of the story. It is argued, expanding on earlier chapters, that the call to royal priesthood, the kingship law, the various positive and negative construals of the king in biblical narrative, and especially the presentation of the ideal kingly reader in the Psalms furnish us with a particular understanding of the virtues as they relate to reading/hearing the Word. While wanting to preserve an emphasis on the pervasiveness of sin's effects and the resultant need for divine deliverance, this account stresses individual aspiration to and cultivation of virtue, as well as readers conforming to the story of God's redemption of his people.[13] Moreover, when referring to virtues or character in interpretation, I am speaking in the way attempted in various parts of this study—of virtue involving disposition, aim, and response, at once addressing internal, personal dispositions, as well as embodied actions and communal practices. Both are determinative of the goodness of readers and their reading. While not addressing or overcoming fundamental concerns about created nature and sin, this approach calls attention to the fact that a right reader of Scripture will embody virtue and good character internally and externally, in her heart and in her deeds, so to speak. Presently, we turn to examine what the interpretive virtues might look like when informed by the themes of royal priesthood and, more essentially, kingship.

When one encounters the many lists of virtues related to the interpreter in the hermeneutical literature, the question immediately arises as to why certain virtues are enumerated and not others. One of the key problems, as Christopher Seitz presents it, is that what counts as an ethical reading of Scripture today may appear unethical at a future time. If, for example, human progress were the highest value for a particular age and context, then readings that promote this end—whether deconstructive or revisionist—would be seen as virtuous, while those that do not—even if faithful to the literal sense—would be immoral. Speaking of Fowl's work, but making a claim applicable to much talk about virtue in interpretation, Seitz concludes strongly: "One searches in vain . . . for any comprehensive, public, agreed-upon statement of what actually counts for virtue, such that we could see it and believe it was under God's

---

13. Treier notably provides a biblical story-formed depiction of the virtues, particularly wisdom and *phronesis*, in *Virtue and the Voice of God*, chap. 2.

providential care as it went about the business of 'engaging scripture.'"[14] While the issue may not be one of comprehensiveness or unanimity, the concern to define (or at least describe) virtues as they relate to readers is an important one. Whether we see the prime interpretive virtues as receptivity, humility, truthfulness, courage, charity, and imagination (so Jones), or repentance, attention, receptivity, delight, freedom, courtesy, and humility (so Webster), or some combination or extension of these, some measure of biblical re-description can only but fortify these proposals.[15] Much of the burden of the third chapter of this study was to provide a measure of such description. Thus I will draw primarily from the findings of that chapter as I offer an(other) account of the interpretive virtues.

There is a cluster of virtues that commonly appears in virtue-oriented hermeneutical proposals, the chief of which are love, humility, wisdom, receptivity, and trust.[16] My account acknowledges and appreciates these virtues as well as others' accounts of them, yet differs on two fronts. First, it will not deal with love, wisdom, trust, or receptivity, but will supplement humility with different virtues that have received less attention. Second, this account is informed primarily by the themes of royal priesthood and kingship vis-à-vis the Word of God. Thus the virtues will, at some points, take on a slightly different hue than in other treatments, even a cognate account like Briggs'. Though a few others could have been listed, the three interpretive virtues I describe are fear of God, humility, and delight, as these are some dominant traits emerging from the study of ideal kingly reading practices primarily. Two of them receive scant treatment in the literature, and the third can be helpfully refined by the biblical picture here presented.[17] Moreover, as virtue

---

14. Seitz, *Figured Out*, 29. Cf. Briggs, *Virtuous Reader*, 30.

15. See Jones, "Formed and Transformed," 32, and Webster, "Hermeneutics in Modern Theology," 80. Webster is reticent to use "virtue" language, but allows for it with sufficient theological qualification (see Webster, *Holy Scripture*, 89).

16. These, in fact, are the very virtues Briggs seeks to address, partially because they are currently *en vogue* (*Virtuous Reader*, 43).

17. The absence of the virtue of "love" is conspicuous, but (1) there is already an abundance of relevant literature; (2) the above virtues provide some specificity to love for God, or that love is expressed concretely as fear, humility, and delight; (3) the royal-priestly reading practices to follow in the next section also add specificity; and, (4) since love is tied closely to obedience (e.g., John 14:15, 23), an account of obedience as it relates to the virtues covers some key (often uncovered) territory.

regarding Scripture reading entails an appropriate response, obedience will be presented as the chief response called for in Scripture, and thus a necessary component in the completion of the virtuous reading act. The above virtues find their fulfillment, so to speak, in acts of obedience.[18]

Fear

The first virtue, *the fear of God*, in some ways overlaps with subsequent interpretive virtues, but still requires separate treatment. By fear we refer to the sense of awe and reverence before the majesty of God. Fear is an *interpretive* virtue when conceived as the ongoing, consistent acknowledgment that one is encountering the living God when one engages Scripture: the Law and Prophets are not mere words, but the very declarations and demands of the Lord, which, therefore, stand over against the reader. Speaking of the nature of Scripture, Webster captures much of this insight: "The Bible as a whole is *address,* the *viva vox Dei* which accosts us and requires attention. God's address is interceptive; it does not leave the hearer in neutrality, or merely invite us to adopt a position vis-à-vis itself and entertain it as a possibility. It allows no safe havens; *it judges.*"[19] Indeed, the reader of the Bible is confronted by the God who speaks in and through it, irrespective of genre. The divine address, Webster notes, is an incident in the slaying and making alive of the sinner. In this event of reading, the reader as sinner becomes undone.[20] Although Webster does not elaborate on fear as such, he points us in that direction through citations of Augustine. Speaking of the relationship between fear and reading, the Bishop of Hippo writes: "It is therefore necessary above all else to be moved by the fear of God towards learning his will: what it is that he instructs us to seek or avoid. This fear will necessarily inspire reflection about our mortality and future death, and by nailing our flesh to the wood of the cross as it were crucify all our presumptuous impulses."[21] The fear of God gives the reader the proper

---

18. To some degree this pattern follows Deut 17:19b–20a ("... that he may *fear* the Lord his God, diligently *observing* all of this law and these statutes, *neither exalting himself* . . .") and Ps 1:2a, which reflects the ideals of Deut 17 ("His *delight* is in the law of the Lord"). Thus reverence, obedience, humility, and delight are those attitudes and responses that characterize the ideal royal reader.

19. Webster, "Hermeneutics in Modern Theology," 75.

20. Ibid., 80.

21. Augustine, *On Christian Teaching*, II.16.

perspective on her status as a creature *coram Deo* and puts to death those wrongful desires that will undoubtedly be expressed in her reading. It is the fear of God that motivates the reader to ponder the judgment of God and act accordingly.[22] The heart of the matter, as we will see, is stated pointedly: "The student who fears God earnestly seeks his will in the holy scriptures."[23] The fear of God rightly orients the reader to Scripture as one who deserves judgment, but who by divine grace is permitted to hear and read the Word of God. As such, fear does not merely provide pause when reading Scripture, but also offers an open gateway, an entry pass, to the wisdom of the Word (Prov 1:7). Those who fear the Lord are invited to drink often and drink deeply from the wells of Scripture. This picture of fear and reading is given specific color in the reading practices of the ideal king of chapter 3.

In the kingship law, we find a purpose clause for the king's prescribed reading activities: ". . . so that he may learn to fear the Lord his God" (Deut 17:19a). When the king takes the throne, he is to write out and carry with him the very law that limits his own powers and prerogatives. The goal of the king's reading is that he would display reverence for the God of Israel and model a submissive attitude to God through adherence to the law. When we come to the story of Jehoiakim (Jer 36) we are presented with the anti-ideal, away from which we are to turn if we desire to have the proper attitude and response to God's words. Six times in this account it is mentioned that the king reacted to God's Word by burning the scroll (Jer 36:23, 25, 27–29, 32). This action displays the ultimate irreverence, the evident lack of awe and dread before the Word of God. The narrator, moreover, records that the king was not "alarmed" by Jeremiah's words of judgment (36:24). This lack of alarm is akin to the absence of fear, which, as we saw in Augustine, should provoke one to take judgment seriously, especially imminent judgment. The casual nature of Jehoiakim's hearing and response to the words of Jeremiah is the very antithesis of reverent reading. He was unmoved by the reality of YHWH, either because he dissociated the words of Jeremiah from the God who gave them, or he simply did not care to heed. Either way, there was no serious inquiry into the truth of the words. He simply got rid of them. The reader that fears knows that the words of Scripture, no matter the human author, are divine words spoken for and against

22. Ibid., II.19.
23. Ibid., III.1.

him. He stands in awe of God and abases himself in the presence of God's revelation, which carries with it God's very presence. In Psalm 19 the royal reader expresses these sentiments poetically when he depicts YHWH as the covenant God who speaks personal words to his covenant people. With the presence of the law comes the presence of the Lord, who blesses those who keep his Word and threatens those who do not (19:11). Psalm 119:20 makes this point clear: "My flesh trembles for fear of you, and I am afraid of your judgments." The NIV renders the last clause: "I stand in awe of your laws." Both the Lord and his law receive the same attitude and response: fear, dread, and awe. God is present in and with his Word. We are therefore called to approach with reverence and fear. There is no other entrée into a right relationship with God's Word. Moreover, if we define wisdom as the rightful application of torah to life, then the fear of God, as the beginning of wisdom, may be seen as the passport to rightly reading the Scriptures. Thus, in light of the kingly reading practices described in chapter 3, the faithful reader of Scripture is the one who fears God and is therefore attentive to every word that proceeds from the mouth of God.

Humility

The second interpretive virtue, *humility*, is variously described by a number of authors. Fowl presents humility as rooted in one's recognition that one is a sinner. To be humble before God and others in a way that leads to faithful interpretation, readers must see themselves as those in desperate need of God's forgiveness.[24] Rogers presents humility as a proper recognition of the limitations of one's interpretation when compared to the exhaustiveness of God's knowledge.[25] William Stacy Johnson defines interpretive humility as that approach which moves beyond foundations and totalizing accounts while being open to the ultimate Other, God.[26] Briggs appeals to Num 12:3 and the example of Moses to offer a Scripture-centered portrait of interpretive humility. He contends that Moses is the self-reputed "most humble man on the face of the earth" because he receives God's words face-to-face, something no one else can claim. Humility in this arrangement refers to "dependence

---

24. Fowl, *Engaging Scripture*, 81–85.
25. Rogers, "How the Virtues of an Interpreter," 71.
26. Johnson, "Reading the Scriptures Faithfully," 109–24.

upon God for any speaking of a divinely authorized word."[27] In contrast to Miriam and Aaron (Num 12:2), who also received words from God, Moses receives the Word of YHWH as the preeminent God-dependent man.[28] For Briggs, humility has little to do with meekness or modesty in this passage. Rather, it is a term that speaks of a dependent disposition toward God and his words that will often be expressed in bold (not self-degrading) speech to God and others. Put differently, to speak for God one must be dependent on God.[29] Translated into the realm of biblical interpretation, humility defined this way implies that one's spiritual life matters for faithful reading. Thus humility is expressed through active pursuit of God via the various spiritual disciplines, especially prayer.[30] By examining one text of Scripture Briggs is able to present a cogent, biblically circumscribed, and specific enough notion of interpretive humility.

When we turn to the kingly reading practices, we are presented with complementary portraits of humility before God's Word. Beginning in Deut 17:20a, the king is to display humility as the proper aim and response with regard to torah reading. Humility here is framed as not "exalting himself above other members of the community." The same covenantal promises and judgments that apply to Israel apply to the king. He is to see himself as equally subordinated to the law of God. Humility thus involves seeing oneself as a graced member of the covenant community, no greater or lesser, regardless of the specific office one holds. This attitude is exemplified in the story of Josiah who, upon hearing the book of the law and realizing his complicity in violating it, humbled himself before YHWH (2 Kgs 22:11, 19). What is noteworthy is that Josiah views himself and his people of the time as one with their ancestors who failed to obey the law. Not only is the king one with his current community, but he is also one with his disobedient forebears. They are all condemned covenant breakers, equally. Interpretive humility, therefore, takes on the character of acknowledging one's solidarity with the sinful covenant community of the present as well as the past. A word spoken long ago is ever a present word because of the common promise and sentence humanity shares across time. Barth gets at this to

---

27. Briggs, *Virtuous Reader*, 59–60.
28. Ibid., 60–61.
29. Ibid., 61–63.
30. Ibid., 67–68.

some extent, writing about the historical distance between and nearness of Abraham and Paul in Rom 4:1–8:

> [H]istorical individuals are a unified whole . . . , a family in one and the same house. They are, admittedly, gradated and differentiated as forerunners, contemporaries, and descendants of the Messiah, according to their special relationship to the great course of prophecy, fulfillment, and completion. But (what is more important than this variation!) they are bound together through their commonality—that in the Messiah the kingdom of God has come near them.[31]

Humanity is united by its common sinfulness and need of divine forgiveness. Abraham is the same as Paul, who himself is the same as the twenty-first century North American Christian, since the kingdom of God stands over against every age and culture. Donald Wood sums up Barth's position: "The fundamental distinction between God and humanity involves the affirmation of a fundamental human solidarity."[32] On Barth's account, a failure to acknowledge this fundamental unity, this solidarity, leads one to miss the very heart of the biblical authors' concerns. On my account, this failure represents a gross lack of humility on the part of readers. Humble readers see all history as the history of God's saving work, "the history of his patience with and creative renewal of *sinful* humanity."[33] Thus, interpretive humility requires that we acknowledge the sinful tendencies we share with all humankind that may distort reading practices, while also glorying in the promise of divine liberation that humanity likewise shares. Humble readers see their practices as simultaneously sinful and righteous.

Moreover, in the Psalter, humility takes on dimensions that complement Briggs' account. For example, many parts of Psalm 119 suggest

---

31. Barth, *Der Römerbrief 1919*, quoted in Wood, *Barth's Theology of Interpre-tation*, 15.

32. Wood, *Barth's Theology of Interpretation*, 13.

33. Ibid., 15. There are implications here for the relative place of historical criticism in the apparatus of theological interpretation. To argue for a unity of history is not to negate what Barth calls the "preparation"—the necessary recognition of the historical and cultural distance between the text and the modern reader—provided by historical criticism. To appreciate fully the depths of historical similarity we must recognize the real difference that exists, even if the solidarity is more fundamental. Thus, there is a place for methods that privilege difference (historical criticism) and for those that privilege sameness (precritical exegesis). See Wood's entire discussion of Barth's critique of historical criticism (ibid., 12–24).

that humility is dependence upon God for every benefit proceeding from his Word. The psalmist regularly implores the Lord to supply what is lacking in his reading of God's law. He asks the Lord to open his eyes (119:18), teach him (119:26, 33, 64, 66, 68, 108, 124), make him understand (119:27, 34, 73, 125, 144, 169), lead him in the paths of God's commandments (119:35), turn his heart to the divine decrees (119:36), incline his heart toward performing God's Word (119:112), and keep him living and hoping in light of God's promise (119:133). These requests by the psalmist point to his recognition that he is insufficient to the task of reading and following the Word of God. His humility is expressed by prayers of dependence upon YHWH, that the Lord would enable him to be a right reader of torah. Prayer becomes something not peripheral but, rather, central to the act of reading Scripture faithfully. Rogers, making reference to Aquinas, suggests similarly:

> The interpreter may never pursue an interest or purpose as though its success or failure depended alone on his or her own efforts. . . . Those who worry about the salubrious or deleterious effects of interpretations will tend, if they follow the Enlightenment, to address their worries in hermeneutics. Those who worry about the effects of interpretation will tend, if they follow Thomas, to address their worries among other places in prayer. . . . And the interpreter who prays well, of course, will find that prayer also improves the interpretation, most of all, perhaps, by leaving the interests and purposes that motivate it changed.[34]

Luther speaks likewise in his emphasis on *Oratio*:

> Kneel down in your little room [Matt 6:6] and pray to God with real humility and earnestness, that he through his dear Son may give you his Holy Spirit, who will enlighten you, lead you, and give you understanding. . . . Although [David] well knew and daily heard and read the text of Moses and other books besides, still he wants to lay hold of the real teacher of the Scriptures himself, so that he may not seize upon them pell-mell with his reason and become his own teacher. For such practice gives rise to factious spirits who allow themselves to nurture the delusion that the Scriptures are subject to them and can be easily grasped with their reason, as if they were *Markof* or Aesop's Fables, for which no Holy Spirit and no prayers are needed.[35]

---

34. Rogers, "How the Virtues of an Interpreter," 80–81.
35. Luther, "Preface to the Wittenburg Edition," 72.

Thus, intrinsic to interpretive humility is the acknowledgement that divine action—not method or unaided reason—is largely determinative of the quality of our reading practices, and this is most readily expressed in dependent prayer. Humility is the recognition that we, of ourselves, can only progress so far as we seek to understand and appropriate God's good words. Thus, the royal reading practices direct us to view interpretive humility as the profession of one's solidarity with the transgressors and the admission of one's inability to read without divine assistance.

Delight

The final virtue, *delight*, is joy or pleasure that both motivates and results from reading. As an interpretive virtue it is surprisingly scarce in the hermeneutical literature, eliciting only brief mention by some, while others suggest distant analogues to it. For example, Webster, here as with other virtues, demonstrates the right instincts regarding the ethics of reading but does not develop the matter, writing, "Attention, astonishment and repentance, together with the *delight* and freedom in which they issue, characterize the reader of Holy Scripture when he or she reads well, that is, with courtesy and humility."[36] Delight in the realm of Scripture reading is a well-formed pleasure, far from what Griffiths calls a "Proustian" mode of engagement.[37] The proper enjoyment of the Bible is not sensual, merely aesthetic, or sexual, nor does it bypass what is there in Scripture or the reality of its divine Author. Rather, it involves pleasure amid reflection and requires a specific orientation. The Psalms furnish us with what such an orientation might entail.

Psalm 1:1–2 provides some substance to the notion of delight in the reading of Scripture. Verse 1 gives the content of what delight in torah is *not*, while verse 2b adds positive details to that account. Delight in the law of the Lord is the opposite of seeking the counsel of those who have no regard for God or his Word. Delight in torah means viewing it as the source of wisdom and life. VanGemeren writes that delight "expresses all that makes the man of God happy." He adds, "The law is more than

---

36. Webster, "Hermeneutics in Modern Theology," 80 (emphasis added).

37. "Proustian readers read in order to be incited to reverie, to be pushed by the catalyst of reading into the internal depths of memory and aesthetic sensibility. Reading is productive of sensual, aesthetic, and (often) properly sexual pleasure . . ." (Griffiths, "Reading as a Spiritual Discipline," 40).

his delight; it is his chief desire."[38] More than the longing to have his ears tickled or to hear what he wants to hear, the royal reader turns his ear to the Word of God. Delight is not a withdrawal from the wicked realities of life, but it does involve a single-minded focus on the counsel that comes from the Lord. Furthermore, delight is expressed in the sounding aloud of or meditating on the law. As we saw in chapter 3, hgh primarily refers to the *quality* of the reading act. It speaks of one being lost in her devotion or deep feelings in her soul.

The word "delight" is not used in Psalm 19, but the idea is there in two forms. First, the speaker expresses his delight in the law by treating it doxologically in 19:7–11. Second, he makes the more explicit claims that the uprightness of YHWH's precepts results in his rejoicing heart (19:8a) and that they are more to be desired than gold (19:10a). The law of God leads one to praise God, even in formal poetry. Thus the result of one's engagement with Scripture is rejoicing. However, delight is not merely the result, but also the motivation, of reading torah. The sense one gets of the speaker is that his heart overflows with pleasure in torah, and this pleasure leads to future engagement, which itself issues in further joy, and so on. Delight in Psalm 19 flows from and is informed by the recognition and actualization of the many benefits of God's Word in the life of the reader. It motivates reading and results in deeper longing. Ultimately, however, this delight is in the covenant God who graciously provides his good Word for the benefit of his people.

In Psalm 119, similar ideas are conveyed at various points. A delighting disposition is expressed, first, by ascribing great value to the Word of God. The law is as delightful as "all riches" (119:14; 162). The reason for such high praise and pleasure may be found in the function the law plays: it is a trustworthy counselor (119:24), connecting us to the presence of God through the Spirit. Second, delight is presented as the opposite of forgetfulness or neglect (119:16). What this suggests is that for one to claim delight in the law, he must also be its practitioner. Delight may not be synonymous with willing observance of the Word, but the former must contain the latter. Third, delight is a disposition that places one in a position to receive the Lord's personal moral instruction and guidance (119:35). Delight, therefore, is related to the reader's concern for the ethical direction of her life. Fourth, delight is rooted in a love for God's commandments that overflows in reverence and meditation

---

38. VanGemeren, *Psalms*, 55.

(119:47-48). What is striking is that the love called for is not directed at God *per se*, but rather his words. Moreover, these verses again make the connection between delight and meditation; that is, the former is expressed in the latter. Where there is no love, there is no delight; where there is no delight, there is no meditation. Fifth, the heart of the one who delights in the law is the opposite of one that is callous and unfeeling (119:70 NIV; "fat and gross," NRSV). A rejoicing heart is a tender and receptive heart, open to God's comfort and rebuke. Finally, delight is tied to hope. Specifically, the speaker credits his perseverance in trials and hope for salvation to his delight in the law (119:92, 143, 172). At stake is the intensity of commitment to the truth of God's promises. Had he not delighted in the law, he would have given up hope. Delight, then, connotes strength of belief in God's Word. As such it is able to empower perseverance to those who display it.

Delight can be the disposition as well as the result and response of one rightly engaging the Scriptures. As a response, it is often expressed as jubilant song and doxological proclamation (119:171-172, 175). Indeed, as a virtue (ἀρετή), delight is about declaring joyfully, musically and poetically even, the virtues (ἀρετάς) of God (1 Pet 2:9). This connection makes sense, particularly in light of C. S. Lewis' observations about his eventual realization of the nature of praise. He writes:

> But the most obvious fact about praise—whether of God or anything—strangely escaped me. I thought of it in terms of compliment, approval, or the giving of honour. I had never noticed that all enjoyment spontaneously overflows into praise . . . My whole, more general, difficulty about the praise of God depended on my absurdly denying to us, as regards the supremely Valuable, what we delight to do, what indeed we can't help doing, about everything else we value . . . I think we delight to praise what we enjoy because the praise not merely expresses but completes the enjoyment; it is its appointed consummation.[39]

Joy cannot be restrained. It must overflow into praise. And this joy will not be full until it performs the climactic acts of singing, shouting, and proclamation. When the royal speaker of Psalm 119 praises the Word of God, he simultaneously brings about the consummation of his delight in that very Word. Lewis then asks the rhetorical question: what would it be like if one could fully praise something to perfection? His response

---

39. Lewis, *Reflections on the Psalms*, 79-81.

is insightful: "Then indeed the object would be fully appreciated and our delight would have attained perfect development. The worthier the object, the more intense the delight would be."[40] Perhaps the torah psalms, particularly Psalm 119, are these very attempts to bring delight in and appreciation of God's Word to perfect development. At the very least, these psalms make it clear that delight, as a disposition and a response, is multi-dimensional and plays an important role in the entire reading act.

Unto Obedience and Holiness

These virtues—fear, humility, and delight—are verified and made complete in the response of *obedience*. Yet, it is interesting that obedience is also underrepresented in hermeneutical literature as an explicitly articulated orientation toward and response to Scripture. This apparent lacuna might be accounted for by the apparent transparency of obedience as an end in any encounter with God. To point out that a reader should be obedient to the Word of God is simply to say that the reader is a disciple or servant of God. However, sometimes what is implicit is soon forgotten if not brought out for (re-)examination. I propose that obedience is a chief goal and response of all Scripture reading. To read the Scriptures and neglect obedience is to miss the point of the Bible altogether and, thus, to be a failure. Obedience is at the heart of a properly theological reading of Scripture. Theologians are, of course, aware of the importance of obedience and indeed imply it in much of what they have to say in their accounts of readers. For example, Billings writes, "Reading Scripture is about being mastered by Jesus Christ through a biblical text that functionally stands over us as the Word of God, not under us as a word we can control, rearrange, and use for our own purposes."[41] We are called to follow the word of Scripture as servants of the Lord Jesus. Much of Vanhoozer's account of readers as disciples, followers, martyrs, witnesses, and so on, similarly points toward obedience as the proper posture and response to Scripture.[42] Almost every strand of the biblical material that we have traversed in this study has directed us along the same lines, while providing some specificity to how obedience might inform an account of readers. A few noteworthy examples will demonstrate how this is the case.

---

40. Ibid., 81.
41. Billings, *Word of God for the People of God*, 203.
42. Vanhoozer, *First Theology*, 201–2; idem, *Is There a Meaning*, 392–441.

When our story begins at the edge of Mount Sinai, the theme of obedient reading is put front and center: "Now therefore, if you *obey* my voice and *keep* my covenant, you shall be my treasured possession, . . . a priestly kingdom and a holy nation" (Exod 19:5–6, italics added). Obedience to the covenant stipulations defines and perpetuates the uniqueness and dignity of the people of Israel over against all the peoples of the earth. To be Israel is to be those who obey the voice of the Almighty. YHWH thus promises blessing to the thousandth generation of those who "keep" his commandments and curses upon those who reject him through disobedience (20:6). From Exodus to Deuteronomy the stress is laid on obedience as that which sets God's people apart. These people are called to have hearts that long to be obedient and hands that carry out the specific demands of the law. Even at the end of the canonical narrative—John's Revelation—obedience to the Word of God characterizes the people of God. It is those who heed the words of John's prophecy (Rev 1:3; 22:7, 9), who keep Christ's word (3:8, 10) and God's command (12:17), even to the point of death, who will reign as kings and priests to God. Often difficult obedience to God's Word separates wheat from chaff presently as well as eschatologically. Although speaking of the Abraham story, Moberly captures the essence of obedience as the heart of biblical religion and as an identity marker for the people of God:

> To the charge that religious people act self-seekingly, as the satan said of Job, and as Abraham himself apparently displays on occasion, the answer is that this is what true religion entails: a trusting obedience of God which means relinquishing to God that which is most precious (sacrifice Isaac, the beloved son); a self-dispossession of that on which one's identity and hopes are most deeply based (sacrifice Isaac, the long-awaited bearer of God's promise and Abraham's hopes for the future); a recognition that response to God may be as costly, or even more costly, at the end of one's life as it was earlier on (Abraham must relinquish his future as once he relinquished his past); a recognition that the outcome of obedience is unknown and cannot be predicted in advance (a test is not "only" a test, but is a real test); and a recognition that the religious community to which one belongs and which tells this as one of its foundation stories can only become complacent at the expense of the essence of its identity.[43]

---

43. Moberly, *Bible, Theology and Faith*, 182.

Trusting obedience lies at the center of true religion, and this obedience is self-divesting, costly, risky, life threatening, and unaware of outcomes. Yet it is this kind of obedience that marks the disciples of Jesus Christ and the faithful readers of Scripture.

The theme of obedience to the Word of God as the chief response is further accented when we look at the depiction of the ideal king as the paradigmatic reader. The kingship law commands that the fear of the Lord be expressed by "diligently observing all the words of this law and these statutes . . . [not] turning aside from the commandment, either to the right or to the left" (Deut 17:19b–20a). The king's primary duty is to obey carefully the command of God, particularly as it pertains to his rule over God's people. The narratives of Josiah and Jehoiakim, in their own ways, highlight obedience as a key criterion for assessing the faithfulness of these rulers. Josiah is introduced as the one who walked in David's ways and did not swerve to the right or left of God's law (2 Kgs 22:2). Obedience is the lens through which the reader is to evaluate Josiah, especially over against prior and subsequent kings. Jehoiakim is accordingly presented as the rejecter of God's Word and, thus, as the epitome of faithless and unfaithful reading. When we come to the Psalter, especially Psalm 119, the evidence is overwhelming that obedience is everything for the ideal reader—it is the longing of the heart, the aim for which he reads, and the result of the act: "O that my ways may be steadfast in keeping your statutes!" (119:5); "I will keep your law continually, forever and ever" (119:44); "I hurry and do not delay to keep your commandments" (119:60).[44] The desire for obedience is *the* primary orientation readers are to have toward the Word of God, while the carrying out of obedient action is *the* cardinal response. Every Bible reading act is abortive that misses, or at least under-emphasizes, this critical outcome.

Perhaps at this point it would be fitting to expand on the importance of suffering as a context for the cultivation of interpretive virtue. First Peter and Revelation emphasized a suffering royal priesthood, who in affliction embody and minister the Word. The royal reader of Psalm 119 ties affliction to faithful engagement with the Word, in fact linking it to delight and obedience: "If your law had not been my delight, I would have perished in my affliction" (Ps 119:92 ESV); "Trouble and anguish have found me out, but your commandments are my delight (119:144 ESV); "Before I was afflicted I went astray, but now I keep your word"

---

44. See also Ps 119:2, 4, 8, 17, 30, 115, 145, and dozens more.

(119:67 ESV); "They have almost made an end of me on earth, but I have not forsaken your precepts" (119:87). Understanding is furthermore linked to affliction: "It is good for me that I was afflicted, that I might learn your statutes" (119:71). Luther sheds light on these connections when he speaks of "agonizing struggle" and "experience" as chief characteristics of a theologian (or reader of Scripture).[45] Agonizing struggle (*tentatio, Anfechtung*) is a faith-filled internal battle instigated by suffering, injustice, and pain. According to Luther, it "teaches you not only to know and understand, but also to experience how right, how true, how sweet, how lovely, how mighty, how comforting God's Word is, wisdom beyond all wisdom."[46] This struggle forces one to pay close attention to Scripture, leading to what he calls "experience"—a sustained personal, oral, and communal *meditatio* on Scripture amid hardship—which may itself produce eventual mastery of the spirit of the text.[47] Adversity becomes a hermeneutical key, touchstone, and perhaps litmus test for faithful reading of the Bible because it enables us to taste and see, test and approve—to experience—the goodness and truth of God's Word in an intimate way. Doubtless Christ modeled the experience of the sustaining goodness of God's Word in his wilderness temptations (Matt 4:1–11). We are likewise summoned to embrace suffering so that we might, in experiencing the Word, cultivate virtues and respond in obedience.

Now obedience—particularly obedience forged in the fires of suffering—points to what would seem to be an overriding category in which to understand the ideal reader, namely, *holiness*—particularly holiness through obedience to God's law. Exodus 19:5–6 hints at this connection between holiness and obedience: obey the divine voice and you will continue to be a royal priesthood and holy nation. God objectively sanctifies the people, and subsequently commands them to display their holiness through obedience to the totality of the covenant stipulations to follow. Holiness is expressed through obedience to the Lord's words. The matter is put similarly in 1 Pet 1:2, where the church is spoken of as those "who have been chosen and destined by God the Father and

---

45. He also names the grace of the Holy Spirit, opportunity, concentrated textual study, and knowledge and practice of the academic disciplines. See Bayer, *Martin Luther's Theology*, 17.

46. Luther, "Preface to the Wittenburg Edition," 73.

47. Bayer, *Martin Luther's Theology*, 21–22. "Yet experience alone makes the theologian" (*Table Talk Recorded by Veit Dietrich, No. 46* [1531], *LW* 54:7). Cf. *Preface to the Complete Edition of Luther's Latin Writings* (1545), *LW* 34:338.

sanctified by the Spirit to be obedient to Jesus Christ." In other words, holiness (objective) leads to holiness (subjective) expressed as obedience to the divine Word. In speaking of the ways which the church manifests its holiness, Webster writes: "The Church's holiness is visible as it hears afresh the promise and command of the gospel."[48] For our concerns, the hearing of the *command* of the gospel is particularly relevant. Webster continues:

> As commandment, the gospel is the declaration of the law, the shape or direction for the life of God's holy people. Hearing the gospel's summons to obedience, the Church is holy, submitting to the gospel's judgement of sin, and setting itself to govern its life by God's commands. In this way, the Church is holy as it stands beneath the final promulgation of the summons to that holiness which corresponds to the divine commitment of election: You shall be my people. How, then, is the Church holy? By attention and submission to the gospel as the indicative of election and the imperative of obedience.[49]

The church manifests its holiness as it commits itself to hear and obey the Word of God. Yet, it is not only obedience that is constitutive of the holiness to which the church is called. Obedience presupposes the virtues addressed earlier and, thus, implies that they are also components of the holy act of reading God's Word. Reverence for God and his law, humility before him, and delight in his commands cannot but lead to obedient action. Thus holiness designates the entire transformation of persons so that they represent the creaturely counterpart to the holiness of God: he is to be feared as the awesome One, exalted as the only God, delighted in as the blessed One, and ultimately obeyed as Lord. The call to be a right reader of Scripture is a call to holiness.

In that light, it is worth asking what an orientation to holiness as obedience might contribute to current accounts of how experience of the Spirit relates to reading the Bible. Holiness is a protest against the values of the cultures of this world. It is a protest against our natural, sinful inclinations. As such, holiness should spark and sustain a healthy initial suspicion of all claims to experiences of the Spirit, especially when these experiences apparently confirm the ever-evolving values of society. The church hears and responds to the voice of the Lord, a voice that very

48. Webster, *Holiness*, 72.
49. Ibid., 73.

often contradicts the ways of the culture, even contradicting the church's practices and calling it to pattern its life after the Holy One who sanctified it. That being the case, we should not expect our reading of Scripture to conform to the prevalent mores of the culture. Rather, we should at least anticipate that faithful reading will often lead to those beliefs and practices that contradict what is most valued in our day. Reading this way is realistic. The call to holiness is also a call to honesty: even as those indwelt by the liberating Spirit, the church is often tempted to return to the bondage of Egypt. The call of God, therefore, is repeatedly: "Come out from among them and be separate" (2 Cor 6:17). To read as those called to separation requires that God's judging grace leads us to exercise a hermeneutic of suspicion against ourselves and our habitual desire to rethink, re-envision, relativize, and make relevant the Scriptures, perhaps especially in how we treat its commands. Most assuredly, the world will pose questions that the church must answer. However, the church's holiness implies a cautious approach to the way that it appropriates the culture's questions, no less its answers, to the church's act of reading Scripture.

God's people, as a royal priesthood of readers, are called to embody the characteristics that make for faithful Scripture reading. These "virtues" are many, but all of them tend toward the goal of obedience as the prime display of holiness. Holiness as the summative characteristic is the ultimate goal and disposition of the reader of Scripture. Holiness is expressed as obedience to God's commands that is rooted in fear, humility, and delight. Without holiness no one looking into the Scriptures will see the One about whom these Scriptures testify (Heb 12:14).

A Preaching Priesthood: Readers as Ministers and Missionaries

To read Scripture in light of the royal priestly dignity and responsibility granted to believers no doubt involves attending to one's character formation. Ethical reading is personal: it enjoins individuals to work out their own reading practices with fear and trembling. However, lest Bible reading dissolve into an entirely personal act, we must be reminded that faithful reading demands an outward orientation. Indeed, the streams of election, sanctification, and covenant terminate at what I would call the ministerial and missionary aspects of reading. As for ministry, much of the official priestly vocation in Israel, for example, was to take the

Word of God and teach, discern, interpret, apply, judge, and bless, for the sake of the community. Priests were those chosen, consecrated, and covenanted to carry out these others-directed tasks within the community of God. Reading as a missionary act also receives much attention in the biblical material. Israel's priestly vocation was to declare to the nations the salvation of YHWH (Isa 59–62); Jesus Christ fulfills his priestly vocation by teaching and proclaiming the Word of God; the *telos* of the church's royal priestly calling is the proclamation of the mighty acts of God (1 Pet 2:9); preaching the gospel, according to Paul, is a priestly calling (Rom 15:16); those who hold on to the Word of God and bear witness to it in the face of suffering will be declared royal priests (cf. Rev 20:6). The election and sanctification of Israel, Jesus Christ, and the church are ordered toward the proclamation of the Word of God. These insights into the ministerial and missionary dimensions of reading converge in and are ably expressed by Luther, as shown in chapter 6. Regarding the ministerial reading of the Word, he argues, first, that all believers are royal priests responsible for ministering the Word of God to one another in the forms of teaching and preaching, the sacraments, and comfort and encouragement, thus contributing to the purification of the church. Second, concerning the missionary reading of the God's Word, Luther underscores that both oral and sacramental forms of the Word are annunciative—they proclaim to the outside world the gospel of a merciful God—and all believers are responsible for this publication. For Luther, the Word has not been read correctly if it is not proclaimed to those who need it. For the remainder of this chapter, therefore, I will attempt to expand on these two important contributions by the German Reformer.

Reading Scripture as Ministry

Luther's insights can be stated in a two-part proposition: *All believers are royal priests who are responsible to minister the Word of God to one another and to proclaim the Word of God to the outside world as witnesses.* *All believers* refers to every Christian in every church and every church in every nation. There is no exception. The dignity and responsibility bestowed by the designation of royal priesthood are given to all equally—Jew or Gentile, American or African, woman or man, poor, middle-class, or rich. The church could not, ultimately, be located in the official priesthood of Luther's day. It had to take seriously the privilege of all the baptized. Fowl and Jones somewhat share this instinct, arguing for the need of a more expansive notion of the church in order to combat potentially sectarian and, thus, unfaithful readings of Scripture. They contend that the "we" who hear Scripture must take into account the voices of supposed outsiders such as homosexuals, those bearing some "family resemblance" (Jews), and cultural and religious foreigners, as these serve to correct our sometimes arrogant and destructive readings.[50] Although one need not follow Fowl and Jones at every turn, they point us to the importance of openness in the reading of Scripture, particularly openness to silenced and neglected voices within the church of Jesus Christ. "All believers" emphasizes that even the un- and under-educated must have a voice. Furthermore, on an inter-ecclesial level, non-Western voices must be heard, appreciated, and appropriated.[51] If all believers are royal priests, then all are responsible to minister the Word. This democratization of priestly privilege does not ignore Hauerwas' concerns about the unformed and individualistic North American Bible reader.[52] Rather, this expansion of the "we" is a wise measure to keep in check potentially parochial and political readings of Scripture. Again, there is a faint echo of Luther's concerns here: when the church ceases hearing the voices of "outsiders," it becomes turned in on itself, falling prey to bias-confirming interpretations and, in many respects, losing its way. Instead, every believer as a royal priest is responsible for the church.

All believers *are responsible to minister the Word of God*. Royal priesthood confers on every Christian the privilege and, therefore, responsibility of "reading" the Word for the sake of others. The biblical-theological overviews of royal priesthood and priestly reading in chapters 2, 4, and 5 provide a picture of the various forms of reading Scripture both complemented and supplemented by Luther's account of the seven forms of the ministry of the Word (teaching/preaching, baptism, the Lord's Supper, absolution, prayer, sacrifice, and judging doctrine). Many of the ministries in the former find rough cognates in

---

50. Fowl and Jones, *Reading in Communion*, 113–34; cf. Jones, "Formed and Transformed," 28.

51. For a helpful introduction to the issues surrounding the intersection of globalization and theological hermeneutics, see Treier, *Introducing Theological Interpretation*, 157–86.

52. See Hauerwas, *Unleashing the Scripture*, 15–18.

Luther's proposal and thus can be narrowed further to two broad categories of priestly reading acts: teaching/preaching and blessing. Faithfully reading the Word as a royal priest requires ministering the Word in these various ways within the community of the church.

The primary ministry of the Word given to the royal priesthood is that of teaching and preaching the Word of God to one another. On a basic level this means that believers are called to instruct one another with the Scriptures whenever the opportunity presents itself. This teaching ministry takes place in every sphere within which Christians operate, even though there will be asymmetries. Parents are called to minister the Word to their children and children to their parents; mature believers are called to instruct the immature and the immature to challenge the mature; ministers are to preach the Word to the congregation regularly and the congregation to remind the minister of God's promises. All are priests, and when they minister the Word of God to one another they truly demonstrate this to be the case.

Furthermore, as priests, we are called to follow in the steps of Ezra, who reinterpreted and applied torah for the community of exiles living many years after the texts were written. Priestly reading involves the wise application of Scripture to ever changing contexts, and this not only for oneself but also for others. Related to this function is the priestly role of judging in matters of clean/unclean, legal (intra-ecclesial) cases, and doctrine (according to Luther). All of these acts require some skill and care in bringing the past into the present, something written into the living and breathing reality of every day. Perhaps this is where current hermeneutical appeals to *phronesis*, or practical reasoning, most fruitfully intersect with this study. *Phronesis* is knowledge of how to act in concrete and ever-changing situations; it is about "doing the right thing in a particular situation—i.e., seeing what is right within the situation and grasping it."[53] *Christian* practical reasoning, according to Fowl, requires a focus on Christ's life as its basis. For any judgment to be recognizably Christian, there must be some measure of continuity with the acts and ways of Jesus. This no doubt echoes the practices outlined in our case study at the end of chapter 4, that priestly reading is principled—it follows trajectories and precedents of prior texts (and persons) in order to be able to make the wise decisions sometimes necessary for living faithfully before the Lord. The history of Jesus is the trajectory and precedent

---

53. Gadamer, *Truth and Method*, 19, 314.

with which we must be in continuity. Christian *phronesis*, moreover, demands that we pay attention to human examples of faithful thinking and living, and imitate them. This imitation is not an exact replication of past and present exemplars, but rather "non-identical repetition." Fowl suggests that practically wise readers will appropriate the practices of those who are more advanced in the process—often those culturally, geographically, and historically distant—bringing their judgments into the present.[54]

Vanhoozer defines *phronesis* as "the canonically nurtured ability to say and do the 'fit in Christ' in relatively singular contexts in ways appropriate to their relative singularity," which requires *perception*—the ability to discern everything theologically relevant in a particular situation—as well as *perspective*—the ability to see things in light of what God has done in Christ (the "theo-drama").[55] *Phronesis* is a Christ-centered sapiential virtue that enables faithful readings in manifold specific situations. In Treier's extensive treatment, he defines the *telos* of *phronesis* as spiritual fruit—supremely love—which displays God's glory to the world; its object is the performance of what is pleasing to God.[56] Moreover, for Treier, practical reasoning is decidedly Christocentric and particularly humble—it is patterned on Christ *and* seeks the good of others.[57] This connection to humility suggests something pertinent about phronetic reading, namely, it is priestly reading in that it focuses on the other. In some way, interpretative *phronesis* is realized when the reader considers the direction of the church and the persons that comprise it. Priestly prudence in reading the Word may require the involvement of all members of the Body directing the gaze of one another to examples of faithful Christian living and together envisioning what "non-identical repetition" might look like in their context. The phronetic reader may sometimes have to render unpopular judgments for the sake of the other. Like the Israelite priest who was concerned for the purity of the people, she may have to offer a word of correction to a fellow pilgrim if she is convinced that the Christian is not reasoning (φρονεῖτε) with the mind of Christ (Phil 2:5) or living consistently with the redemptive story of which he or she is a participant.

54. Fowl, *Engaging Scripture*, 196–99.
55. Vanhoozer, *Drama of Doctrine*, 332–35.
56. Treier, *Virtue and the Voice of God*, 57.
57. Ibid., 51–52.

The concern for judgment and proper application in reading directs us to Griffiths' account of the function of commentaries within religious traditions. He notes that a key purpose of commentaries is to recommend how the work commented upon should be used or applied. He writes:

> Commentarial acts motivated by the need to apply will most often issue in exhortation or recommendation. For most contemporary speakers of English, the most culturally familiar forms of commentary in which application dominates are probably the sermon and the judicial opinion. Explanation may often be present in both of these, but exhortation (in the former case) and apodictic ruling (in the latter) always is.[58]

Commentary closely resembles the priestly reading acts of applying the Word of God and rendering judgments about one's use or appropriation of it. As a reading act it is concerned about the patterns of behavior that should follow from reading the work being commented upon—something characteristic of many sermons and application commentaries. In addition, Griffiths points out that the commentarial application may also have to do with patterns of behavior directed toward the sacred text itself. The commentarial act commends to the reader or hearer how he should use the work being commented on, rather than how to use what it tells him.[59] Much of the current literature on the theological interpretation of Scripture might fit loosely into this category. These are concerned with instructing readers on how to approach the Bible—technically as well as dispositionally. With these observations, Griffiths raises the important issue of the proper forms of public-oriented Bible reading or, more generally, theological interpretation of Scripture. What his study at least demonstrates is that religious traditions—Christian and otherwise—have continually deemed it appropriate, indeed natural, to produce commentaries on their holy books. It is with these application-oriented commentaries that their scriptures are brought into the present and appropriately deployed therein. Since the priestly reading of Scripture is concerned with the same matters, it may be rightly labeled commentarial. This conclusion suggests, therefore, that the production of commentaries, hermeneutical texts, and sermons is not merely something intended to fatten the pockets of publishers or fulfill a Sunday

---

58. Griffiths, *Religious Reading*, 90.
59. Ibid., 90–91.

morning ritual, but rather may be seen as a necessary, or at least appropriate, expression of the priestly calling of the Christian.

Deuteronomy 31:9–13 reminds us that another priestly task was the regular reading of the law to the people so that successive generations of Israelites "may hear and learn to fear the Lord your God" (31:13). What kind of practice would resemble such reading in light of the universal priesthood of believers? Once again, Griffiths' study proves helpful, particularly his examination of anthologies and quotation. He writes: "Quotation, whatever the conventions governing it in a particular case, has most fundamentally the purpose of superimposing the past upon the present, or of representing the past to the present. This, which is now being quoted, was said before and is now being said again."[60] If public reading is an extended form of quotation, then whatever quotation accomplishes generally is amplified by its protracted cognate. Public reading, whether in a congregational setting or one-to-one encounter, forces the past upon the present. It declares that what was said before by Moses, Isaiah, Paul, or John is now being said afresh. The task of the priestly reader is to give the past a new hearing in the present by taking the words of God on her lips and reiterating them to her fellow priests. Priestly reading requires giving voice to the words of Scripture, not simply because they are wise words (which they are), but because they are the ever-relevant words of God that must be heard.

The second broad category of ministerial reading acts is related to blessing. Chapter 4 described blessing as the assurance that the Lord would keep his promises to his people in their everyday lives; it is a pronouncement of God's will and pledge to bless his covenant people in an ongoing way, particularly as they walk faithfully before him. Although teaching and blessing have some overlap, the latter is a distinct type of reading act. A blessing is an *effective* word spoken; it brings about what it promises. This dynamic nature of blessing is captured by Luther's account of the priestly right of all Christians to absolve fellow believers of their sins. The reformer, we might recall, describes absolution as the announcement of the forgiveness of sins that draws its power from Christ's words to the church about binding and loosing (Matt 18:18). Put another way, the announcement of forgiveness is plainly the proclamation of the gospel, the declaration that God in Christ no longer holds the

---

60. Ibid., 101.

believer's sins against her.[61] In this light, priestly blessing takes the form of preaching the good news to one another, especially those burdened by their sins. Thus, the appeal of some popular authors to "preach the gospel to ourselves" takes a communal turn.[62] Believers, as priests, are called to summon fellow priests to trust in the promises of God and, thus, the God who makes the promises. Both the speaker and hearer must trust in the faithfulness of God. Absolution points to the distinctive nature of divine promises.

Anthony Thiselton offers a number of theses on the nature of promises, some of which might illuminate the present discussion. First, he observes that promises in the Bible presuppose "institutional facts," such as the covenant and death of Christ. Without such prior facts, a promise could not be construed as a promise nor could it be viewed as trustworthy.[63] Second, "acts of promise bring to light most clearly the commitments and responsibilities of agents of promise within an inter-subjective public, extra-linguistic world of ethical undertaking and address."[64] What Thiselton highlights is that promises (1) oblige the agent of promise to fulfill the promise, (2) are strong indicators of commitment on the part of the agent, and (3) call attention to the status of the agent, that is, his power, right, and integrity to perform this promise.[65] With respect to God, these three features are intended to provide confidence to the recipient of God's blessing: "Believers can know where they stand with God and receive assurance: his promissory illocutions are liberative."[66] Finally, promise is a paradigmatic case of how words can transform the world of reality.[67] Contrasting promises and assertions, Thiselton notes: "Characteristically promise shapes world-to-word, assertion shapes word-to-world." The former is an act that shapes a state of affairs, the latter declares a certain state of affairs to be true; one determines reality, the other is determined by reality.[68] A discussion of the nature of promises, particularly of the divine sort, intersects

---

61. See *LW* 40:28.
62. See, e.g., Bridges, *The Gospel for Real Life*, 11 passim.
63. Thiselton, "More on Promising," 124.
64. Ibid., 126.
65. Ibid., 126–27.
66. Ibid., 127.
67. Ibid., 129.
68. Thiselton, *New Horizons*, 298; cf. idem, "More on Promising," 129.

with an account of readers when readers are conceived as enlisted or commissioned agents of promise. On the basis of God's character, the reality of the covenant in Jesus Christ, the Word of God in Scripture, and the divine commission to kingly-priestly ministry, readers confidently declare God's effective and reality-transforming promise to the afflicted. Blessing, then, is promise, and the promise is not vacuous; it is a pledge of the very presence of God. And since all God's promises find their "Yes!" in Jesus Christ (2 Cor 1:20a), we are ever directed to him as the content and guarantor of the divine blessing. Whether we conceive of blessing as the promise of divine favor (as in chapter 4) or as the promise of forgiveness (as in Luther), it is undoubtedly the good news of Jesus Christ.[69] Thus, to be others-oriented readers of Scripture, believers must take seriously the power of divine promises, especially as they have come to us in Jesus, and find ways to make them a regular part of their daily and weekly discourse with one another. In doing this, we strengthen the church by directing its attention to the trustworthiness of God.

Reading Scripture is a ministry of the Word of God involving a variety of tasks directed at those within the Christian community. Instruction, judgment, application, interpretation, reading, and blessing are merely modes of fulfilling the others-oriented *telos* of the incarnate Word and thus the scriptural Word. As royal priests, believers in Jesus find themselves situated in a drama in which faithful performance is measured partially, although significantly, by whether and how well they use Scripture to aid the faithful performances of others. Thus, reading Scripture is ministry.

Reading Scripture as Mission

The second part of the opening proposition claims that all believers are royal priests who are responsible *to proclaim the Word of God to the outside world as witnesses*. It is common in missiological discussions to see the church as a missionary church. Taking its cue from the *missio Dei* and, as we saw in Barth, the election of God's community, the church is by definition missionary:

---

69. "God has shown himself faithful or trustworthy by uttering in Jesus the single word: Yes! In that one word the many words of the scriptural promises are summed up and fulfilled" (Watson, "An Evangelical Response," 289).

> Mission is so much at the heart of the Church's life that, rather than think of it as one aspect of its existence, it is better to think of it as defining its essence. The Church is by nature missionary to the extent that, if it ceases to be missionary, it has not just failed in one of its tasks, it has ceased being Church. Thus, the Church's self-understanding and sense of identity (its ecclesiology) is inherently bound up with its call to share and live out the Gospel of Jesus Christ to the ends of the earth and the end of time.[70]

If mission is the essence of the church, then all of the church's practices must conform to this essence. Thus, the reading of Scripture, as a central practice, must reflect the missionary nature of the church. In that light, reading Scripture is a centrifugal act directed toward those separated from the community of Christ.

Few authors have connected reading specifically with mission in their treatments. In his study, Billings notably argues that the church's reading of Scripture must be missional, but not merely as evangelism and social programs. Rather, the church is on mission by living up to its identity as those who belong to Jesus Christ. Thus, the missional use of Scripture is centered on the formation of the community. "Scripture," he writes, "is the means by which the living Christ instructs, builds up, and continually converts the church to be a people of his mission and his way by the Spirit's enabling power."[71] According to Billings, we must avoid simply using Scripture for church growth and outreach, whether to motivate for evangelism or to attract outsiders. Instead, he counters, "there is no activity more missional than Christ-centered, Spirit-empowered worship, which speaks, hears, smells, and tastes the great drama of the gospel."[72] Thus, he connects our previous discussions of interpretive virtue and ministerial reading to the mission of the church. As we encourage one another through the use of Scripture to be shaped

---

70. Kirk, *What is Mission?*, 30.

71. Billings, *Word of God for the People of God*, 222–23.

72. Ibid., 223. Similar points are being made by many in current missional church conversations. Darrell Guder, for example, writes: "The evangelizing congregation is continuously being evangelized . . . Evangelization as the heart of ministry means that the gospel-centered community encounters and celebrates Christ. This is the purpose and witness of public worship . . . Our worship is therefore the first demonstration before the world of our sentness, as we respond to God's grace in the good news of Jesus Christ" (Guder, *Continuing Conversion of the Church*, 151–55).

in a Christ-like direction, and actually do reflect the way of Jesus, we *are* witnesses.

Vanhoozer moves in a similar direction when he describes the missionary role of the church:

> Preaching, teaching, and evangelism are the means by which the gospel becomes that all-encompassing framework that allows us to think and experience truth, goodness, and beauty in light of the history of Jesus Christ. The ministry of the Word involves more than communicating a few truths; it involves transmitting a whole way of thinking and experiencing. *Preaching and teaching should be "evangelistic," then, in the sense of enabling people to indwell the gospel* (=evangel) *as the primary framework for all that they say and do.*[73]

The church's missionary proclamation is evangelistic inasmuch as it forms a community that indwells the gospel. This more community-focused aspect of mission certainly echoes God's calling of Israel as a royal priesthood and holy nation (Exod 19:5–6). As the people of God reflect their difference and distinctiveness to the nations, God is shown to be the wise, holy, and gracious One. Similarly, as God through Scripture shapes us, the outside world will become cognizant of the work of the triune God in our midst. Surely Vanhoozer (and, for that matter, Billings) would say more about the church's evangelistic and missionary preaching, but in this context he emphasizes the missionary church as one that lives out the gospel and in that way witnesses to God's saving work in Christ.[74]

However, focusing solely on this aspect of the missionary reading of Scripture may lead to a neglect of the more active and evangelistic aspect, the proclamatory component. The biblical authors give us pause: "But you are a chosen race, a royal priesthood, a holy nation, God's own people, *in order that you may proclaim* the mighty acts of him who called you out of darkness into his marvelous light" (1 Pet 2:9). Although Peter will call Christians to conduct their lives in a manner that demonstrates

---

73. Vanhoozer, *Drama of Doctrine*, 74 (italics added).

74. For example, Billings, speaking about the various practices of the church, writes: "Why are worship, Christian education, and the overall ministry of the word and sacrament so important? Ultimately, it is because the church, in these acts, holds forth the gospel of the triune drama of salvation to us—*and to the world*" (*Word of God for the People of God*, 220 [emphasis added]). His emphasis, however, is on the embodiment of Scripture as the primary mode of missionary Scripture use.

their new identity as royal priests (2:10ff), he declares to them the goal of their identity change: proclamation of God's mighty deeds, particularly those recorded in Scripture and experienced in real life. Like the survivors of Isa 66:18–21, God's people are to perform the priestly task of making his name famous to those who have not heard of his deeds. Evangelism as a vital part of the whole mission of the church is an expression of its reading practices.

David Bosch, in seeking to provide a nuanced description of evangelism, provides a number of considerations that, when taken together, are helpful for envisioning reading as evangelistic.[75] First, "evangelism involves witnessing to what God has done, is doing, and will do." Thus evangelism is the publication of what God has done in human history through Jesus Christ. Evangelistic reading, then, at its most basic level requires viewing Scripture as a missionary book and communicating its message, one centered on Jesus Christ the Liberator. Second, "evangelism is always invitation"; it has to do with the proclamation of a positive message and the summons to experience the joy of liberation. Since the message of Scripture is a message of joy for all peoples, reading should inevitably issue in the invitation to others to experience that joy. Finally, though evangelism is not only verbal, in that it involves our actions and character, it must inevitably include some words. Bosch writes, "The deed without the word is dumb; the word without the deed is empty. Words interpret deeds and deeds validate words."[76] Although Bosch refers to Christian deeds, his point is all the more true if we speak of *the* divine deed—the life and work of Jesus. Not only do we not have independent epistemic access to the divine deeds, but also we could not interpret these deeds apart from the words of Scripture. To read evangelistically is to construe what God has done and is doing in the world in light of Scripture. Evangelistic reading is therefore interpretative; it is, at least partially, the royal-priestly teaching ministry *ad extra*. Luke hints at the church's apostolic call: "Thus it is written, that the Messiah is to suffer and to rise from the dead on the third day, and that repentance and forgiveness of sins is to be proclaimed in his name to all nations, beginning from Jerusalem. You are witnesses of these things" (Luke 24:46). When the church proclaims the need for repentance and the reality of forgive-

---

75. He provides eighteen considerations before offering a summary definition of evangelism. See Bosch, *Transforming Mission*, 411–20.

76. Ibid., 412, 413, 420.

ness in Jesus, it is announcing the scriptural Word—both as promise and fulfillment. To be a witness is to proclaim the promised Christ and his finished work as preserved in Scripture. Moreover, it could be said that evangelism is the consummation or completion of the entire reading act, indeed as the achievement of one of Scripture's chief perlocutionary effects. As Luther remarked repeatedly, the New Testament gospel comes to full flower when it is proclaimed in the world by believers. Following Scott's dictum that interpretation is practice, the church's verbal declaration of the good news, as a reading act, is the performed meaning of the missionary scriptural Word. Faithful reading is proclamation, publication, declaration. In sum, reading is missionary work as the church embodies Scripture and announces its central message—Jesus Christ—to the world.

Sounds and Speech as Theological Interpretation: On the Role of Orality

The many vocal reading practices highlighted throughout this study suggest that orality is an important consideration when trying to depict readers and the requisite practices that make for faithful Scripture reading. Meditation, recitation, singing, preaching, teaching, blessing, even the sacraments, are oral practices that in some way contribute to, comprise, or complete the act of reading. A consideration of orality as it relates to reading Scripture is certainly in order. Since an exhaustive treatment of this suggestive topic would require its own full-length study, I will limit this final section to some brief observations about the nature of orality and its relationship to the Bible, then offer some implications and suggestions for further study.

ORALITY AND READING

The most obvious thing about Scripture is that it is *graphē*, writing in the most basic sense of the term. Yet, like many other written artifacts, it originates in the realm of the oral:

> Written texts all have to be related somehow, directly or indirectly, to the world of sound, the natural habitat of language, to yield their meanings. "Reading" a text means converting it to sound, aloud or in the imagination, syllable-by-syllable in slow reading or sketchily in the rapid reading common to high-technology

cultures. Writing can never dispense with orality... Oral expression can exist and mostly has existed without any writing at all, writing never without orality.[77]

This observation appears commonplace among anthropologists, linguists, and sociologists, who, moreover, call attention to the predominance of oral reading throughout the history of the West. William Graham, for example, writes: "Oral speech remains the intrinsic form of human communication, and for most literate peoples of history outside our society in recent times, reading has normally been a vocal, physical activity, even for the solitary reader."[78] Western reading practices into the nineteenth century were primarily oral. Relating this phenomenon to the reading of religious books, Graham adds: "The sacred books carried both the special authority of the written page and the living immediacy of oral reading and recitation. Oral reading and recitation were the primary means through which the written word was apprehended and reflected upon, as well as communicated, not only among the illiterate but also among the educated members of the community."[79] Even among the literate, vocal recitation was the primary mode of reading scripture.

Yet these observations have not received a great deal of attention among advocates of the theological interpretation of Scripture. When speaking about reading the Bible, conversations often tend to assume the silent reading of written material—a decidedly modern notion. If, however, oral forms of reading have been the dominant mode of engagement with written texts, including Scripture, then some account must be given of how orality might shape our depictions of readers and reading.

The Psychodynamics of Orality

The worlds of the biblical authors and their audiences were oral. Therefore, how they might have recorded their writings and expected their readers to appropriate them could be instructive to contemporary readers of Scripture. Walter Ong has shown that the psychodynamics of oral cultures differ from literate (or print) cultures in a number of relevant ways.[80]

77. Ong, *Orality and Literacy*, 8.
78. Graham, *Beyond the Written Word*, 33. For his extended discussion of oral reading practices throughout history, see ibid., 30–44.
79. Ibid., 123.
80. See Ong, *Orality and Literacy*, 31–77.

First, oral peoples believe words to have power. Spoken words are events; hence the dual meaning of the Hebrew term *dabar* as "word" and "event." Sounds, especially words, are dynamic and living; they are modes of action. For writing cultures, words are things, not actions, and as such are dead. However, as Ong notes, these dead words are "subject to dynamic resurrection."[81] For readers of Scripture, this resurrection may occur when the written words of God are vocalized, thus reinforcing that God is a speaking God who must always be heard. This suggestion might help strengthen the force of Paul's injunction to Timothy that he *read* Scripture publicly (1 Tim 4:13).

Second, since in an oral culture conceptualized knowledge that is not repeated aloud soon vanishes, oral societies try hard to repeat constantly what has been learned through the ages. This tendency fosters a state of mind that restrains intellectual experimentation. Writing tends to devalue those who can repeat the past stories in favor of those who might discover new things.[82] The preservation of biblical truth in an oral culture, therefore, would inhibit theological novelty and may help to preserve the Christian identity of the community. For readers, these insights suggest the traditioning role of reading Scripture aloud and retelling Scripture's stories, especially in a communal setting, as these help to safeguard the identity of the church.

Third, and related, knowing in oral cultures "means achieving close, empathetic, communal identifications with the known." Writing, conversely, "separates the knower from the known and thus sets up conditions for 'objectivity,' in the sense of personal disengagement or distancing."[83] Graham states the issue in terms of participation/non-participation in the stories that are told:

> Where memory collapses time spans, writing tends to fix events temporally and heighten the sense of their distinctiveness as well as their "pastness," or separation from the present and the individual person. The sense of participation in the events narrated becomes more difficult . . . In other words, literacy changes the relationship between a society and its traditions, as well as that between individuals and their past, because it fixes traditions and that past in a way that distances both from the present.[84]

---

81. Ibid., 32–33.
82. Ibid., 41–42.
83. Ibid., 45–46.
84. Graham, *Beyond the Written Word*, 16.

Oral practices foster a sense of self-involvement or participation in the events narrated. Of course vocalizing stories does not guarantee participatory hearing, but it can mitigate some of the distancing effects of silent reading. These observations are all the more important for Christians, who must recognize the history of Adam, Israel, and Jesus Christ as their own history. A distancing from the stories is a distancing from the life-altering realities these stories communicate.

Finally, spoken words help bring people together, forming close-knit communities. When a speaker addresses an audience, they are unified under the same spoken word—speaker with the audience, audience members with one another. On the other hand, Ong writes, "If the speaker asks the audience to read a handout provided for them, as each reader enters into his or her own private reading world, the unity of the audience is shattered, to be reestablished only when oral speech begins again. Writing and print isolate."[85] Vocal modes of reading Scripture, therefore, might be one way to address the concern for communal and non-individualistic reading practices in the church. In these and many other ways, studies on orality open up ways of thinking about Scripture reading that remain somewhat unexplored.

It would, of course, be naïve to crusade for a return to a primarily oral society, as this would indeed be impossible. Nevertheless an understanding of orality is important because (1) for most communities in history, interaction with the sacred text has been oral/aural and (2) a focus on orality encourages our apprehension of the relational dynamics of reading Scripture, such as that which occurs in blessing and benediction.[86] What is more realistic than a full-fledged return to orality, then, is a recognition that oral forms of reading might open up avenues for encountering the Word of God in fresh (or forgotten) ways. Thus, the church should consider making them a more prominent part of its reading and, therefore, worship life. Suggestions of what specific practices the above observations might imply comprise the final part of this study.

Implied Practices and Areas for Further Exploration

As alluded to above, a number of the reading practices discussed at different stages of this study are oral. Since many of them were discussed

---

85. Ong, *Orality and Literacy*, 74.
86. See Graham, *Beyond the Written Word*, 159–60.

above in relation to ministry and mission, I will seek only to make explicit connections between these practices and orality, and offer them as areas for further exploration. First, meditation was presented in chapter 3 as a multifaceted vocal act expressing a certain quality of devotion. Graham contends that personal and communal (vocal) meditative reading, recitation, and memorization of Scripture lead to greater spiritual intimacy than silent reading.[87] Cultures that neglect these practices see a decline in spiritual piety, while spiritual fervor and renewal are linked to groups that persist in these practices. Thus, oral modes of reading that foster the memorization and interiorizing of Scripture such as catechism, reading and praying Psalms aloud, even Bible memory activities for kids (with some qualifications) should be given more attention in churches.

Second, and related, the public reading of Scripture in the church needs a facelift. Reading Scripture out loud, Stephen Webb contends, is both a theological and practical act: theological, in that it enables us better to understand God as the living and life-giving Word; practical, in that it brings to life certain portions of Scripture, such as Jesus' conversations or his stilling of the storm. Yet, Webb argues, much public Scripture reading—if it happens at all—serves to de-dramatize the text rather than revivify it. Instead, public reading as oral performance should involve many of the skills actors bring to a script. If more attention in public reading were given to enlivening the text by accenting its dramatic character, perhaps deeper understanding and appropriation would follow.[88] Dramatic readings may also help decrease the perceived distance between the situation of readers and hearers and the narrated situation. Oral performance sweeps hearers into the world of the text and may help foster the kind of solidarity that is constitutive of humility.

Third, Luther's insight into the annunciative character of the gospel is represented by the increasingly common insight that, historically speaking, most theological interpretation occurred in sermons, rather than the commentary or monograph, as is currently en vogue. In a way, the recurrent plea for concrete examples of theological interpretation in action has been answered by the inclusion of sermons in texts like Hays' and Davis' *The Art of Reading Scripture* or the publication of volumes of

---

87. Ibid., 160–61.
88. See Webb, *Divine Voice*, 206–12.

sermons by contemporary theologians.[89] Moreover, Webb's entire study on Christian acoustemology is a sustained argument that the sermon is the most appropriate medium for understanding the Bible.[90] Certainly the theological reading of Scripture—as the complex interplay between God the Word, readers, concrete situations, and the Bible—lends itself to the more fluid and dynamic environment embodied by the event of Christian proclamation. In this light, Fowl's words are apt: "A challenge for the future of theological interpretation concerns how and in what ways sermons can become a mode for serious scholarly theological interpretation."[91] Indeed, the place of the sermon in the overall apparatus of learning and appropriating the Bible is a question that all Christians and churches must consider.

Finally, sacramental action deserves some mention. Luther pointed us to the important place of the sacraments as visible *and* vocal words in the presentation of the gospel to God's people. When the elements of the Lord's Supper, for example, are combined with the scriptural words of institution, the signs themselves preach Christ. As such, the sacraments *are* the faithful performance of Scripture because they proclaim the very heart of the biblical message—Christ crucified and resurrected for us and our salvation. Vanhoozer hints at this relationship between faithful reading and the sacraments:

> The sacraments, like the proclaimed word, are "real presentations" of the gospel of Jesus Christ. . . . The sacraments facilitate *a theo-dramatic participation in the eschatological action* through faith's attestation of the work of Son and Spirit. Through baptism and the Lord's Supper, Christ *presents* himself to believing communicants via a *real presentation* of the climactic events of redemptive history. By performing the biblical words and the sacramental actions, we are *really* drawn into the ongoing theo-dramatic action by the Spirit.[92]

If the sacraments truly present the scripturally mediated gospel, then they are Scripture reading practices in the truest sense. However, they

---

89. See the six sermons by Davis and Hays in *Art of Reading Scripture*, 277–325. See also, for example, Gunton, *Theology Through Preaching*; idem, *The Theologian As Preacher*.

90. Webb, *The Divine Voice*, especially 24–29.

91. Fowl, *Theological Interpretation of Scripture*, 73.

92. Vanhoozer, *Drama of Doctrine*, 412.

are reading practices as God's Word of promise accompanies them. Webb argues that, though the Reformers viewed the sacraments as more than verbal, they never viewed them as less. The sacraments are always verbal. "The Word makes the sacrament," he writes, "not the other way around. The sacraments are an effective means of divine communication because they are the most privileged shapes of the divine sound."[93] The sacraments are the embodiment of the oral Word, which itself is the vocalization of the scriptural Word. Thus through the sacraments we are directed away from the prominence of silent reading toward the centrality of oral reading practices, while affirming (even elevating) tangible and symbolic elements as effective means of proclaiming and hearing the Word of God. Faithful reading, then, is an oral and physical, or better, an oral-physical act.

This list of four practices suggested by considerations of orality is far from exhaustive, but it points in a direction future conversations in the theological interpretation of Scripture might take, particularly as we seek to understand the proper responses and responsibilities of readers of Scripture.

Conclusion: A Royal Priesthood of Readers

This study sought not to provide an entirely new theological hermeneutic but to resource, reframe, and reorder already substantive and largely persuasive proposals regarding readers of Scripture. Much of its burden was to explore how concrete and extensive engagement with biblical texts, focusing on *one* theme—the royal priesthood of believers, informed by ideal notions of torah-centered kingship and priesthood—can provide a robust and well-balanced theological and ethical depiction of the readers and their reading of Scripture. Along much of the way, contemporary hermeneutical voices were somewhat suppressed while, from a number of angles, I tried to develop this case patiently. What resulted is a portrait, maybe more impressionistic than exact, of readers as those situated within a community that is itself situated within the redemptive story initiated by God's actions of election, sanctification, and covenant making. Those readers are called simultaneously to respond by manifesting holiness and committing themselves to particular ministerial and missionary reading practices. At heart, royal priesthood, and

---

93. Webb, *The Divine Voice*, 43–44.

all it entails for reading Scripture, finds its definitive expression in Jesus Christ. Only by his work are we initiated into his priesthood and reign; only by his Spirit are we enabled to embody the way of *the* royal priestly reader and so fulfill a substantial part of our calling as a royal priesthood of readers.

Bibliography

Achtemeier, Paul J. *1 Peter: A Commentary on First Peter*. Hermeneia. Minneapolis: Fortress, 1996.
Allen, Leslie C. *Psalms 101–150*. Word Biblical Commentary 21. Waco: Word, 1983.
Althaus, Paul. *The Theology of Martin Luther*. Translated by Robert C. Schultz. Philadelphia: Fortress, 1970.
Aquinas, Thomas. *Summa Theologiae*. London: Blackfriars, 1964–1976.
Ashley, Timothy R. *The Book of Numbers*. New International Commentary on the Old Testament. Grand Rapids: Eerdmans, 1993.
Auffret, Pierre. *The Literary Structure of Psalm 2*. Translated by David J. A. Clines. Journal for the Study of the Old Testament: Supplement Series 3. Sheffield: JSOT, 1977.
Augustine. *On Christian Teaching*. Translated by R. P. H. Green. World's Classics. Oxford: Oxford University Press, 1997.
Barth, Karl. *Church Dogmatics*. Edited and translated by G. W. Bromiley and T. F. Torrance. 4 vols. London: T. & T. Clark, 2009.
Bauckham, Richard. "The Throne of God and the Worship of Jesus." In *The Jewish Roots of Christological Monotheism: Papers from the St. Andrews Conference on the Historical Origins of the Worship of Jesus*, edited by Carey C. Newman, James R. Davila, and Gladys S. Lewis, 43–69. Leiden: Brill, 1999.
Bavinck, Herman. *Reformed Dogmatics*. Vol. 4, *Holy Spirit, Church, and New Creation*. Edited by John Bolt. Translated by John Vriend. Grand Rapids: Baker Academic, 2008.
Bayer, Oswald. *Martin Luther's Theology: A Contemporary Interpretation*. Translated by Thomas H. Trapp. Grand Rapids: Eerdmans, 2008.
Beale, G. K. *The Book of Revelation*. New International Greek Testament Commentary. Grand Rapids: Eerdmans, 1999.
Beasley-Murray, Paul. "Romans 1:3f: An Early Confession of Faith in the Lordship of Jesus." *Tyndale Bulletin* 31 (1980) 147–54.
Bénétreau, Samuel. *L'Epitre aux Hebreux*. 2 vols. Commentaire Evangelique de la Bible. Paris: Edifac, 1989–1990.
———. *La Premiere Epitre de Pierre*. Commentaire Evangelique de la Bible. Vaux-sur-Seine: Edifac, 1992.
Berkhof, Hendrikus. *Christian Faith: An Introduction to the Study of the Faith*. Translated by Sierd Woudstra. Rev. ed. Grand Rapids: Eerdmans, 1991.
Best, Ernest. "Spiritual Sacrifice: General Priesthood in the New Testament." *Interpretation* 14 (1960) 273–99.
Betts, T. J. *Ezekiel the Priest: A Custodian of Torah*. Studies in Biblical Literature 74. New York: Peter Lang, 2005.
Biddle, Mark E. *Deuteronomy*. Smyth and Helwys Bible Commentary. Macon, GA: Smyth & Helwys, 2003.
Bigg, Charles. *A Critical and Exegetical Commentary of the Epistles of St. Peter and St. Jude*. International Critical Commentary. Edinburgh: T. & T. Clark, 1969.

Billings, J. Todd. *Calvin, Participation, and the Gift: The Activity of Believers in Union with Christ*. Changing Paradigms in Historical and Systematic Theology. Oxford: Oxford University Press, 2007.

———. *Union with Christ: Reframing Theology and Ministry*. Grand Rapids: Baker Academic, 2011.

———. *The Word of God for the People of God: An Entryway to the Theological Interpretation of Scripture*. Grand Rapids: Eerdmans, 2010.

Blenkinsopp, Joseph. *Ezekiel*. Interpretation. Louisville: John Knox, 1990.

———. *Ezra-Nehemiah: A Commentary*. Old Testament Library. Philadelphia: Westminster, 1988.

———. *Isaiah 56–66*. Anchor Bible 19b. New York: Doubleday, 2003.

———. *Religious and Intellectual Leadership in Ancient Israel*. Library of Ancient Israel. Louisville: Westminster John Knox, 1995.

Block, Daniel I. *The Book of Ezekiel: Chapters 1–24*. New International Commentary on the Old Testament. Grand Rapids: Eerdmans, 1997.

———. "The Burden of Leadership: The Mosaic Paradigm of Kingship [Deut. 17:14–20]." *Biblioteca Sacra* 162 (2005) 259–78.

Bock, Darrell L. *Luke 1:1–9:50*. Baker Exegetical Commentary on the New Testament. Grand Rapids: Baker, 1999.

Bockmuehl, K. "Sanctification." In *New Dictionary of Theology*, edited by Sinclair B. Ferguson and David F. Wright, 613–16. Downers Grove: InterVarsity, 1988.

Bockmuehl, Markus. *Seeing the Word: Refocusing New Testament Study*. Studies in Theological Interpretation. Grand Rapids: Baker Academic, 2006.

Boecker, Hans Jochen. *Die Beurteilung der Anfange des Konigtums in den deuteronomistischen Abschnitten des I. Samuelbuches: Ein Beitrag zum Problem des "deuteronomistischen Geschictswerks."* Wissenschaftliche Monographien zum Alten und Neuen Testament 31. Neukirchen-Vluyn: Neukirchener, 1969.

Bosch, David J. *Transforming Mission: Paradigm Shifts in Theology of Mission*. American Society of Missiology 16. Maryknoll: Orbis, 1992.

Botterweck, G. Johannes, Helmer Ringgren, and Heinz-Josef Fabry, eds. *Theological Dictionary of the Old Testament*. Translated by J. T. Willis, G. W. Bromiley, D. E. Green, and D. W. Stott. 15 vols. Grand Rapids: Eerdmans, 1974–2006.

Bowald, Mark Alan. "The Character of Theological Interpretation of Scripture." *International Journal of Systematic Theology* 12/2 (2010) 162–83.

———. *Rendering the Word in Theological Hermeneutics: Mapping Divine and Human Agency*. Burlington, VT: Ashgate, 2007.

Bridges, Jerry. *The Gospel for Real Life: Turn to the Liberating Power of the Cross . . . Every Day*. Colorado Springs: NavPress, 2003.

Briggs, Richard S. *The Virtuous Reader: Old Testament Narrative and Interpretive Virtue*. Studies in Theological Interpretation. Grand Rapids: Baker Academic, 2010.

Bright, John. *Jeremiah: A New Translation with Introduction and Commentary*. Anchor Bible 21. New York: Doubleday, 1965.

Broadhead, Edwin K. "Christology as Polemic and Apologetic: The Priestly Portrait of Jesus in the Gospel of Mark." *Journal for the Study of the New Testament* 47 (1992) 21–34.

Brox, Norbert. *Der erste Petrusbrief*. Evangelisch-katholischer Kommentar zum Neuen Testament 21. Zurich: Benzinger, 1979.

Bruce, F. F. *The Epistle to the Hebrews*. New International Commentary on the New Testament. Grand Rapids: Eerdmans, 1973.

Brueggemann, Walter. *A Commentary of Jeremiah: Exile and Homecoming*. Grand Rapids: Eerdmans, 1998.

———. *Deuteronomy*. Abingdon Old Testament Commentary. Nashville: Abingdon, 2001.

———. *1 & 2 Kings*. Smyth and Helwys Bible Commentary. Macon, GA: Smyth & Helwys, 2000.

———. *To Build, To Plant: A Commentary of Jeremiah 26–52*. International Theological Commentary. Grand Rapids: Eerdmans, 1991.

Budd, Philip J. *Numbers*. Word Biblical Commentary 5. Waco: Word, 1984.

———. "Priestly Instruction in Pre-Exilic Israel." *Vetus Testamentum* 23 (1973) 1–14.

Bullock, C. Hassell. *Encountering the Book of Psalms: A Literary and Theological Introduction*. Grand Rapids: Baker Academic, 2001.

Cahill, Lisa Sowle. "Christian Character, Biblical Community, and Human Values." In *Character and Scripture: Moral Formation, Community, and Biblical Interpretation*, edited by William P. Brown, 3–17. Grand Rapids: Eerdmans, 2002.

Calloud, Jean, and Francois Genuyt. *La Premiere Epitre de Pierre: Analyse Semiotique*. Lectio divina 109. Paris: Cerf, 1982.

Calvin, John. *Commentaries on the Catholic Epistles*. Edited and Translated by John Owen. Grand Rapids: Eerdmans, 1948.

———. *Commentaries on the Prophet Jeremiah and the Lamentations 1*. Translated by John Owen. Grand Rapids: Eerdmans, 1950.

———. *Institutes of the Christian Religion*. Translated by John T. McNeill. Louisville: Westminster John Knox, 2006.

———. *Institutes of the Christian Religion, 1536 Edition*. Translated by Ford Lewis Battles. Rev. ed. Grand Rapids: Eerdmans, 1986.

Carson, D. A. *The Gospel According to John*. Grand Rapids: Eerdmans, 1992.

Cassuto, U. *A Commentary on the Book of Exodus*. Translated by Israel Abrahams. Jerusalem: Magnes, 1997.

———. *A Commentary on the Book of Genesis, Part 1: From Adam to Noah*. Translated by Israel Abrahams. Jerusalem: Magnes, 1961.

Cheung, Alex T. M. "The Priest as the Redeemed Man: A Biblical-Theological Study of the Priesthood." *Journal of the Evangelical Theological Society* 29/3 (1986) 265–75.

Childs, Brevard S. *The Book of Exodus: A Critical, Theological Commentary*. Old Testament Library. Philadelphia: Westminster, 1974.

———. *Introduction to the Old Testament as Scripture*. Philadelphia: Fortress, 1979.

Christensen, Duane L. *Deuteronomy 1:1—21:9, Revised*. Word Biblical Commentary 6a. Nashville: Thomas Nelson, 2001.

Clines, D. J. A. "The Tree of Knowledge and the Law of Yahweh [Psalm XIX]." *Vetus Testamentum* 24 (1974) 8–14.

Cody, Aelred. *A History of Old Testament Priesthood*. Analecta biblica 35. Rome: Pontifical Biblical Institute, 1969.

Cogan, Mordechai, and Hayim Tadmor. *II Kings: A New Translation with Introduction and Commentary*. Anchor Bible 11. New York: Doubleday, 1988.

Craigie, Peter C. *The Book of Deuteronomy*. New International Commentary on the Old Testament. Grand Rapids: Eerdmans, 1976.

———. *Psalms 1–50*. Word Biblical Commentary 19. Waco: Word, 1983.

Cranfield, C. E. B. *The Gospel According to St. Mark*. 4th ed. Cambridge Greek Testament Commentary. New York: Cambridge, 1972.

Bibliography

Croft, Steven J. L. *The Identity of the Individual in the Psalms*. Journal for the Study of the Old Testament: Supplement Series 44. Sheffield: JSOT, 1987.

Daube, David. "One from Among Your Brethren Shall You Set King Over You." *Journal of Biblical Literature* 90 (1971) 480–81.

Davies, John A. *A Royal Priesthood: Literary and Intertextual Perspectives on an Image of Israel in Exodus 19:6*. Journal for the Study of the Old Testament: Supplement Series 395. London: T. & T. Clark, 2004.

Davis, Ellen F., and Richard B. Hays, eds. *The Art of Reading Scripture*. Grand Rapids: Eerdmans, 2003.

De la Potterie, Ignace. *La Vérité dans Saint Jean*. Vol. 1. 2nd ed. Analecta Biblica 73. Rome: Editrice Pontificio Istituto Biblico, 1999.

De Vaux, Roland. *Ancient Israel: Its Life and Institutions*. Translated by John McHugh. New York: McGraw Hill, 1961.

Dohmen, Christoph. *Exodus 19–40*. Herders theologischer Kommentar zum Alten Testament. Freiburg: Herder, 2004.

Driver, S. R. *A Critical and Exegetical Commentary on Deuteronomy*. 3rd ed. International Critical Commentary. Edinburgh: T. & T. Clark, 1996.

Dumbrell, William J. *Covenant and Creation: A Theology of Old Testament Covenants*. Grand Rapids: Baker, 1993.

———. *The Search for Order: Biblical Eschatology in Focus*. Grand Rapids: Baker, 1993.

Dunn, James D. G. *Christology in the Making: A New Testament Inquiry into the Origins of the Doctrine of the Incarnation*. 2nd ed. Grand Rapids: Eerdmans, 1996.

Durham, John I. *Exodus*. Word Biblical Commentary 3. Waco: Word, 1987.

Eagleton, Terry. "The Revolt of the Reader." *New Literary History* 13 (1982) 449–52.

Eastwood, Cyril. *The Priesthood of All Believers: An Examination of the Doctrine from the Reformation to the Present Day*. Minneapolis: Augsburg, 1962.

Eaton, John H. *Kingship and the Psalms*. Naperville, IL: Allenson, 1976.

———. *The Psalms: A Historical and Spiritual Commentary with an Introduction and New Translation*. London: T. & T. Clark, 2003.

Eddleman, H. Leo. "Word Pictures of the Word: An Exposition of Psalm 19." *Review and Expositor* 49 (1952) 413–24.

Edwards, James R. *The Gospel According to Mark*. Pillar New Testament Commentary. Grand Rapids: Eerdmans, 2002.

Elliot, John H. *Conflict, Community, and Honor: 1 Peter in Social-Scientific Perspective*. Cascade Companions. Eugene, OR: Cascade, 2007.

———. *The Elect and the Holy: An Exegetical Examination of I Peter 2:4–10 and the Phrase* Basileion Ierateuma. Novum Testamentum Supplements 12. Leiden: Brill, 1966.

———. *I Peter: A New Translation with Introduction and Commentary*. Anchor Bible 37b. New York: Doubleday, 2000.

Engnell, Ivan. *Studies in Divine Kingship in the Ancient Near East*. Oxford: Blackwell, 1969.

Enns, Peter. *Exodus*. New International Version Application Commentary. Grand Rapids: Zondervan, 2000.

Eusebius. *Ecclesiastical History* I.3. Fathers of the Church 19. Translated by Roy Deferrari. New York: Fathers of the Church, 1953.

Evans, Craig A. "Images of Christ in the Canonical and Apocryphal Gospels." In *Images of Christ: Ancient and Modern*, edited by Stanley E. Porter, Michael A. Hayes, and David Tombs, 34–72. Sheffield: Sheffield Academic, 1997.

Fee, Gordon D. *Pauline Christology: An Exegetical-Theological Study*. Peabody, MA: Hendrickson, 2007.

———. *Paul's Letter to the Philippians*. New International Commentary on the New Testament. Grand Rapids: Eerdmans, 1995.

Fensham, F. Charles. *The Books of Ezra and Nehemiah*. New International Commentary on the Old Testament. Grand Rapids: Eerdmans, 1982.

Fletcher-Louis, Crispin H. T. "Jesus as the High Priestly Messiah: Part 1." *Journal for the Study of the Historical Jesus* 4 (2006) 155–75.

———. "Jesus as the High Priestly Messiah: Part 2." *Journal for the Study of the Historical Jesus* 5 (2007) 57–79.

Floor, Lambertus. "The General Priesthood of Believers in the Epistle to the Hebrews." In *Ad Hebraeos: Essays on the Epistle to the Hebrews*, 72–82. Pretoria: Die Nuwe-Testamentiese Werkgemeenskap van Suid-Afrika, 1971.

Fowl, Stephen E. *Engaging Scripture: A Model for Theological Interpretation*. Challenges in Contemporary Theology. Malden, MA: Blackwell, 1998.

———. *Theological Interpretation of Scripture*. Cascade Companions. Eugene, OR: Cascade, 2009.

———. "Virtue." In *Dictionary for Theological Interpretation of the Bible*, edited by Kevin J. Vanhoozer, 837–39. Grand Rapids: Baker Academic, 2005.

Fowl, Stephen E., and L. Gregory Jones. *Reading in Communion: Scripture and Ethics in Christian Life*. Grand Rapids: Eerdmans, 1991.

France, R. T. *The Gospel of Mark*. New International Greek Testament Commentary. Grand Rapids: Eerdmans, 2002.

Freedman, David Noel. *Psalm 119: The Exaltation of Torah*. Biblical and Judaic Studies 6. Winona Lake, IN: Eisenbrauns, 1999.

Fretheim, Terence E. *Exodus*. Interpretation: A Bible Commentary for Teaching and Preaching. Louisville: John Knox, 1991.

Gadamer, Hans-Georg. *Truth and Method*. Translated by Joel Weinsheimer and Donald G. Marshall. 2nd rev. ed. New York: Continuum, 1994.

Gerhardsson, Birger. *The Testing of God's Son (Matt 4:1–11 & Par) An Analysis of an Early Christian Midrash*. Coniectanea biblica: New Testament Series 2. Lund: CWK Gleerup, 1966.

Gerrish, Brian A. "Priesthood and Ministry in the Theology of Luther." *Church History* 34 (1965) 404–22.

Goppelt, Leonhard. *A Commentary on I Peter*. Edited by Ferdinand Hahn. Translated by John E. Alsup. Grand Rapids: Eerdmans, 1993.

Goulder, Michael D. *The Psalms of the Return (Book V, Psalms 107–150)*. Journal for the Study of the Old Testament: Supplement Series 258. Sheffield: Sheffield Academic, 1998.

Gounelle, André. "Le sacerdoce universel." *Études Théologiques et Religieuses* 63 (1988) 429–34.

Grabbe, Lester L. *Priests, Prophets, Diviners, Sages: A Socio-Historical Study of Religious Specialists in Ancient Israel*. Valley Forge, PA: Trinity, 1995.

Graham, William A. *Beyond the Written Word: Oral Aspects of Scripture in the History of Religion*. Cambridge: Cambridge University Press, 1987.

Grant, Jamie A. *The King as Exemplar: The Function of Deuteronomy's Kingship Law in the Shaping of the Book of Psalms*. Society of Biblical Literature Academia Biblica 17. Atlanta: Society of Biblical Literature, 2004.

———. "The Psalms and the King." In *Interpreting the Psalms: Issues and Approaches*, edited by David Firth and Philip S. Johnston, 101–18. Downers Grove: InterVarsity, 2005.

Gray, Timothy C. *The Temple in the Gospel of Mark: A Study in Its Narrative Role*. Wissenschaftliche Untersuchungen zum Neuen Testament, Second Series 242. Tübingen: Mohr Siebeck, 2008.

Green, Joel B. *Seized By Truth: Reading the Bible as Scripture*. Nashville: Abingdon, 2007.

Greenberg, Moshe. *Ezekiel 21–37: A New Translation with Introduction and Commentary*. Anchor Bible 22a. New York: Doubleday, 1997.

Griffiths, Paul J. "Reading as a Spiritual Discipline." In *The Scope of Our Art: The Vocation of the Theological Teacher*. edited by L. Gregory Jones and Stephanie Paulsell, Pages 32–47. Grand Rapids: Eerdmans, 2002.

———. *Religious Reading: The Place of Reading in the Practice of Reading*. New York: Oxford University Press, 1999.

Guder, Darrell L. *The Continuing Conversion of the Church*. Gospel and Our Culture. Grand Rapids: Eerdmans, 2000.

Guelich, Robert A. *Mark 1—8:26*. Word Biblical Commentary 34a. Dallas: Word, 1989.

Gunkel, Hermann, and Joachim Begrich. *Introduction to Psalms: The Genres of the Religious Lyric of Israel*. Translated by James D. Nogalski. Macon, GA: Mercer University Press, 1998.

Gunton, Colin E. *Intellect and Action: Elucidations on Christian Theology and the Life of Faith*. Edinburgh: T. & T. Clark, 2000.

———. *The Theologian As Preacher: Further Sermons from Colin Gunton*. London: T. & T. Clark, 2004.

———. *Theology Through Preaching: The Gospel and the Christian Life*. London: T. & T. Clark, 2001.

Halpern, Baruch. *The Constitution of the Monarchy of Israel*. Harvard Semitic Monographs 25. Chico, CA: Scholars, 1981.

Hart, Trevor. "Tradition, Authority, and a Christian Approach to the Bible as Scripture." In *Between Two Worlds: Spanning New Testament Studies and Systematic Theology*, edited by Joel B. Green and Max Turner, 183–204. Grand Rapids: Eerdmans, 2000.

Hartley, John E. *Leviticus*. Word Biblical Commentary 4. Dallas: Word, 1992.

Hauerwas, Stanley. *Unleashing the Scripture: Freeing the Bible from Captivity to America*. Nashville: Abingdon, 1993.

Hawthorne, Gerald F. *Philippians*. Word Biblical Commentary 43. Waco: Word, 1983.

Healy, Mary. *The Gospel of Mark*. Catholic Commentary on Sacred Scripture. Grand Rapids: Baker Academic, 2008.

The Heidelberg Catechism. Translated by the Christian Reformed Church of North America and the Reformed Church of America. Grand Rapids: Faith Alive Christian Resources, 2011.

Heil, John Paul. "Jesus as the Unique High Priest in the Gospel of John." *Catholic Biblical Quarterly* 57 (1995) 729–45.

Hengel, Martin. *Studies in Early Christology*. Edinburgh: T. & T. Clark, 1995.

Heppe, Heinrich. *Reformed Dogmatics: Set Out and Illustrated from the Sources*. Edited by Ernst Bizer. Translated by G. T. Thomson. Grand Rapids: Baker, 1984.

Hill, Andrew E. *Malachi*. Anchor Bible 25d. New York: Doubleday, 1998.

Hobbs, T. R. *2 Kings*. Word Biblical Commentary 13. Waco: Word, 1985.

Holt, Else K. "Word of Jeremiah—Word of God: Structures of Authority in the Book of Jeremiah." In *Uprooting and Planting: Essays on Jeremiah for Leslie Allen*, edited by John Goldingay, Pages 172–89. Library of Hebrew Bible/Old Testament Studies 459. New York: T. & T. Clark, 2007.

Holwerda, David E. *Jesus and Israel: One Covenant or Two?* Grand Rapids: Eerdmans, 1995.

Hurtado, Larry W. *Lord Jesus Christ: Devotion to Jesus in Earliest Christianity.* Grand Rapids: Eerdmans, 2003.

Isbell, Charles D. "2 Kings 22:3–23:24 and Jeremiah 36: A Stylistic Comparison." *Journal for the Study of the Old Testament* 8 (1978) 33–45.

Jacobs, Alan. *A Theology of Reading: The Hermeneutics of Love.* Boulder, CO: Westview, 2001.

Jansen, John F. *Calvin's Doctrine of the Work of Christ.* London: Camelot, 1956.

Jewett, Robert. *Romans: A Commentary.* Hermeneia. Minneapolis: Fortress, 2007.

Jobes, Karen H. *1 Peter.* Baker Exegetical Commentary on the New Testament. Grand Rapids: Eerdmans, 2005.

Johnson, William Stacy. "Reading the Scriptures Faithfully in a Postmodern Age." In *The Art of Reading Scripture*, edited by Ellen F. Davis and Richard B. Hays, 109–24. Grand Rapids: Eerdmans, 2001.

Jones, L. Gregory. "Formed and Transformed by Scripture: Character, Community, and Authority in Biblical Interpretation." In *Character and Scripture: Moral Formation, Community, and Biblical Interpretation*, edited by William P. Brown, 18–33. Grand Rapids: Eerdmans, 2002.

Keener, Craig S. *The Gospel of John: A Commentary.* 2 vols. Peabody, MA: Hendrickson, 2005.

Kennedy, Joel. *The Recapitulation of Israel: Use of Israel's History in Matthew 1:1–4:11.* Wissenschaftliche Untersuchungen zum Neuen Testament. Second Series 257. Tübingen: Mohr Siebeck, 2008.

Keown, Gerald L., Pamela J. Scalise, and Thomas G. Smothers. *Jeremiah 26–52.* Word Biblical Commentary 27. Dallas: Word, 1995.

Kirk, J. Andrew. *What is Mission? Theological Explorations.* London: Darton, Longman and Todd, 2002.

Kistemaker, Simon J. *Exposition of the Epistles of Peter and of the Epistle of Jude.* New Testament Commentary. Grand Rapids: Eerdmans, 1987.

Kittel, G., and G. Friedrich, eds. *Theological Dictionary of the New Testament.* Translated by G. W. Bromiley. 10 vols. Grand Rapids: Eerdmans, 1964–1976.

Knierim, Rolf P., and George W. Coats. *Numbers.* Forms of the Old Testament Literature 4. Grand Rapids: Eerdmans, 2005.

Knoppers, Gary N. "The Deuteronomist and the Deuteronomistic Law of the King." *Zeitschrift für die alttestamentliche Wissenschaft* 108 (1996) 329–46.

Koester, Craig R. *Hebrews: A New Translation with Introduction and Commentary.* Anchor Bible 36. New York: Doubleday, 2001.

Kolb, Robert. *Martin Luther: Confessor of the Faith.* Christian Theology in Context. Oxford: Oxford University Press, 2009.

Kort, Wesley A. *Take, Read: Scripture, Textuality, and Cultural Practice.* University Park: Pennsylvania State University, 1996.

Kraus, Hans-Joachim. *Psalms 1–59: A Commentary.* Translated by Hilton C. Oswald. Minneapolis: Augsburg, 1988.

———. *Psalms 60–150: A Continental Commentary*. Translated by Hilton C. Oswald. Minneapolis: Fortress, 1993.

Kynes, William L. *A Christology of Solidarity: Jesus as the Representative of His People in Matthew*. Lanham, MD: University Press of America, 1991.

Lane, William L. *The Gospel According to Mark*. New International Commentary on the New Testament. Grand Rapids: Eerdmans, 1974.

———. *Hebrews 1–8*. Word Biblical Commentary 47a. Dallas: Word, 1991.

LeFebvre, Michael. "Torah-Meditation and the Psalms: The Invitation of Psalm 1." In *Interpreting the Psalms: Issues and Approaches*, edited by David Firth and Philip S. Johnston, 213–25. Downers Grove: InterVarsity, 2005.

Legasse, Simon. *L'Évangile de Marc*. Vol. 1. Lectio divina 5. Paris: Cerf, 1997.

Leithart, Peter J. *The Priesthood of the Plebs: A Theology of Baptism*. Eugene, OR: Wipf & Stock, 2003.

Levering, Matthew. *Participatory Biblical Exegesis: A Theology of Biblical Interpretation*. Reading the Scriptures. Notre Dame: University of Notre Dame Press, 2008.

Levinson, Bernard M. *Deuteronomy and the Hermeneutics of Legal Innovation*. Oxford: Oxford University Press, 1998.

———. "The Reconceptualization of Kingship in Deuteronomy and the Deuteronomistic History's Transformation of Torah." *Vetus Testamentum* 51 (2001) 511–34.

Lewis, C. S. *Reflections on the Psalms*. Glasgow: Collins, 1978.

Lieberg, Helmut. *Amt und Ordination bei Luther und Melanchthon*. Forschungen zur Kirchen-und Dogmengeschichte 11. Göttingen: Vandenhoeck & Ruprecht, 1962.

Liebreich, Leon J. "The Songs of Ascent and the Priestly Blessing." *Journal of Biblical Literature* 74 (1955) 33–36.

Lohfink, Norbert. *Studien zur biblischen Theologie*. Stuttgarter biblische Aufsatzbände 16. Stuttgart: Katholisches Bibelwerk, 1993.

Lohse, Bernhard. *Martin Luther's Theology: Its Historical and Systematic Development*. Edited and Translated by Roy A. Harrisville. Minneapolis: Fortress, 1999.

Lull, Timothy F., ed. *Martin Luther's Basic Theological Writings*. 2nd ed. Minneapolis: Augsburg Fortress, 2005.

Lundbom, Jack R. *Jeremiah 1–20: A New Translation with Introduction and Commentary*. Anchor Bible 21a. New York: Doubleday, 1999.

MacIntyre, Alasdair. *After Virtue: A Study in Moral Theory*. 2nd ed. Notre Dame: University of Notre Dame Press, 1984.

Maier, Johann. "Self-Definition, Prestige, and Status of Priests Towards the End of the Second Temple Period." *Biblical Theology Bulletin* 23 (1993) 139–50.

Malchow, Bruce V. "A Manual for Future Monarchs." *Catholic Biblical Quarterly* 47 (1985) 238–45.

Marshall, I. Howard. *The Gospel of Luke: A Commentary on the Greek Text*. Grand Rapids: Eerdmans, 1978.

Mays, James Luther. *The Lord Reigns: A Theological Handbook to the Psalms*. Louisville: Westminster John Knox, 1994.

———. *Psalms*. Interpretation: A Bible Commentary for Teaching and Preaching. Louisville: Westminster John Knox, 1994.

McConville, J. G. *Deuteronomy*. Apollos Old Testament Commentary 5. Downers Grove: InterVarsity, 2002.

———. "King and Messiah in Deuteronomy and the Deuteronomistic History." In *King and Messiah in Israel and the Ancient Near East: Proceedings of the Oxford Old*

Testament Seminar, edited by John Day, 271–95. Journal for the Study of the Old Testament: Supplement Series 270. Sheffield: Sheffield Academic, 1998.

Merrill, Eugene H. *Deuteronomy*. The New American Commentary 4. Nashville: Broadman & Holman, 1994.

———. *Kingdom of Priests: A History of Old Testament Israel*. Grand Rapids: Baker, 2005.

Meyers, Carol L., and Eric M. Meyers. *Haggai and Zechariah 1–8*. Anchor Bible 25b. Garden City, NY: Doubleday, 1987.

Michaels, J. Ramsey. *The Gospel of John*. New International Commentary on the New Testament. Grand Rapids: Eerdmans, 2010.

———. *1 Peter*. Word Biblical Commentary 49. Waco: Word, 1988.

Milgrom, Jacob. *Leviticus 1–16: A New Translation with Introduction and Commentary*. Anchor Bible 3. New York: Doubleday, 1991.

———. *Numbers*. Jewish Publication Society Torah Commentary. Philadelphia: Jewish Publication Society, 1990.

Miller, Patrick D. "The Beginning of the Psalter." In *The Shape and Shaping of the Psalter*, edited by J. Clinton McCann, 83–92. Journal for the Study of the Old Testament: Supplement Series 159. Sheffield: JSOT, 1993.

———. "The Blessing of God: An Interpretation of Numbers 6:22–27." *Interpretation* 29 (1975) 240–51.

———. "Deuteronomy and Psalms: Evoking a Biblical Conversation." *Journal of Biblical Literature* 118 (1999) 3–18.

———. "Kingship, Torah Obedience, and Prayer: A Theology of Psalms 15–24." In *Neue Wege der Psalmenforschung*, edited by K. Seybold and E. Zenger, 127–42. Freiburg: Herder, 1995.

Moberly, R. W. L. *The Bible, Theology, and Faith: A Study of Abraham and Jesus*. Cambridge Studies in Christian Doctrine 5. Cambridge: Cambridge University Press, 2000.

———. *Prophecy and Discernment*. Cambridge Studies in Christian Doctrine 14. Cambridge: Cambridge University Press, 2006.

Moo, Douglas. *The Epistle to the Romans*. New International Commentary on the New Testament. Grand Rapids: Eerdmans, 1996.

Moran, William L. "A Kingdom of Priests." In *The Bible in Catholic Thought*, edited by John L. McKenzie, 7–20. New York: Herder and Herder, 1962.

Morris, Leon. *The Epistle to the Romans*. Pillar New Testament Commentary. Grand Rapids: Eerdmans, 1988.

Motyer, J. Alec. *The Prophecy of Isaiah: An Introduction and Commentary*. Downers Grove: InterVarsity, 1993.

Nelson, Richard D. *Deuteronomy: A Commentary*. Old Testament Library. Louisville: Westminster John Knox, 2002.

———. *First and Second Kings*. Interpretation: A Bible Commentary for Teaching and Preaching. Louisville: John Knox, 1987.

———. *Raising Up a Faithful Priest: Community and Priesthood in Biblical Theology*. Louisville: Westminster John Knox, 1993.

O'Brien, Peter T. *The Epistle to the Philippians*. New International Greek Testament Commentary. Grand Rapids: Eerdmans, 1991.

O'Collins, Gerald, and Michael Keenan Jones. *Jesus Our Priest: A Christian Approach to the Priesthood of Christi*. Oxford: Oxford University Press, 2010.

Ong, Walter J. *Orality and Literacy: The Technologizing of the Word*. New York: Routledge, 2005.
Osborne, Grant R. *Revelation*. Baker Exegetical Commentary on the New Testament. Grand Rapids: Baker, 2002.
Oswalt, John N. *The Book of Isaiah: Chapters 1–39*. New International Commentary on the Old Testament. Grand Rapids: Eerdmans, 1986.
———. *The Book of Isaiah: Chapters 40–66*. New International Commentary on the Old Testament. Grand Rapids: Eerdmans, 1998.
Paddison, Angus. "Scriptural Reading and Revelation: A Contribution to Local Hermeneutics." *International Journal of Systematic Theology* 8 (2006) 433–48.
Patrick, Dale. "The Covenant Code Source." *Vetus Testamentum* 27 (1977) 145–57.
Peterson, David. *Engaging with God: A Biblical Theology of Worship*. Downers Grove: InterVarsity, 1992.
———. *Haggai and Zechariah 1–8*. Old Testament Library. Philadelphia: Westminster, 1984.
———. *Possessed by God: A New Testament Theology of Sanctification and Holiness*. New Studies in Biblical Theology 1. Grand Rapids: Eerdmans, 1995.
Peterson, Eugene H. "Caveat Lector." *Crux* 32 (1996) 2–12.
———. "Eat This Book: The Holy Community at Table with the Holy Scripture." *Theology Today* 56 (1999) 5–17.
Preus, Herman A. "Luther and the Universal Priesthood and the Office of the Ministry." *Concordia Journal* 5 (1979) 55–62.
Pritchard, James B., ed. *Ancient Near Eastern Texts Relating to the Old Testament*. 3rd ed. Princeton: Princeton University Press, 1969.
Ricoeur, Paul. "The Task of Hermeneutics." In *Hermeneutics and the Human Sciences: Essays on Language, Action and Interpretation*, edited and translated by John B. Thompson, 43–62. Cambridge: Cambridge University Press, 1981.
Rogers, Eugene F., Jr. "How the Virtues of an Interpreter Presuppose and Perfect Hermeneutics: The Case of Thomas Aquinas." *Journal of Religion* 76 (1996) 64–81.
Sabourin, Leopold. *Priesthood: A Comparative Study*. Studies in the History of Religions (supplement to Numen) 25. Leiden: Brill, 1973.
Sailhamer, John H. *The Pentateuch as Narrative: A Biblical-Theological Commentary*. Grand Rapids: Zondervan, 1992.
Sarna, Nahum. *Exodus*. Jewish Publication Society Torah Commentary. New York: Jewish Publication Society, 1991.
Schaff, Philip, and David S. Schaff, eds. *The Creeds of Christendom*. Vol. 3. 6th ed. Grand Rapids: Baker, 1983.
Schelke, Karl Hermann. *Die Petrusbriefe—Der Judasbrief*. Herders Theologischer Kommentar zum Neuen Testament 13/2. Freiburg: Herder, 1965.
Schleiermacher, Friedrich. *The Christian Faith*. Edited by H. R. Mackintosh and J. S. Stewart. Edinburgh: T. & T. Clark, 1968.
Schmitt, Hans-Christoph. "Redaktion des Pentateuch im Geiste der Prophetie: Beobachtungen zur Bedeutung der 'Glaubens'-Thematik innerhalb der Theologie des Pentateuch." *Vetus Testamentum* 32/2 (1982) 170–89.
Scholer, John M. *Proleptic Priests: Priesthood in the Epistle to the Hebrews*. Journal for the Study of the New Testament: Supplement Series 49. Sheffield: Sheffield Academic, 1991.
Schreiner, Thomas R. *1, 2 Peter, Jude*. New American Commentary 37. Nashville: Broadman & Holman, 2003.

———. *Romans*. Baker Exegetical Commentary on the New Testament 6. Grand Rapids: Baker Academic, 1998.

Schüssler Fiorenza, Elisabeth. *Priester für Gott: Studiem zum Herrschafts- und Priestermotiv in der Apokalypse*. Neutestamentliche Abhandlungen 7. Münster: Aschendorff, 1972.

Schwarz, Reinhard. "Geistliche Vollmacht: Luther über allgemeines Priestertum und kirchliches Amt [1523]." *Luther* 77 (2006) 74–82.

Scott, David. "Speaking to Form: Trinitarian-Performative Scripture Reading." *Anglican Theological Review* 77 (1995) 137–59.

Seerveld, Calvin. *How to Read the Bible to Hear God Speak: A Study in Numbers 22–24*. Toronto: Toronto Tuppence, 2003.

Seitz, Christopher R. *Figured Out: Typology and Providence in Christian Scripture*. Louisville: Westminster John Knox, 2001.

Silva, Moisés. *Philippians*. 2nd ed. Baker Exegetical Commentary on the New Testament. Grand Rapids: Baker, 2008.

Soll, Will. *Psalm 119: Matrix, Form, and Setting*. Catholic Biblical Quarterly Monograph Series 23. Washington, DC: Catholic Biblical Association of America, 1991.

Sonnet, Jean-Pierre. *The Book within the Book: Writing in Deuteronomy*. Biblical Interpretation 14. Leiden: Brill, 1997.

Spicq, C. *L'Épitre aux Hebreux*. Vol. 2. Études Bibliques. Paris: Librairie Lecoffre, 1953.

———. *Les Epitres de Saint Pierre*. Sources Bibliques. Paris: Librairie Lecoffre, 1966.

Spinks, D. Christopher. *The Bible and the Crisis of Meaning: Debates on the Theological Interpretation of Scripture*. T. & T. Clark Theology. London: T. & T. Clark, 2007.

Stein, Robert H. *Mark*. Baker Exegetical Commentary on the New Testament. Grand Rapids: Baker Academic, 2008.

Taylor, Richard A., and E. Ray Clendenen. *Haggai-Malachi: An Exegetical and Theological Exposition of Holy Scripture*. New American Commentary. Nashville: Broadman & Holman, 2004.

Terrien, Samuel. *The Psalms: Strophic Structure and Theological Commentary*. Grand Rapids: Eerdmans, 2003.

Thiselton, Anthony C. "More on Promising: 'The Paradigm of Biblical Promise as Trustworthy, Temporal, Transformative Speech-Acts.'" In *Thiselton on Hermeneutics: Collected Works with New Essays*, 117–29. Grand Rapids: Eerdmans, 2006.

———. *New Horizons in Hermeneutics: The Theory and Practice of Transforming Biblical Reading*. Grand Rapids: Zondervan, 1992.

———. *The Two Horizons: New Testament Hermeneutics and Philosophical Description with Special Reference to Heidegger, Bultmann, Gadamer, and Wittgenstein*. Grand Rapids: Eerdmans, 1984.

Throntveit, Mark A. *Ezra-Nehemiah*. Interpretation: A Bible Commentary for Teaching and Preaching. Louisville: John Knox, 1992.

Tigay, Jeffrey H. *Deuteronomy*. Jewish Publication Society Torah Commentary. Philadelphia: Jewish Publication Society, 1996.

Torrance, T. F. *Royal Priesthood*. Scottish Journal of Theology Occasional Papers 3. London: Oliver and Boyd, 1955.

Treier, Daniel J. "Biblical Theology and/or Theological Interpretation of Scripture?" *Scottish Journal of Theology* 61 (2008) 16–31.

———. *Introducing Theological Interpretation of Scripture: Recovering a Christian Practice*. Grand Rapids: Baker Academic, 2008.

———. *Virtue and the Voice of God: Toward Theology as Wisdom*. Grand Rapids: Eerdmans, 2006.

Trigg, Jonathan D. *Baptism in the Theology of Martin Luther*. Studies in the History of Christian Thought 56. Leiden: Brill, 1994.

Turretin, Francis. *Institutes of Elenctic Theology*. Edited by James T. Dennison Jr. Translated by George M. Giger. Phillipsburg, NJ: P & R, 1994.

VanGemeren, Willem A. *Psalms*. Expositor's Bible Commentary 5. Grand Rapids: Zondervan, 1991.

Vanhoozer, Kevin J. *The Drama of Doctrine: A Canonical-Linguistic Approach to Christian Theology*. Louisville: Westminster John Knox, 2005.

———. *First Theology: God, Scripture and Hermeneutics*. Downers Grove: InterVarsity, 2002.

———. "Imprisoned or Free? Text, Status, and Theological Interpretation in the Master/Slave Discourse of Philemon." In *Reading Scripture with the Church: Toward a Hermeneutic for Theological Interpretation*, edited by A. K. M. Adam et al., 51–93. Grand Rapids: Baker Academic, 2006.

———. *Is There a Meaning in this Text? The Bible, the Reader, and the Morality of Literary Knowledge*. Grand Rapids: Zondervan, 1998.

Venema, G. J. *Reading Scripture in the Old Testament: Deuteronomy 9-10, 31, 2 Kings 22-23, Jeremiah 36, Nehemiah 8*. Oudtestamentische Studien. Leiden: Brill, 2004.

Verhoef, Pieter A. *The Books of Haggai and Malachi*. New International Commentary on the Old Testament. Grand Rapids: Eerdmans, 1987.

Visser't Hooft, W. A. "Jesus is Lord: The Kingship of Christ in the Bible." *Theology Today* 4 (1947) 177–89.

Vogt, Peter T. *Deuteronomic Theology and the Significance of Torah: A Reappraisal*. Winona Lake, IN: Eisenbrauns, 2006.

Wagner, J. Ross. "From the Heavens to the Heart: The Dynamics of Psalm 19 as Prayer." *Catholic Biblical Quarterly* 61 (1999) 245–61.

Wainwright, Geoffrey. *For Our Salvation: Two Approaches to the Work of Christ*. Grand Rapids: Eerdmans, 1997.

Waltke, Bruce K., and Charles Yu. *An Old Testament Theology: An Exegetical, Canonical, and Thematic Approach*. Grand Rapids: Zondervan, 2007.

Walton, John H. *Ancient Near Eastern Thought and the Old Testament: Introducing the Conceptual World of the Hebrew Bible*. Grand Rapids: Baker Academic, 2006.

Watson, Francis. "Authors, Readers, Hermeneutics." In *Reading Scripture with the Church: Toward a Hermeneutic for Theological Interpretation*, edited by A. K. M. Adam et al., 119–23. Grand Rapids: Baker Academic, 2006.

———. "An Evangelical Response." In *The Trustworthiness of God: Perspectives on the Nature of Scripture*, edited by Paul Helm and Carl R. Trueman, 285–89. Grand Rapids: Eerdmans, 2002.

———. *Text and Truth: Redefining Biblical Theology*. Grand Rapids: Eerdmans, 1997.

———. *Text, Church and World: Biblical Interpretation in Theological Perspective*. Grand Rapids: Eerdmans, 1994.

Watts, Rikki E. *Isaiah's New Exodus in Mark*. Biblical Studies Library. Mohr Siebeck, 1997. Repr., Grand Rapids: Baker Academic, 2000.

Webb, Stephen H. *The Divine Voice: Christian Proclamation and the Theology of Sound*. Grand Rapids: Brazos, 2004.

Webster, John. "Hermeneutics in Modern Theology: Some Doctrinal Reflections." In *Word and Church: Essays in Christian Dogmatics*, 58–97. Edinburgh: T. & T. Clark, 2001.

———. *Holiness*. Grand Rapids: Eerdmans, 2003.

———. *Holy Scripture: A Dogmatic Sketch*. Current Issues in Theology. Cambridge: Cambridge University Press, 2003.

———. "Resurrection and Scripture." In *Christology and Scripture: Interdisciplinary Perspectives*, edited by Andrew T. Lincoln and Angus Paddison, 138–55. New York: T. & T. Clark, 2008.

Wells, Jo Bailey. *God's Holy People: A Theme in Biblical Theology*. Journal for the Study of the Old Testament: Supplement Series 305. Sheffield: Sheffield Academic, 2000.

Wengert, Timothy J. *Priesthood, Pastors, Bishops: Public Ministry for the Reformation and Today*. Minneapolis: Fortress, 2008.

Wenham, Gordon J. *The Book of Leviticus*. New International Commentary on the Old Testament. Grand Rapids: Eerdmans, 1979.

Westcott, Brooke Foss. *The Epistle to the Hebrews*. Grand Rapids: Eerdmans, 1950.

Westerholm, Stephen. *Jesus and Scribal Authority*. Coniectanea biblica: New Testament Series 10. Lund: CWK Gleerup, 1978.

Westermann, Claus. "Creation and History in the Old Testament." In *The Gospel and Human Destiny*, edited by Vilmos Vajta, 11–38. Minneapolis: Augsburg, 1972.

———. *Praise and Lament in the Psalms*. Translated by Keith R. Crim and Richard N. Soulen. Atlanta: John Knox, 1981.

Wilson, Gerald H. *The Editing of the Hebrew Psalter*. Society of Biblical Literature Dissertation Series 76. Chico, CA: Scholars, 1985.

———. "Shaping the Psalter: A Consideration of Editorial Linkage in the Book of Psalms." In *The Shape and Shaping of the Psalter*, edited by J. Clinton McCann, 72–82. Journal for the Study of the Old Testament: Supplement Series 159. Sheffield: JSOT, 1993.

———. "The Structure of the Psalter." In *Interpreting the Psalms: Issues and Approaches*, edited by David Firth and Philip S. Johnston, 229-46. Downers Grove: InterVarsity, 2005.

Witherington, Ben, III. *The Gospel of Mark: A Socio-Rhetorical Commentary*. Grand Rapids: Eerdmans, 2001.

Wolff, Hans Walter. *Haggai: A Commentary*. Translated by Margaret Kohl. Minneapolis: Augsburg, 1988.

Wood, Charles M. *The Formation of Christian Understanding: An Essay in Theological Hermeneutics*. Philadelphia: Westminster, 1981.

Wood, Donald. *Barth's Theology of Interpretation*. Barth Studies. Burlington, VT: Ashgate, 2008.

Work, Telford, *Living and Active: Scripture in the Economy of Salvation*. Sacra Doctrina. Grand Rapids: Eerdmans, 2001.

Woudstra, Marten H. *The Book of Joshua*. New International Commentary on the Old Testament. Grand Rapids: Eerdmans, 1981.

Wright, Christopher J. H. *The Message of Ezekiel*. The Bible Speaks Today. Downers Grove: InterVarsity, 2001.

Wright, N. T. "How Can the Bible Be Authoritative? (The Laing Lecture for 1989)." *Vox Evangelica* 21 (1991) 7–32.

General Index

absolution, 149–51, 153–54, 157, 161–62, 219, 223–24
aims (in reading), 3, 4n11, 8n25, 13, 20–21, 51–53, 57–59, 74, 77–81, 95, 167, 181, 197–98, 201, 206, 214
Althaus, Paul, 153, 158–59
Aquinas, Thomas, 13, 105, 208
attitudes (in reading), 20, 21n70, 51–53, 74, 77, 79, 81, 167, 198, 203n18, 204–6
Augustine, 3, 18n63, 149n54, 199n8, 203–4

Barth, Karl, 104n1, 111–15, 136, 176–80, 206–7, 225
Bauckham, Richard, x, 117n56
Bavinck, Herman, 185–86
Beale, G. K., 42n51, 43
Berkhof, Hendrikus, 180–81
biblical theology, ix–xi, 19, 22–24, 115
Billings, J. Todd, ix, 4n12, 107n16, 188n54, 212, 226, 227
bless, blessing (as a reading act), 22, 34–36, 82–88, 92–95, 99, 167, 218, 220, 223–25, 229, 232
Bosch, David, 228
Bowald, Mark, 6–7, 174, 184
Briggs, Richard, 12–13, 19, 170, 199, 202, 205–7
Brueggemann, Walter, 54, 63–67

Calvin, John, 41n50, 88, 106–7, 180, 191–92
canon
  biblical, 1, 11, 21n71
  law, 141, 160
canonical, 19n65, 70–80, 125, 189, 193n68, 194, 213, 221
character, 4n12, 6, 13, 17n62, 42, 50, 91, 185–87, 199–201, 217, 225, 228
character indelibilis. See indelible character
charity, 12–18, 186–87, 202
Christensen, Duane, 53, 56n20
church, 2–6, 8–16, 18–20, 23, 27, 39–51, 95, 100, 104n1, 106, 108, 110–11, 116, 138–41, 146, 155–62, 166–70, 175, 178–81, 183–88, 190, 194, 197n1, 215–21, 223–29, 231–34
covenant, x–xi, 4n12, 6, 11, 20, 22–23, 72, 132, 136, 217–18, 224, 235
  Mosaic, Old, 28–30, 33–36, 40, 44–45, 49, 54–57, 62n49, 63–64, 66, 81, 87, 89–94, 97, 103, 129, 166, 170, 175, 182, 205–6, 210, 213, 215
  New, 42, 47, 112, 114, 130, 169, 187–97, 225

democratic, democratize, 2–3, 148, 161, 183

David (King), 38, 59–62, 68–72, 75–79, 83n3, 117, 121, 125, 131–32, 195, 208, 214
Davies, John, 29–34, 83–84
delight, x, 21n70, 72–75, 77, 79–81, 202, 203n18, 209–12, 214, 216–17
dignity (of God's people), 27, 30–32, 34, 37, 40, 49, 51, 72, 84, 110, 143, 146, 159, 162, 168, 173, 175–77, 213, 217–18
dispositions (also see attitudes), 3–4, 10, 21n70, 52–53, 59, 63–64, 79n114, 149, 152, 172, 197–98, 200–201, 206, 210–12, 217, 222
divine action, agency, x, 3–13, 19, 23, 151, 165, 169, 170n6, 174–75, 181, 184–85, 187, 193, 197
drama, dramatic, x, 4n12, 171–73, 181

election, 20, 23, 27, 49, 109, 159, 169, 173–82, 185, 187, 197, 216–18, 235
  of church, 37–40, 42, 47, 143, 178–79, 225
  of Israel, 29–34, 36, 40, 55, 166, 175, 178
  of Jesus Christ, 39–40, 110, 130, 176
  of king, 51, 55, 72, 175
  of priests, 83, 175
Elliot, John, 32n18, 40n45
ethics, ethical, 3–4, 12, 17, 19, 23, 27, 49–50, 52, 137, 165, 167, 171–72, 176, 185, 187, 197–236
Eusebius of Caesarea, 104
Ezra, 88n22, 91–92, 95–97, 220

fear, x, 18n63, 66–67, 70, 78–79, 81, 91, 95, 129, 202–5, 212, 214, 216–17, 223

figural reading. *See* typology
Fletcher-Louis, Crispin, 119–21
Fowl, Stephen, ix, 14–19, 52–53, 177–79, 184–87, 200–201, 205, 219–21, 234
freedom
  divine, 5–6, 10–11, 34, 72, 176–78,
  human, 14–15, 97, 158, 169, 193, 202, 209
  of Word of God, 161–62

Gadamer, Hans-Georg, 1, 220
gospel, 37–42, 47–49, 106–13, 140–41, 144, 148–50, 153, 155n80, 156–62, 178, 186, 216, 218, 223–29, 234
Gospels, 15, 19n66, 22, 104, 116–36, 167, 175, 183, 193–94, 196
grace, 11, 37, 44, 46, 48, 100, 105, 110, 118, 135, 139–40, 146, 149, 151, 169–71, 174–79, 181, 186, 188, 191–92, 197n1, 200, 204, 206, 215n45, 217, 226n72
Graham, William, 230–33
Grant, Jamie, 58n34, 68–79
Green, Joel, ix, 4n11
Griffiths, Paul, x, 17n63, 209, 222–23
Gunton, Colin, 180, 234n89

habits, 2, 5, 13–15, 52, 73, 170, 200, 217
Halpern, Baruch, 60–61
Hart, Trevor, 6, 18, 172
Hauerwas, Stanley, 2–3, 200, 219
hear, hearing, x, 4n12, 6, 10–11, 20n68, 43, 63–69, 74, 77, 88, 95, 99, 123, 149–53, 161–62, 169–71, 189–90, 196, 201–6, 210, 216, 219, 222–24, 228, 231–35

Heppe, Heinrich, 107n18, 108n24, 110n34
hermeneutic, hermeneutical, hermeneutics, ix–x, 1, 3–4, 6–10, 14, 17–19, 23, 27, 168–71, 174, 177–78, 187–91, 194–97, 200–3, 208–9, 212, 215, 217, 222, 235
holiness, 82–87, 94–95
  of God, x, 182, 198, 216
  of Jesus Christ, 108, 120, 130, 133–35, 217
  of priests, 92, 98–99
  of readers, 18n63, 20, 27–40, 42, 46, 49, 80, 84, 87–88, 100, 146, 159, 166, 173, 180–87, 199, 213, 215–17, 227, 235
  of sacraments, 141, 149
  of tabernacle/temple, 44–45, 98–99, 121–22
humility, 12, 14, 18, 21n70, 58, 63, 67, 80–81, 176–77, 202–9, 212, 216, 221, 233

indelible character, 139–41, 159, 183
individualism, 2, 161, 219, 232

Jehoiakim, 59, 61, 64–67, 173, 204, 214
Jesus Christ
  as Israel, 22, 103–4, 125–30
  as king, 103–18, 119n60, 135–36, 175, 188, 191–95
  as mediator, 22, 44, 103–16, 122, 124, 136, 168, 187–95
  as priest, 22, 44–46, 103–16, 118–25, 130, 133, 135–36, 143–46, 148, 167–68, 188, 191–93, 196
  as subject matter, 104, 132, 136, 188, 191, 193–94
  threefold office, x–xi, 22, 23n73, 103–16, 192

Jones, L. Gregory, 13–14, 172, 177–78, 185, 200, 202, 219
Josiah, 59–67, 173, 206, 214
judge, judging, 21–22, 82, 85–87, 90–91, 95, 99, 123, 132–33, 154–58, 167, 218–22, 225
justification, 112, 192

Keener, Craig, 118
Kennedy, Joel, 126–29
"kingdom of priests," 29n6, 31–33, 177
kingship law, 21, 53–62, 71–72, 78, 81, 167, 172, 175, 204, 214
Kynes, William, 126

Leithart, Peter, 123n72–75
Lewis, C. S., 2, 211–12
love
  God's, 30, 40, 42, 143, 177–78, 181,
  reader's, 11–12, 17n63, 21, 34n22, 41–42, 45, 71, 73–74, 78, 81, 115, 129, 133, 187, 192, 202, 210–15, 221
Luther, Martin, 23, 80n116, 137–62, 168, 172n17, 183, 208, 215, 218–20, 223, 225, 229, 233–34

MacIntyre, Alasdair, 20n68, 52
McConville, Gordon, 61, 90
mediation, x, 13n44, 36, 56, 84, 120, 130, 136, 138, 144, 156, 161n100, 166, 188, 190–91, 200, 234
meditation, 36–37, 57n26, 61, 69–70, 72–80, 175, 210–11, 215, 229, 233
Melchizedek, 109–10, 144
Michaels, J. Ramsey, 118
Miller, Patrick, 75, 94

ministry
  of God's people, x, 32, 35–37,
    43–48, 84–85, 89, 92, 98, 148,
    154–58, 161–62, 166–67,
    173, 179, 183, 193n67, 199,
    214, 217–20, 223, 225–28,
    233, 235
  of Jesus Christ, 104, 107–8, 110–
    16, 119–25, 130, 135–36,
    168, 188n55
  of ordained, 138–43, 145
mission, missionary, 23, 59, 118,
    130, 162, 166, 168, 173, 179,
    183, 199, 217–18, 225–29,
    233, 235
Moberly, R. W. L., 19n66, 172, 213
Moses, 12, 28, 36, 54, 57, 59, 62, 64,
    66–67, 70, 87, 91, 95, 97, 99,
    120n64, 123, 126, 128–29,
    178, 182, 187, 193, 205–6,
    208, 223
munux triplex Christi. See Jesus
    Christ, threefold office

oral, orality, x–xi, 23, 58, 74,
    148–54, 161–62, 168, 199,
    215, 218, 229–35
obedience, 4n12, 5, 9, 11, 20–22,
    27, 29–35, 40, 42, 46, 54,
    58–59, 63–67, 71–81, 84,
    90–91, 96–97, 103, 109, 112,
    115, 118, 125–26, 128–30,
    135–36, 166–69, 173, 175,
    179–83, 188, 195, 199,
    202–3, 212–17
Ong, Walter, 229–32
Oswalt, John, 36–37, 91

Paddison, Angus, 5–6
participation (*see also* union with
    Christ), x–xi, 4n12, 110n34,
    172, 181, 185, 188, 191–93,
    196, 197n1, 231–32, 234
penance, 150–51

Pentateuch, 31, 33–34, 53–54, 57,
    62n49, 85, 92
Peterson, David, 182–86
Philo, 31, 57, 87n19
phronesis (*see also* wisdom), 4n12,
    19n66, 220–21
politics, political, 2–3, 219
practices, x–xi, 2–6, 8, 11, 14–18,
    20n68, 22–23, 50, 52–53, 61,
    67, 81, 82, 85–100, 160–62,
    167, 170–72, 178n23, 180,
    186–88, 191–209, 217–36
prayer, x–xi, 10, 13, 18, 44, 46,
    74–81, 93, 106, 108n24, 144,
    146–48, 154, 156–57, 193,
    206, 208–9, 219, 233
preaching, 20n68, 46–47, 108–9,
    113–15, 125n80, 141, 146–
    58, 161–62, 217–20, 224,
    227, 229, 234
privilege, xi, 20, 23, 27–29, 32–35,
    40, 46, 79n113, 83, 130,
    132, 159, 165–66, 168, 175,
    177–78, 180, 189, 219
proclamation, 4, 20, 23, 29, 36–37,
    41–49, 80–81, 89, 108, 110,
    113, 115–17, 123, 135–37,
    146, 148–61, 166, 168, 175,
    177, 179, 181, 183, 188n55,
    193, 196, 199, 211, 218,
    223–29, 234–35
promise(s), 34n22, 35–37, 39–42,
    44, 49, 54n10, 55, 59, 66, 70,
    80, 91–94, 99, 110, 114–15,
    118, 125, 128–29, 138–39,
    150–54, 157, 161–62, 166,
    170, 189n57, 190, 206–8,
    211, 213, 216, 220, 223–25,
    229, 235

Rogers, Eugene, 13, 200, 205, 208

sacraments, 23, 137–41, 146n39,
    149–52, 154, 161–62, 168,
    218, 229, 234–35

General Index

sacrifice(s), 38, 43, 45–49, 83–84, 98, 106–7, 109–12, 115–16, 118, 120, 122–24, 135, 138n1, 143–44, 147–48, 151, 154, 157–58, 176, 193, 213, 219

salvation, 5–6, 10, 40–41, 78, 105, 108–11, 124, 127, 153–54, 162, 171–75, 177–81, 184, 211, 218, 227n74, 234

sanctification, 20, 23, 27, 30–31, 34, 37–40, 45, 47, 49, 83, 85n12, 112–13, 130, 143, 159, 166, 169, 173–74, 176, 181–87, 192, 197, 215–18, 235

Schleiermacher, F. D. E., 111n37

Scott, David, 197–98, 229

Seitz, Christopher, 201–2

sermons, 149, 150n57, 153, 222, 233–34

sin, 10, 14–15, 21n70, 43, 76, 88–90, 107–8, 120, 140, 150–51, 161–62, 171, 173, 183, 185–86, 193, 200–1, 216

Sonnet, J. P., 56–59

soteriology (*see also* salvation), 5, 24, 104n1, 122

sovereignty, divine (*see also* freedom, divine), xi, 5–6, 10, 43, 59, 110n33, 118n57, 135, 169, 178, 181

speech acts, 189–90, 193, 198, 224, 229

suffering, 27, 37–40, 42, 46, 48–49, 66, 80, 122n71, 130, 151, 195–96, 214–15, 218, 228

Spinks, D. Christopher, 18n64, 53n4, 198n4

Spirit, Holy, 4n12, 6, 9, 11, 16–18, 38–39, 48, 105–8, 110, 114, 122–23, 127, 139–41, 144–45, 149n54, 150, 152n67, 158, 181, 183–84, 186, 188–92, 208, 210, 216–17, 226, 234, 236

Stände, 138–39, 159, 176

teach, teaching, x, 22–23, 36, 45–47, 49, 82–100, 105–8, 113–16, 121–25, 130, 133–36, 139, 143–48, 154–60, 167, 188, 196, 218–20, 223, 227–29

theological interpretation of Scripture, 4n12, 7, 19n65, 24, 50, 165, 174, 179, 207n33, 222, 229–31, 233–35

Thiselton, Anthony, 224

Tigay, Jeffrey, 54–57

Torrance, T. F., 84, 135

"treasured possession," 29, 33, 175, 182

Treier, Daniel, ix–xi, xiv; 4n11, 19n65, 19n66, 201n13, 219n51, 221

Trinitarian, x, 4, 7, 11, 110n33

Turretin, Francis, 107–11

typology, 194

union with Christ, xi, 49, 188n54, 191–93

Vanhoozer, Kevin, ix, 2, 4n12, 18n64, 19n66, 52, 53, 169n3, 171, 172, 177, 188–90, 193n68, 194, 195, 200, 212, 221, 227, 234

Venema, G., 19n66, 62–65

virtue(s), x, 10, 12–21, 23, 41, 49, 51–53, 59, 61, 67–68, 74, 77, 81, 105, 135, 160, 170, 172–73, 176–77, 185–86, 190, 198–217, 221, 226

Watson, Francis, ix, 18n63, 195, 225n69

Webb, Stephen, 233–35

Webster, John, 7–12, 168–71, 178, 181, 184, 188n55, 202–3, 209, 216
Wells, Jo Bailey, 30
Wilson, Gerald, 69–72
wisdom, 12, 18–19, 22, 54, 74–76, 80, 90, 99, 106, 108, 122, 123n73, 201n13, 202, 204–5, 209, 215
witness, 4n12, 43, 46, 84, 106, 112, 114, 119, 135, 190, 212, 218, 225–29

www.ingramcontent.com/pod-product-compliance
Lightning Source LLC
Chambersburg PA
CBHW050343230426
43663CB00010B/1969